THE PRACTICE OF INTERCESSION

ZACHARIAS TANEE FOMUM

books4
revival.com

Copyright © 1989 by Zacharias Tanee Fomum
All rights reserved.

No part of this book may be reproduced in any form or by any electronic or mechanical means, including information storage and retrieval systems, without written permission from the author, except for the use of brief quotations in a book review.

Published by

books4revival.com

A division of the Book Ministry of Christian Missionary Fellowship International

info@books4revival.com

To

EVERLYNE NGO HONYO

a woman of God and an intercessor

FOREWORD

DON'T GET ON YOUR KNEES WITHOUT IT!

This book is the sequel and companion to The Art of Intercession. The current volume, as its title suggests, focuses on the more practical aspects of intercession: the use of time, discipline, goals, fasting, resisting the devil, the use of the Bible and knowledge of facts.

From a practical perspective, Professor Fomum leads us through the levels of intercession - from the beginner to the advanced. He goes on to give practical lessons on high level spiritual warfare against principalities and powers - for those who are called into this ministry. There are sections on intercessory prayer chains and a full-time ministry of intercession. All this from the pen of one who has himself advanced through the school of calloused knees.

If God is calling you to be an intercessor, this is the single best, most practical manual to get you started or advancing on your knees.

CONTENTS

Introduction ix

PART 1
1. Prayer 3
2. Prayerlessness 15
3. Intercession 19

PART 2
4. The Intercessor And The Use of Time 31
5. The Intercessor And Discipline 43
6. The Intercessor And Hard Work 53
7. The Intercessor And Courage 67
8. The Intercessor And The Devil 87
9. The Intercessor And Burden 99
10. The Intercessor And Fasting 107
11. The Intercessor And Personal Holiness 113
12. The Intercessor And Goals 123
13. The Intercessor And Urgency 127
14. The Intercessor And His Bible 133
15. The Intercessor And Personal Revelation 141
16. The Intercessor And Secrecy 145
17. The Intercessor And a Knowledge of Facts 149
18. The Intercessor And World Conquest For Christ 155
19. The Intercessor And His Needs 161
20. The Intercessor And The Sovereign Will of God 167
21. The Intercessor And Intercessors 175
22. The Intercessor And Prayer Retreats 183
23. The Intercessor And Gratitude 201

PART 3
24. Levels Of Intercession 207
25. A Beginner In The School Of Intercession 213

26. Making Progress In The School Of Intercession	221
27. The Advanced Intercessor	227

PART 4
28. The Intercessor And The Overthrow of Principalities And Powers	237
29. Intercession Against a Principality or Prince - 1	247
30. Intercession Against A Principality Or Prince - 2	261

PART 5
31. An Intercessional Prayer Chain	285

PART 6
32. Intercession For an Individual - 1	299
33. Intercession For an Individual - 2	307
34. Intercession For a Family	313
35. Intercession For an Assembly (Church)	321
36. Intercession For a City	327
37. Intercession For a Nation	335
38. Intercession For a Continent	383
39. Intercession For Planet Earth	391

PART 7
40. A Full-Time Ministry of Intercession	407
41. Intercession	411
Very Important!!!	413
Thank You	417
About the Author	419
Also by Z.T. Fomum	425
Distributors of ZTF Books	433

INTRODUCTION

This book is a continuation of our other book, *The Art of Intercession*, which is already in circulation. We had intended to write one book titled *The Ministry of Intercession*, but we found that what God had to say to us could not be contained in one medium-size book. We therefore stopped the book at a convenient point and gave the first part the title ***The Art of Intercession***, and this second part, which is more on the practical aspects of the ministry of intercession; we have titled **The Practice of Intercession**.

There is not much that I want to say about the book before you. I only ask that you read all of it, chapter by chapter. However, I want to share with you what the Lord has done for me in the course of the eighteen months during which I have worked on writing the two books on intercession. By the time I started writing ***The Art of Intercession***, I was praying, on the average, three hours and spending one six-hour period on a prayer chain, a day. By the time I finished the book, I had been forced by the evidence of what I saw in the Bible about intercession, to increase my daily praying to an average of four hours a day and to maintain the six-hour period of praying on the prayer chain. During the ten months in which I have worked on the present volume, my being has been stirred beyond measure to keep on praying. It has meant that this book, which was scheduled to be finished by September last year, has dragged on until today when the last chapter was written. During the last ten months, I have been forced by what I saw in the Bible and by what the Lord spoke to my heart, to work further on increasing the time I spend in prayer to an average of four hours daily, three six-hour periods on the prayer chain, every first week-end of each month given to prayer according to the schedule I have shared with you in this book, and one fifteen-day period of praying ten hours a day. This will be the way I will run my prayer life for the rest of my life.

Prayer is the most important work on earth. Intercessors are the most important people on earth. Today, knowing what I know, if the Lord of the harvest were to leave the choice with me (He has not), I would stop everything else and give myself to eighteen to twenty hours of prayer every day and thereby do the greatest good to the Kingdom of God, the Church, the world, the continent of Africa, this nation, this city, the church of Yaounde, my family, and myself.

God has, however, not left the choice with me. He has called me to do other things in addition to prayer in general and intercession in particular. I will faithfully do these things, but from this day on, I will give prayer a place of priority in my life and ministry. I will pray and I will do everything I can to pray. I will do everything I can to call men, women, and children to pray. I will labour to remove anything in my life that will hinder or weaken prayer. I will pour out my all to God in prayer.

This book is written in such a way that, in a sense, each chapter can be read on its own, for each is fairly complete. However, we plead that each chapter be read so as to have the overall picture. If you can lay hands on our other books,

- The Way of Victorious Praying,
- The Ministry of Fasting,
- The Art of Intercession, and
- The Way of Christian Service,

read them. We believe God has a message in them that will encourage, bless, and challenge you.

We will be glad to have your reactions to the subject matter in this book (via **ztfbooks@cmfionline.org**).

To the Lord Jesus, the interceding Lord of the Church, may there be glory, honour, majesty, power, and dominion for ever and ever.

Amen.

PART 1

1
PRAYER

1. We are seeking to make the Church asleep and silent, to be the Church revived and militant. We are seeking to call God's people back to the old paths, to get people to pray fervently, fast frequently, and work mightily for the Lord and the lost. We want to get people to pray before dawn and after dark for a soul-stirring, heaven-sent, Holy Ghost-inspired revival that will turn the tide in our pleasure-loving, spiritually slumbering age. God wants His children hot-hearted and not lukewarm or cold. He wants soldiers, not sleepers. He wants life service and not lip service, He wants total commitment, not token commitment. He wants the church to be an evangelistic centre, not a social rendezvous. He wants Christians on their knees in prayer, and then on their toes for the lost (Fred D. Javis, *Herald of His Coming*, vol. 46, no. 5 [May 1987]).
2. In each generation those who focus on God and hunger to know Him stand as spiritual giants. But God's call to know Him extends to all believers regardless of time, pressure, and obligations. The apostle Paul not only

travelled frequently, founded numerous churches, and wrote much of the New Testament, but he also supported himself by tent making: David was a busy king", but he still sought God constantly, and his prayers, recorded in the Psalms, bless us today. Jesus ministered to people all day long but still found time for an extensive prayer life. Begin where you are. Ask the Lord to give you great hunger and thirst for Him. Tell him that you want to be changed. As you learn to focus on Him, recording your priorities will become easier, until you can say with Paul: *"I count everything as loss compared to the surpassing greatness of knowing Christ Jesus my Lord" (Philippians 3:8)*. (Hannelore Bozeman. *The Message of the Cross,* vol. 51 [May-June 1981]).

3. Surprisingly, Satan, our adversary, wants the men of vision most of all dead or alive! Trapped in the nets of immorality, suffocating in materialism, stifled by indifference and deadness—whatever the means, Satan doesn't care, as long as men of vision are prevented from leading God's people to the evangelistic and missionary triumphs easily within reach. Where are the men of vision God is calling to do great exploits for Him? Sadly, many are lost (Mike Crow, *The Message of the Cross,* vol. 51 [November-December 1987]). Will you intercede so that the Lord should raise them up? Will you pray that they should be protected from immorality, materialism, indifference, and "deadness?" Will you pray that they should be protected from discouragement? Please pray. Israel did not pray and Saul went astray. Again she did not pray and David was trapped in immorality. Still, she would not pray and Solomon went astray!

4. Beyond a doubt, one of the great secrets of the dissatisfaction and superficiality, unreality and temporary character of many of our modern so-called revivals is that

so much dependence is put upon man's machinery and so little upon God's power, sought and obtained by the earnest, persistent, believing prayer that will not take no for an answer. We live in a day characterized by the multiplication of man's machinery and the diminution of God's power. The great cry of our day is work, work, work; organize, organize, organize; give us some new society; tell us some new methods; devise some new machinery; but the great need of our day is prayer, more prayer, and better prayer . . . Great revivals always begin in the hearts of a few men and women whom God arouses by His Spirit to believe in Him as a living God, as a God who answers prayers, and upon whose hearts He lays a burden from which no rest can be found except in importunate crying unto God. Oh, may He by His Spirit lay such a burden upon our hearts today (R.A. Torrey, *The Power of Prayer* [Grand Rapids: Zondervan Publication, 1982]).

5. Every true revival, from the beginning, has had its earthly origin in prayer. "The Great Awakening" under Jonathan Edwards in the eighteenth century began with his famous call to prayer and he carried it forward by prayer. It has been recorded of Jonathan Edwards that he "so laboured in prayer that he wore the hard wooden boards into grooves where his knees pressed so often and so long ..." The marvellous work of grace among the North American Indians under David Brainerd, Jonathan Edwards's son-in-law, in 1743 and the following years, had its origin in the days and nights that Brainerd spent before God in prayer for an enduement of power from on high for his work (R. A. Torrey, *The Power of Prayer*).

6. "Then they returned to Jerusalem from the mount called Olivet. . . they went up to the upper room, where they

were staying, Peter, John . . . All these with one accord devoted themselves to prayer ..." (Acts 1:12-14).

7. "And they devoted themselves to the apostles' teaching and fellowship, to the breaking of bread and to prayer" (Acts 2:42).

8. "And when they heard it they lifted their voices together to God and said, Sovereign Lord, who didst make the heaven and the earth and the sea and everything in them . . . And now O Lord, look upon their threats, and grant to thy servants to speak thy word with boldness, while thou stretchest out thy hand to heal, and signs and wonders are performed through the name of thy holy servant Jesus. And when they had prayed, the place in which they were gathered was shaken, and they were all filled with the Holy Spirit and spoke the word of God with boldness" (Acts 4:24-31).

9. And as they were stoning Stephen, he prayed, Lord Jesus, receive my spirit. And he knelt down and cried with a loud voice. Lord, do not hold this sin against them" (Acts 6:59-60).

10. The next day, as they were on their journey and coming near the city, Peter went up on the house-top to pray, about the sixth hour. And he became hungry and desired something to eat; but while they were preparing it, he fell into a trance" (Acts 10:9-10).

11. *"And* Cornelius said, Four days ago, about this hour, I was keeping the ninth hour of prayer in my house and behold, a man stood before me in bright apparel, saying, Cornelius, your prayer has been heard and your alms have been remembered before God" (Acts 10:30-31).

12. "About that time Herod the king laid violent hands upon some who belonged to the Church. He killed James the brother of John with the sword; and when he saw that it pleased the Jews, he proceeded to arrest Peter also. This

was during the days of unleavened Bread. And when he had seized him, he put him into prison, and delivered him to four squads of soldiers to guard him, intending after the Passover to bring him out to the people. So Peter was kept in prison, but earnest prayer for him was made to God by the Church" (Acts 12:1-5).

13. "When he realized this, he went to the house of Mary, the mother of John whose name was Mark, where many were gathered together praying" (Acts 12:12).
14. "Now in the church at Antioch there were prophets and teachers ... While they were worshipping the Lord and fasting, the Holy Spirit said, 'Set apart for me Barnabas and Saul for the work to which I have called them.' Then after fasting and praying they laid their hands on them and sent them off (Acts 13:1-3).
15. "And when they had appointed elders for them in every church, with praying and fasting, they committed them to the Lord in whom they believed" (Acts 14:23).
16. "As we were going to the place of prayer ..." (Acts 16:16).
17. "Having received this charge, he put them into the inner prison and fastened their feet in the stocks. But about mid night Paul and Silas were praying and singing hymns to God, and the prisoners were listening to them, and suddenly there was a great earthquake, so that the foundations of the prison were shaken, and immediately all the doors were opened and every one's fetters were unfastened" (Acts 16:24-26).
18. And when he had spoken this, he knelt down and prayed with them all" (Acts 20:36).
19. "Great men of prayer are all great givers, that is, great givers according to their ability. George Mueller, of Bristol, England, was, as we know, one of the greatest men of prayer of the last generation. He obtained the English equivalent of more than £ 7,200,000 by prayer.

For about sixty years he carried on a most marvellous work in supporting and training the orphans of England, oftentimes housing two thousand or more orphans at one time, feeding them three meals a day. Yet every penny that came for the support of the orphans, and for the support of the other work for which he felt responsible, came in answer to prayer. No appeal was ever made to anyone, no collectings or offerings were ever taken, and yet the money never failed. Sometimes it seemed up to almost the last moment as if it would fail, but it always came. He would ask God for a hundred pounds sterling, and it would come and he would pass it on. He would ask for sixty thousand pounds sterling, and it would come and he would pass it on. In all, as we have already stated, he asked for over £ 7,200,000 and it came and he passed it on. None of it stuck to his fingers. And when he came to die at the advanced age of ninety-two or ninety-three years, he had just enough left to pay his funeral expenses. We ask and we get and we keep, and so God ceases to give" (R. A. Torrey, *The Power of Prayer*).

20. "There is no spiritual blessing that any believer enjoys that may not be yours. It belongs to you now; Christ purchased it by His atoning death and God has provided it in Him. It is there for you; but it is your part to claim it; to put out your hand and take it. God's appointed way of claiming blessings, or putting out your hand and appropriating to yourself the blessings that are procured for you by the atoning death of Jesus Christ, is by prayer. Prayer is the hand that takes to ourselves the blessings that God has already provided in His Son."

21. "All that God is, and all that God has, is at the disposal of prayer. But we must use the key. Prayer can do anything that God can do, and as God can do anything, prayer is omnipotent. No one can stand against the man who

knows how to pray and who meets all the conditions of prevailing prayer and who really prays. 'The Lord God Omnipotent' works for him and works through him" (R. A. Torrey, *The Power of Prayer*).

22. Samuel Taylor Coleridge says, in *The Necessity of Prayer* by F. M. Bounds, The act of praying is the very highest energy of which the human mind is capable; praying, that is, with the total concentration of the faculties. The great mass of worldly men and of learned men are absolutely incapable of prayer."

23. William Bramwell is famous in Methodist annals for personal holiness and for his wonderful success in preaching and for the marvelous answers to his prayers. For hours at a time he would pray. He almost lived on his knees. He went over his circuits like a flame of fire. The fire was kindled by the time he spent in prayer. He often spent as much as four hours in a single session of prayer in retirement.

24. "Bishop Andrewes spent the greatest part of five hours every day in prayer and devotions. Sir Henry Havelock always spent the first two hours of each day alone with God."

25. "Dr Judson's success in prayer is attributed to the fact that he gave much time to prayer. He says on this point, 'Arrange the affairs, if possible, so that thou canst leisurely devote two or three hours every day not merely to devotional exercises but to the very act of secret prayer and communion with God. Endeavour seven times a day to withdraw from business and company and lift up thy soul to God in private retirement. Begin the day by rising after midnight and devoting some time amid the silence and darkness of the night to this sacred work. Let the hours of opening dawn find thee at the same work. Let the hours of nine, twelve, three, six and nine at night

witness the same. Be resolute in His cause. Make all practical sacrifices to maintain it. Consider that thy time is short, and that business and company must not be allowed to rob thee of thy God.' Impossible, say we, fanatical directions! Dr. Judson impressed an empire for Christ and laid the foundations of God's kingdom, with imperishable granite in the heart of Burma. He was successful, one of the few men who mightily impressed the world for Christ. Many men of greater gifts and genius and learning than he have made no such impression; their religious work is like footsteps in the sands, but he has engraven his work on the adamant. The secret of its profundity and endurance is found in the fact that he gave time to prayer. He kept the iron red-hot with prayer, and God's skill fashioned it with enduring power. No man can do a great and enduring work for God who is not a man of prayer, and no man can be a man of prayer who does not give much time to praying" (E. M. Bounds, *Power Through Prayer* [Grand Rapids: Baker Book House, 1979]).

26. "How glibly we talk of praying without ceasing! Yet we are quite apt to quit, if our prayer remained unanswered but one week or month! We assume that by a stroke of His arm or an action of His will, God will give us what we ask. It never seems to dawn on us, that He is the master of nature, as of grace, and that, sometimes He chooses one way, and sometimes another in which to do His work. It takes years sometimes, to answer a prayer and when it is answered, and we look backward we can see that it did. But God knows all the time, and it is His will that we pray, and pray, and still pray, and so come to know, indeed and of a truth, what it is to pray without ceasing" (Bounds, *The Necessity of Prayer*),

27. "Two thirds of the praying we do, is for that which would

give us the greatest possible pleasure to receive. It is a sort of spiritual self-indulgence in which we engage, and as a consequence is the exact opposite of self-discipline. God knows all this, and keeps His children asking. In the process of time - His time - our petitions take on another aspect, and we, another spiritual approach. God keeps up praying until, in His wisdom, He designs to answer. And no matter how long it may be before He speaks, it is, even then, far earlier than we have right to expect or hope to deserve" (Bounds, *The Necessity of Prayer*).

28. No amount of praying today will exempt us of the need to pray tomorrow. No intentions to pray tomorrow will meet our need of today.

29. Resolutions to pray that are not translated into action are self-deception. A timetable that includes prayer hours that are ignored with impunity, is evidence of spiritual malady.

30. The only people who are honest are those who decide to pray and actually pray. Good intentions, on their own, are useless.

31. "To pray is the greatest thing we can do: and to do it well there must be calmness, time, and deliberation; otherwise it is degraded into the littlest and meanest of things. True praying has the greatest capacity for good, and poor praying, the least. We cannot do too much of real praying; we cannot do too little of the sham. We must learn anew the worth of prayer. There is nothing that takes more time to learn. And if we learn this wondrous art, we must not give a fragment here and there. 'A little talk with Jesus,' as the tiny saintlets sing, but we must demand and hold with an iron grasp the best hours of the day, for God and prayer, or there will be no praying worth the name" (Bounds, *Power Through Prayer*).

32. If our prayer is only for the purpose of accomplishing our

plans and expectations, it does not have much value in the spiritual realm. Prayer must originate from God and be responded to by us. Such alone is meaningful prayer, since God's work is controlled by prayer (Watchman Nee in *Let Us Pray* [New York: Christian Fellowship Publishers, 1977]).

33. We read of men in past times who spent whole nights of agony, pleading for the salvation of the lost, of men who wept tears of grief, because they believed somebody was in danger of eternal damnation. But it is only as God the Spirit with draws the veil from our eyes, as He makes the things of the spiritual realm real to us, and enables us to anticipate the future, that we shall be able to realize these tremendous truths of the Scripture, and be able to pray (T. T. Shields in *Herald of His Coming*, vol. 46, no. 5 [May 1987]).

34. Prayer can sway not only individuals but also great audiences. Catherine Booth knew the effect and power of prayer. She saw the weight of a simple heartfelt prayer moving God to influence great audiences. She wrote of her observations in early Salvation Army meetings in her "Papers of Godliness." "I have seen, at the bottom of a great hall or theater, or in the gallery, a lot of the roughest men conceivable, behaving in the most unseemingly manner, arrested by the influence of prayer. Perhaps, when the rowdyism had been ready to break into open tumult, a little woman has stretched out her hands over the congregation, and said, 'Now, let us pray.' And I have seen the whole mass of men assume an attitude of quietness and reverence. I have watched the aspect of the congregation, and have seen great, rough fellows get their heads down, and sometimes wipe their eyes; and when we have got up to sing, there has been no more disorderly conduct, but they have settled down with the solemnity

of death to listen. Hundreds of them were convicted of sin while under that prayer. It was the Holy Ghost wrestling for those souls in the heart of that woman that struck them with conviction *(Herald of His Coming,* vol. 46, no. 5 [May 1987]).
35. In our day, "the goddess of sleep and ease" is worshipped. Prayer nights have disappeared from the spiritual scene in many nations. Oh, for the return of God's people to prayer!
36. "Continue steadfastly in prayer, being watchful in it with all thanksgiving" (Colossians 4:2).
37. "Pray at all times in the Spirit, with all prayer and supplication. To that end keep alert with all perseverance, making supplication for all the saints" (Ephesians 6:18).
38. Watch and pray.
39. In all things give thanks!
40. Praise the Lord!

2
PRAYERLESSNESS

1. Prayerlessness is manifested by no praying at all.
2. Prayerlessness is also manifested by too little praying.
3. Prayerlessness is also manifested when old believers pray like babies in Christ.
4. Prayerlessness is also indicated by the fact that too little is invested in it.
5. How many things the Lord desires to do, yet He does not perform them because His people do not pray. He will wait until men agree with Him, and then He will work (Watchman Nee, *Let Us Pray* [New York: Christian Fellowship Publishers, 1977]).
6. To the apostle Paul it was pray or perish; intercede or others perish. He knew too well that although God had given him a great ministry and he was in the centre of God's will and was labouring with all his might, if he did not pray, he would obviously fail.
7. The prayerless spirit saps a people's moral strength because it blunts their thought and conviction of the Holy. It must be so if prayer is such a moral blessing and such a shaping power, if it pass, by its nature, from the

vague volume and passion of devotion to formed petition and effort. Prayerlessness is an injustice and damage to our own soul, and therefore to its history, both in what we do and what we think. The root of deadly heresy is prayerlessness (P. T. Forsythe, "The Refiner's Fire," *World Challenge,* vol. 1).

8. Elders who have lost spiritual direction, hold their meetings and spend countless hours in discussion and then briefly pray for fifteen minutes at the end to ease their consciences. They are not frightened about meetings in which God has no central position. Although they know that God can only be brought in by violent praying and righteous living, they prefer to discuss, scheme, and act instead *of* praying. They are unaware that their meetings are assemblies of sin in sin.
9. The prayer meeting of prayerless believers lasts one hour. Of that hour, fifteen minutes are spent on putting the believers into the right mood. The next fifteen minutes are spent in joyous singing of lighthearted songs and choruses. The next thirty minutes are spent on a "mini" sermon from the leader and the last fifteen minutes are shared between throwing a few empty phrases at God and then the announcements.
10. A prayerless man thinks, desires, plans, and acts. He then asks God to bless what he has done "in the name of Jesus and for His sake."
11. The devil loves prayerless believers. They do more to expand and establish his kingdom and his glory than unbelievers.
12. The enemy gloats over prayerless churches because they are his workshop. He rejoices as many more such churches are established and is never as happy as when more prayerless people are added to their numbers.
13. The only work for the Lord that will last is a work

conceived in prayer, carried out in prayer, and consummated in prayer. All else is wood, hay, stubble.

14. Any preacher who does not set aside two hours every day for intense violent praying for himself, his family, and the people of God under his leadership is a politician, religious organizer, deceiver of himself, and ultimately a traitor of the people of God. The Kingdom of God will do better if all such men disappear from positions of responsibility in the Church of the One who lives to intercede for us.
15. Prayerlessness is not an accident. It is a deliberate attempt to frustrate the purposes of God.
16. Prayerlessness is the normal life of gluttonous eaters of meat, fish, and other delicacies.
17. " This, however, is not a day of prayer. Few men there are who pray. Prayer is defamed by preacher and priest. In these class of hurry and bustle, of electricity and steam, men will not take time to pray. Preachers there are who 'say prayers' as a part of their programme, on regular or state occasions, but who 'stirs himself up to take hold of God? Who prays as Jacob prayed - till he is crowned as a prevailing princely intercessor? Who prays as Elijah prayed till all the locked-up forces of nature were unsealed and a famine-stricken land blooms as the Garden of God? Who prayed as Jesus Christ did out upon the mountain when he 'Continued all night in prayer to God'? The apostles 'gave themselves to prayer' - the most difficult thing men or preachers do. Laymen there are who will give them money - some of them in rich abundance - but they will not 'give themselves' to prayer, without which their money is but a curse. There are plenty of preachers who will preach and deliver great and eloquent addresses on the need of revival and the spread of the kingdom of God but not many who will do

that without which all preaching and organizing are worse than vain - pray. It is out of date, almost a lost art, and the greatest benefactor this age could have is the man who will bring the preachers and the church back to prayer" (Bounds, *Power Through Prayer*).

18. Salvation never finds its way into a prayerless heart (ibid.).
19. The Holy Spirit never abides in a prayerless spirit (ibid.).
20. The gospel cannot be projected by a prayerless preacher (ibid.).
21. Preaching never edifies a prayerless soul (ibid.).
22. Gifts, talents, education, eloquence, God's call, cannot abate the demand of prayer but only intensify the necessity for the preacher to pray and be prayed for (ibid.).
23. A preacher may preach in an official, entertaining, or learned way without prayer, but between this kind of preaching and sowing God's precious seed with holy hands and prayerful weeping hearts there is immeasurable distance (ibid.).
24. A prayerless ministry is the undertaker for all God's truth and for God's Church. He may have the most costly casket and the most beautiful flowers, but it is a funeral, notwithstanding the charmful array (ibid.).
25. The Church that does not pray for her pastor will soon reap what she has sown - a nation-shaking scandal!
26. Watch and pray!
27. Pray without ceasing.
28. Make prayer your number one priority.

3
INTERCESSION

1. Abraham stood, a lonely figure against the smoke of dying Sodom, but his prayer brought deliverance to Lot. I know of a cynical father of several sons and daughters who, like him, shrugged off the Christian faith. Yet the day came when the whole family turned to Christ. There was a wife and mother in that family who broke her heart in agonies of intercession. One by one the family came to the Lord. When they were all Christians, one daughter said, "What this unworthy family owes to my mother is beyond knowing. How kindly God must think of her to bring us back from our insane wanderings!" Who knows what vast debts the careless multitudes owe to those few whose unflagging faith will not surrender the unsaved to the enemy? Committed intercessors hold back the judgments that strain to consume the earth! What saving elements in human society are greater than those of Christian character and intercession? Once, my own life was being consumed in a reckless abandonment to evil. My aunt and uncle prayed for me - although I did not

know it at the time. They prayed daily for me, and their prayers were answered. I became not only a Christian but a minister of the gospel - which I have now delivered for more than half a century. I have never been able to shake off the conviction that without the prayers of that committed couple I might never have been redeemed. Once the apostle Paul had undergone a trial so fierce that he felt he was under "the sentence of death" (2 Corinthians 1:9). But he fairly shouted that God had delivered him from his "deadly peril." Then he added, "He will continue to deliver us, as you help us by your prayers. Then many will give thanks on our behalf for the gracious favour granted us in answer to the prayers of many" (2 Corinthians 1:10,11). We speak often of Paul's achievements, but he himself was aware that his success depended on the petitions of those who loved him and his Lord. One supreme fact concerning the power of prayer and goodness in our world must never be forgotten. There is a Presence in the universe who keeps our world from tumbling into judgment. He is, in fact, the one saving element in creation. There is a man before the cosmic throne who "always lives to intercede for [us]" (Hebrews 7:25). He came to this position by way of the cross, and His death stands between us and our own eternal dying. Rejected by millions, He is still there, pleading for a ruined world. And many, now under sentence of death, will find everlasting aliveness through His mediation. The Word insists that the prayer of a righteous man is powerful and effective" (James 5:16). All the computers of earth cannot total up what is accomplished for the human race through the prayers of the Man who went to Calvary—or through the lives and prayers of those who follow Him (Lon Woodrum, *The Message of the Cross,* vol. 51 [May-June 1987]).

2. The first characteristic of the prayer that is in the Holy Spirit is intense earnestness. This we see in Romans 8:26 KJV: "And in like manner, the Spirit also helpeth our infirmity: for we do not know how to pray as we ought; but the Spirit himself maketh intercession for us with groanings which cannot be uttered." As we saw in studying Acts 12:5, the prayer that prevails with God is the prayer into which we throw our whole heart, the prayer of intense earnestness; and it is the Holy Spirit who inspires us to that intense earnestness in prayer. Oh, how cold and formal we are in many of our prayers. How little intense longing there is in our souls to obtain the thing that we ask. We pray even for the salvation of the lost with much indifference, though we ought to realize that if our prayers are not heard, they are going to spend eternity in hell. But men and women whose prayer life is under the control of the Holy Spirit pray with intense earnestness, then cry mightily to God; there is a great burden of prayer in their hearts, they pray sometimes with groanings that cannot be uttered. Mr. Finney told us about a man named Abel Clary. He said of him, "He had been licensed to preach, but his spirit of prayer was such, he was so burdened with the souls of men, that he was not able to preach much, his whole time and strength being given to prayer. The burden of his soul would frequently be so great that he was unable to stand, and he would writhe and groan in agony. I was well acquainted with him, and knew something of the wonderful spirit of prayer that was upon him. He was a very silent man, as almost all are who have the powerful spirit of prayer." Abel Clary was of great assistance to Mr Finney, simply by praying, in his work in Rochester, New York, where a revival sprang up, the report of which resulted in revivals all over the country, and which, it is said, brought in a

hundred thousand souls to Christ in a year. Of Mr. Clary's work in Rochester, Mr. Finney wrote, "The first I knew of his being in Rochester, a gentleman who lived about a mile West of the city called on me one day and asked me if I knew a Mr. Abel Clary, a minister. I told him that I knew him well. 'Well,' he said, 'he is at my house, and has been there for some time, and I do not know what to think of him.' I said, 'I have not seen him at any of our meetings.' 'No,' he replied, 'he cannot go to meetings, he says. He prays nearly all the time, day and night, and in such agony of mind that I do not know what to make of it. Sometimes he cannot even stand on his knees, but will lie prostrate on the floor, and groan and pray in a manner that quite astonishes me.' I said to the brother, 'I understand it; please keep still. It will all come out right; he will surely prevail'." Mr. Finney said of Mr. Clary in another place, "I think it was the second Sabbath that I was at Auburn. At this time I observed in the congregation the solemn face of Mr. Clary. He looked as if he was borne down with an agony of prayer. Being well acquainted with him, and knowing the great gift of God that was upon him, the spirit of prayer, I was glad to *see* him there. He sat in the pew with his brother, the doctor, who was also a professor of religion, but who had nothing, by experience, I should think, of his brother Abel's great power with God. At intermission, as soon as I came down from the pulpit, Clary, with his brother, met me at the pulpit stairs, the doctor invited me to go home with him and spend the intermission and get some refreshment. I did so. After arriving at his home we were soon summoned to the dinner table. We gathered about the table, and Dr Clary turned to his brother and said, 'Brother Abel, will you ask the blessing?' Brother Abel bowed his head and began, audibly, to ask a blessing. He had uttered but a sentence or two when he broke instantly down, moved suddenly back from the table, and fled to his chamber. The doctor supposed he had been taken suddenly ill, and rose up and followed him. In a few moments he came down and said, 'Mr Finney, Brother Abel wants to see you.' Said I, 'What ails him?' Said he, 'I do not know but he says you know. He appears in great distress, but I think it is the state of his mind.' I understood it in a moment, and went to his room. He lay groaning upon the bed, the Spirit making intercession for him, and in him, with groanings that could not be uttered. "I had barely entered the room when he made out to say, 'Pray, Brother Finney.' I knelt down and helped him in prayer, by leading his soul for the conversion of sinners. I continued to pray until his distress passed away, and then I returned to the dinner table. A wonderful revival broke out in Auburn; hundreds of souls were converted in six weeks" (R. H. Torrey, *The Power of Prayer* [Grand Rapids, Mich.: Zondervan Publishing House, 1982]).

3. Moses' ministry was mainly a ministry of intercession, which meant that he had to have a place with God so complete and so utter that his own reasonings did not come in; his own feelings did not come in, nothing about himself came in. He was right there with God, and although God told him to do things which seemed altogether contrary to God, and certainly contrary to his own best judgment, he obeyed. He knew it would work out. He could not understand why the Lord was doing it; it was going to be disaster, it seemed to be a contradiction. But he obeyed! We cannot have power with God unless God has got us into a place like that (T. Austin-Sparks, "The Refiner's Fire." *World Challenge*, vol. 1).

4. A prayer is also a promise. Every true prayer carries with it a vow. If it does not, it is not in earnest. It is not of a piece with life. Can we pray in earnest if we do not in the act commit ourselves to do our best to bring about the answer? Can we escape some kind of hypocrisy? This is especially so with intercession. What is the value of praying for the poor if all the rest of our time and interest is given only to becoming rich? Where is the honesty of praying for our country if in our most active hours we are chiefly occupied in making something out of it, if we are strangers to all sacrifice for it? Prayer is one form of sacrifice, but if it is the only form, it is vain oblation. If we pray for our child that he may have God's blessing, we are really promising that nothing shall be lacking on our part to be a divine blessing to him. . . . To pray for God's kingdom is also to engage ourselves to service and sacrifice for it. To begin our prayer with a petition for the hallowing of God's name and to have no real and prime place for holiness in our life or faith is not sincere. The prayer of the vindictive for forgiveness is mockery, like the prayer for daily bread from a wheat-corner. No such man could say the Lord's prayer but to his judgment . . . "Thy will be done." Unless that were the spirit of our prayer, how should we have courage to pray if we know ourselves at all or if we have come to a time when we can have some retrospect on our prayers and their fate? Without this committal to the wisdom of God, prayer would be a very dangerous weapon in proportion as it was effective (ibid.).

5. The Christian soldier is to pray at all seasons, and under all circumstances. His praying must be arranged so as to cover his times of peace as well as his hours of active combat. It must be available in his marching and his fighting. Prayer must diffuse all effort, impregnate all

ventures, decide all issues. The Christian soldier must be as intense in his praying as in his fighting. For his victories will depend very much more on his praying than on his fighting. Fervent supplication must be added to steady resolve, prayer and supplication must supplement the armour of God. The Holy Spirit must aid the supplication with His own strenuous plea. And the soldier must pray in the Spirit. In this, as in other forms of warfare, eternal vigilance is the price of victory, and thus, watchfulness and persistent perseverance must mark the every activity of the Christian warrior. The soldier-prayer must reflect its profound concern for the success and well-being of the whole army. The battle is not altogether a personal matter; victory cannot be achieved for self alone. There is a sense in which the entire army of Christ is involved. The cause of God, His saints, their woes and trials, their duties and crosses, all should find a voice and pleader in the Christian soldier, when he prays. He dare not limit his praying to himself. Nothing dries up spiritual secretions so certainly and completely; nothing acts in such deadly fashion, as selfish praying (E. M. Bounds, *The Necessity of Prayer* [Grand Rapids: Baker House, 1984]).

6. Because God will accomplish all His purpose; because He will accomplish only what He has purposed; because He brings the counsel of the nations to nought and frustrates the plans of the peoples, all who want to intercede must first of all find out what the mind of God is about the matter about which they want to intercede. (Z. T. Fomum, *The Art of Intercession,* [New York: Vantage Press, 1989)).

7. There are too many people who intend to do things but never get down to doing them. A man may be qualified before God to intercede; he may know the Bible grounds

for intercession and he may plan to intercede or desire to intercede or talk about intercession but all of this is to no avail until he actually gets down to interceding (Ibid.).
8. An intercessor is a person who takes the needs of another on himself, then takes those needs to God and labours relentlessly until they are met by the Lord.
9. An intercessor must be able to remain calm when others around him are losing their heads. He must not be carried away by what is carrying the others away. He must be in control of himself. This personal control must come out of the unshakeable faith that the Lord is in control of all that is happening.
10. An intercessor must know how to present the situation clearly to God. He must have a clear mind and right words. In presenting his case to God, he is to act as if God knows nothing about it. He must be as detailed as possible. He must present a clear, detailed report of what the situation is. It is no use for him to say, "God, you know the situation. I do not need to bother You with the details because nothing is hidden from You. Act as You see fit." Such a person might as well never pray because God knows all that he needs! Although God knows the details, he wants the intercessor to present them to Him. Although He knows what ought to be done, He wants man to tell Him [God] what he [man] wants Him [God] to do (Fomum, *The Art of Intercession.*)
11. There is a sense in which all believers can intercede. There is a sense in which all believers can come with boldness into the presence of God.
12. There is a plane of communion with God that is opened only to those who pay a special price.
13. The intercessor is a great man. He is so great that he can lift others to greatness without thought for himself. He must truly die to the self-life. Such a spirit that is

completely dead to the self-life is precious in God's sight and makes its possessor a beloved of God. The beloved of God intercedes from a plane that other believers have not yet attained.

14. All who seek to make progress in the School of Intercession must also make progress in the School of Blamelessness.

15. The ministry of intercession is not just words. It is a life lived out before God. It is a life delivered from sin and self. It is a live lived in victory. It is a life poured out to God. It is a life that seeks the glory of God and the glory of God alone. Out of such a life, intercession will flow out to God from the heart through the mouth, in prayer.

16. The power of intercession will always be proportional to the quality of the relationship between the intercessor and God. Those who are deeply united to God will flow accordingly.

17. Every intercessor must grow in union with God. He must grow in the knowledge of God in his heart. He must also grow in the exercise of the mind of Christ that he has received. In that way, his mind will help his spirit to flow forth in power with the appropriate words.

18. If a person who has depth in the Lord does not find the words that are necessary to communicate what is flowing forth from his heart to God, he will limit his potential as an intercessor.

19. If a person without spiritual depth uses his head to gather thoughts and ideas from the prayers of others and repeats them before God, he is not interceding but deceiving himself.

20. The extent of a person's leadership is measured by the extent to which he intercedes. A person is the leader of those he carries in his heart and intercedes for. Where there is no intercession, there is no leadership.

21. An intercessor must believe that God is able. He must also believe that without God man is not able. He must whole heartedly turn from man who is not able on his own, to God who is able.
22. Amen.

PART 2

THE INTERCESSOR AND THE USE OF TIME

SOME THOUGHTS ON TIME

1. Time is one of the greatest gifts that God has given to man.
2. God is so good that He has given every human being the same number of hours each day.
3. God has no favourites as far as time is concerned. He has not given some people ten hours a day, others fifteen, and others twenty-four.
4. Time is a very perishable gift.
5. People may vary in natural and spiritual endowments, but what ultimately makes a difference between them at the human level is how they use the time God gave them.
6. Your time is not yours. It is God-given. It is God-vested.
7. Each person meets each second, minute, hour, and day twice. He meets it the first time when it comes upon him. He will meet it the second time at the judgment seat of Christ to give account for that second, minute, hour and day.

8. Much money can be gained in a short time. Time cannot be gained that way.
9. Every second, minute, hour, or day that is lost is lost for ever.
10. A fool may waste money but the greatest fool wastes time.
11. The easiest way to lose time is to do it one second at a time,
12. I once met a fool, a great fool, the greatest fool. He wasted a second every second and soon found out that in a month of thirty days, he had wasted 2,592,000 seconds!
13. The Enemy ensures that he steals your time one second at a time and in that way prevents you from realizing it. It is neat and skilfull stealing.
14. The person who wastes fifteen minutes every hour will waste twenty-five years if he lives to be one hundred.
15. A man who sleeps eight hours a day and lives to be seventy-five has actually spent one-third of his entire life sleeping, that is, twenty-five years.
16. The believer who tithes his time should give God 2.4 hours every day and 16.8 hours every week.
17. The believer who is taking God more seriously should give God not only a tithe or ten percent of his time but also an offering of five percent of his time. In this way, he will give God 3.6 hours each day.
18. The believer who gives God a tithe or 10 percent of his time and an offering of 5 percent of his time still has 20.4 hours each day left for him to decide how to invest.
19. The believer who gives God less than 2.4 hours of his time a day is stealing from God.
20. Those believers who do not tithe time and money are robbing God. If they tithe only time, they rob God. If they tithe only their money, they rob God.
21. "Will a man rob God? Yet you are robbing me. But you

say, How are we robbing thee? In your tithes and offerings. You are cursed with a curse for robbing me; the whole nation of you" (Malachi 3:8-9).

22. God cannot demand a tithe and an offering from a man which does not include a tithe and an offering of his time.

23. Those who give God a tithe of their time and an offering of it will find that they are blessed, for God has said, "Bring the full tithes into the storehouse, that there may be food in my house, and thereby put me to the test, says the Lord of hosts, if I will not open the windows of heaven for you and pour down for you an overflowing blessing. I will rebuke the devourer for you, so that it will not destroy the fruit of your soil; and your wine in the field shall not fail to bear, says the Lord of hosts. Then all the nations will call you blessed, for you will be a land of delight, says the Lord of host" (Malachi 3:10-12).

24. Those who give God a tithe and an offering of their time are putting God to the test positively. God will respond to the test and do the following for them:

25. He will open heaven for them and pour down an overflowing blessing on them in all ways possible.

26. He will rebuke the devourer for them: the devourer through sickness during which they cannot work; the devourer through accidents that waste time and every other type of devourer of time. All will be rebuked so that the remaining time is safe.

27. He will rebuke the destroyer of your soil so that you do not invest where you will not harvest; so you will not serve employers who will not pay you; so that you do not farm on land that will not yield crops; so that you will not waste time going to see people who are not at home. He will rebuke the destroyer of people coming to loiter in your home. He will rebuke the destroyer of your wife,

children, friend, friends and relatives getting sick so that you have to spend time going to the hospital and the like.
28. He will bless the time you give Him so that abundant fruit accrues from it for the coming kingdom and glory.
29. He will bless the rest of your time in such a way that your concentration and capacity to understand are improved. You will be able to do in one hour what would normally have needed two, three, or four hours. You may be able to do in one hour what may take one year, five years, or even ten years to do. I will illustrate. If God intervenes supernaturally, a man could, in one minute, receive the formula for improving his business and moving from the red to the black, a thing that by working at the current rate he might not have been able to do in ten years. A Christian scientist may be given an idea in one minute that could cause him to move ten years ahead in his researches. A believer could be given the spiritual gift that he needs in a matter of seconds and with that gift, he could accomplish in one month what he might never have accomplished in twenty years. God could send someone to bring the answer to you that you have sought for years and which will immediately open doors of spiritual blessing.
30. He will bless you with good health. You could be sick and unproductive for a long time. God's blessings of health mean that He has given you more time for work.
31. He will make you young and strong even in your old age. I was privileged to meet and fellowship with that prince of God, Dr. Lester Sumrall. He was strong and healthy at seventy-six and still putting in over fourteen hours of hard work each day. Perpetual youthfulness and perpetual strength are in the Lord's hands. He gives them to whom He wills. He reserves them for those who have put Him to the test.

32. He will give you long life. You could die at twenty, thirty, forty, fifty, sixty, seventy, eighty, ninety, one hundred.... Who makes the final decision? God of course! If instead of dying at fifty, He lets you live in perpetual youthfulness until you are one hundred, then He has doubled your lifespan. God will be no one's debtor. He has promised to bless. He will bless. He must bless. He says, "Put me to the test." Put Him and see if He will fail. He cannot fail. No! He cannot. Glory be to His holy name.
33. Wiser people give God first a tithe of their time, then a second tithe, then a third tithe, and so on. In that way they make even greater progress.

SOME THOUGHTS ON PLANNING AND USING TIME

1. God is a master planner.
2. God planned the salvation of the world from the foundations of the world.
3. God has a fixed time for everything. The Bible says, "For everything there is a season and a time for every matter under heaven" (Ecclesiastes 3:1).
4. The Lord Jesus followed a predetermined time schedule. He said, "My time has not yet come, but your time is always here" (John 7:6).
5. All who want to be like God plan their time even as He has planned His.
6. Those who do not plan their time have decided that time, events, and circumstances will rule them. They are like a tree whose branches and leaves are open to be moved in any direction by any wind coming from any direction, at whatever intensity, for whatever duration, and at whatever hour. They are like a branch at sea, totally at the mercy of the waves.

7. God plans His time and keeps to it.
8. Those who want to be like God plan their time before God, and having planned it, keep to it.
9. Those who plan their time have decided to succeed.
10. Those who do not plan their time have decided to fail.
11. Satan labours to ensure that he has a great portion of all time that is not planned.
12. Those who plan to succeed have a clearly defined order of priorities written down.
13. Those who succeed give the majority of their time to their priority project(s).
14. Those who succeed give the best hours to their priority project; they, therefore, give the best and the largest portion of their time to their priority project(s).
15. The priority project of Jesus was prayer.
16. *Jesus gave His best hours to His priority project. The Bible says, "And in the morning, a great while before day, he rose and went out to a lonely place, and there he prayed" (Mark 1:35).*
17. To tell what or whom a man worships, look at the distribution of his time. His god has the largest share.
18. Sleep is the god of most people and they have planned it to be so. They protect their sleeping hours with full force. They hardly do a thing to protect the other things and when something does not happen they convert the time to sleeping time.
19. There are others whose god is idleness.
20. Each person faithfully keeps the appointment he makes with the god of his life. He does everything to be at the appointment. No one misses an appointment with his god without deep regret and pain.
21. In order to know who a man's god is, find out whose appointment he will not break.
22. To know a man's real priority, from his inner being, find

out that he will not fail doing except under extremely impossible circumstances.
23. Those who worship the goddess Sleep give her the largest portion of their time.
24. Those who worship idleness give the goddess Idleness many hours each day.
25. Idleness is defined as the time that is not put into useful work.
26. Any time that cannot be accounted for is wasted.
27. *Those who walk close to the Lord redeem the time because the days are evil. They simply obey the command, "Look carefully then how you walk not as unwise men but as wise, making the most of the time, because the days are evil. Therefore do not be foolish, but understand what the will of the Lord is" (Ephesians 5:15—17).*
28. Those who understand the will of God redeem time.
29. Those who do not redeem time do not understand what the will of the Lord is.
30. Wisdom is measured in part by whether or not a man redeems time.
31. Greater wisdom is manifested in part by a greater amount of time redeemed.
32. The real evidence that a project is on a man's heart, that it is a priority project, is that he will invest all his "free" time in it.
33. Fools have no priority projects.
34. Losers may plan well but they leave out their priority project and get carried away with secondary, tertiary, and quaternary issues.
35. Losers leave the issues on their programme and get carried away by new issues that seem more exciting.
36. Winners stick to the priority issue.
37. Winners draw timetables.
38. Winners put the priority issue on the timetable.

39. Winners then look at the timetable and ask, "Is there anything I can do to give more time to my priority issue?"
40. Winners ask, "What secondary or tertiary issue can I take off my timetable so that the time allocated to it may be added to that already given to my priority issue?" He asks, looks at the timetable, weighs things, strikes off some things, and gives the time initially programmed for them to the priority project.
41. Winners ask, "How can I cut down my sleeping time in order to increase the time available for my priority project?" He may then say, "I sleep six hours. I will teach my body to be satisfied with five hours of sleep and then I will increase the amount of time available for my priority project by one hour." If a person is investing eight hours a day on a project that should take ten years, and decides to give away one hour of sleep to the project and therefore invests nine hours a day on the project, he will accomplish the project in 8.9 years. He has saved 1.1 year with which to plan and get another project started! This is really great!

This, of course, requires discipline but we know that the world belongs to the disciplined. The apostle Paul believed in discipline and confessed,

"I pommel my body and subdue it" (1 Corinthians 9:27).

Everyone can pommel his body and subdue it. There is no body that cannot be subdued. There is no one (except those who are already sleeping for two or three hours a day) who cannot cut down their sleeping time and invest it in their priority project.

1. Winners, after they have done all they can to have all the time they can find to give to the priority project on their

timetables, cry out to God, "Show me what else I can do to increase the time available to satisfy Your heart."
2. God will show the winner some other modifications that can help him gain time.
3. The winner then finalizes the timetable and then seals it with God and nothing will move him from it. Without this capacity to keep to a timetable with strict discipline, the making of timetables is a waste of time.
4. Losers make timetables and then put them aside with a calm conscience.
5. The devil labours to ensure that believers do not keep to their timetables for fear that they may accomplish their priority projects to his undoing.
6. Jesus gave His time only to the "musts" of His life. At the age of twelve He said, "I must be in my Father's house" (Luke 2:49). At the height of His ministry He said, "We must work the works of him who sent me, while it is day, night comes, when no one can work" (John 9:4). Towards the end of His life, He said, "The Son of man must suffer many things and be rejected by the elders and the chief priests and Scribes, and be killed, and on the third day be raised" (Luke 9:22). In fact, the entire life of the Lord Jesus was one unending chain of "musts." The Bible says: "From that time Jesus began to show his disciples that *he must* go to Jerusalem and suffer many things from the elders, and chief priests and scribes, and be killed, and on the third day be raised" (Matthew 16:21). But he said to them, "I *must* preach the good news of the kingdom of God to the other cities also; for I was sent for this purpose" (Luke 4:43). "Nevertheless I *must go* on my way today and tomorrow and the day following; for it cannot be that a prophet should perish away from Jerusalem" (Luke 13:33). And when Jesus came to the place, he looked up and said to him, "Zacchaeus, make haste and come

down, for I *must* stay at your house today" (Luke 19:5). "The Son of man *must* be delivered into the hands of sinful men, and be crucified, and on the third day rise" (Luke 24:7). Then he said to them, "These are my words which I spoke to you, while I was still with you, that everything written about me in the law of Moses and the prophets and the psalms *must* be fulfilled" (Luke 24:44). "And as Moses lifted up the serpent in the wilderness, so *must* the Son of man be lifted up, that whosoever believes in him may have eternal life" (John 3:14-15). "And he *must* needs go through Samaria" (John 4:4 KJV). "And I have other sheep that are not of this fold; I *must* bring them also, and they will heed my voice. So there shall be one flock, one shepherd" (John 10:16). Jesus was a total success because He was sold to the "musts" of His life.

THE INTERCESSOR AND THE USE OF TIME

The intercessor, being called to the most important business on earth must do the following:

1. Decide that intercession is the most important business on earth.
2. Decide that intercession is the priority of priorities.
3. Decide that he will never stop interceding because something else is drawing him away from it, unless he has settled the issue over which he was interceding with God.
4. Decide to make a timetable.
5. Make one.
6. Give time on the timetable to intercession.
7. Drop other issues of secondary importance and give their time over to intercession.
8. Cut down sleeping time and thereby increase the amount of time available for intercession.

9. Ask of God and receive more time to add to that for intercesion .
10. Finalize the timetable
11. Present it to God and receive God's' approval of it.
12. Commit himself to intercession according to the timetable, come shine or come rain.
13. Close his ears to all who make negative comments about the time he is giving to intercession.
14. Close his ears to all comments about what he is neglecting by giving himself to intercession.
15. Close his ears to all who say that he is not a "balanced" Christian. No intercessor can ever be balanced in the eyes of the world or in the eyes of believers whose eyes are not opened to the priority of priorities. When Mary came and broke her alabaster box of very costly ointment and poured it on the head of the Lord Jesus, the Bible says: *"But when the disciples saw it, they were indignant. Why this waste? For this ointment might have been sold for a large sum, and given to the poor." But Jesus, aware of this, said to them, "Why do you trouble the woman? For she has done a beautiful thing to me. For you always have the poor with you, but you will not always have me. In pouring this ointment on my body she has done it to prepare me for burial. Truly, I say to you, wherever this gospel is preached in the whole world, what she has done will be told in memory of her" (Matthew 26:8-13)*. There will always be indignant disciples, frowning, rebuking, and blaming the intercessor who is totally sold to the Lord Jesus. There will always be those who bring logical arguments and even quote the Bible to back up what they are saying. However the intercessor is tuned in to the Lord Jesus, and the Lord Jesus whispers to him, "You have done a beautiful thing." Is that not enough? Sure it is!

5

THE INTERCESSOR AND DISCIPLINE

"Do you not know that in a race all the runners compete, but only one receives the prize? So run that you may obtain it. Every athlete exercises self-control in all things. They do it to receive a perishable wreath, but we are imperishable. Well, I do not run aimlessly, I do not box as one beating the air; but I pommel my body and subdue it lest after preaching to others I myself should be disqualified" (1 Corinthians 9:24 - 27).

"No soldier on service gets entangled in civilian pursuits, since his aim is to satisfy the one who enlisted him. An athlete is not crowned unless he competes according to the rules" (2 Corinthians 2:4-5).

"A man without self-control is like a city broken into and left without walls" (Proverbs 25:28),

Nowhere in the Christian life is discipline more required than in the ministry of intercession. The reason is obvious - the intercessor decides the destiny of men, families, towns, nations, continents, and the world.

He is, therefore, constantly under attack by the enemy. If the smallest opening is allowed, Satan will use it fully. Knowing this, all who want to make progress must wage war against indiscipline. There are a number of areas in which discipline must specially be applied. These include:

1. Time,
2. Food, and
3. Relationships.

TIME

No one will ever make progress in the School of Intercession who did not apply himself rigidly to the use of time. The saintly Paul E. Billheimer wrote,

> *"To become prayerful saints, we must pray by the clock, at fixed times. This is very important. You will never become a praying saint if you depend upon impulse to call you to prayer. You will never become a praying saint unless you discipline yourself to a fixed programme of prayer. To depend upon impulse as a guide to prayer will probably end in not praying at all"*
>
> — *PAUL E. BILLHEIMER, OVERCOMERS THROUGH THE CROSS [SUSSEX, ENGLAND: KINGSWAY PUBLICATION, 1982]*

The intercessor will consequently plan his time. If he decides to spend four hours each day in intercession, he will make a timetable for the week and on that timetable fit in four hours every day as time for intercession. He will ensure that he gives the best hours of each day to the most important business that anyone can do for God and for man - intercede. Having fitted those hours on his timetable, he will seal them up, that is, he will consider them as a covenant between him and the Lord. He will know that he dares not break his covenant with God.

He will watch over those hours jealously and ensure that nothing on earth interrupts them. He will of course do everything, day or night, with those hours in view. For example, he will ensure that he prepares for those hours. He will keep himself separated from sin and from anything that is questionable so that he would have a clear conscience before God. He will ensure that all his appointments end two hours before the time of intercession. If he is not yet able to stand four hours of God's presence, he might divide his four hours into two periods of two hours.

He will then choose the place where to withdraw and intercede. If it is possible to go away from his own dwelling, he will do that preferentially. If not, he will lock himself up in his room and leave instructions that he has an appointment with the God of heaven and consequently all other persons must wait. For the intercessor who will make progress, it is inevitable that he turns down anyone who wants to see him when he must meet God. If his earthly boss wants to see him, the earthly boss must wait.

If someone is sick and needs to be taken to the hospital, he must wait.

If there is some problem in the neighbourhood and his attention is demanded, the problem must wait. The Lord cannot be kept waiting.

Every serious intercessor knows that the Lord cannot be kept waiting. This is a most serious matter. Any serious intercessor knows that if he had to start interceding at 6:00 and at 5:50 p.m. he had the most important man in the nation call upon him, he will excuse himself, leave the most important man in the nation in order to attend to the God of the universe. The person who leaves God waiting so that he may attend to man has failed utterly. In a sense, it betrays the fact that God is not Lord of his life, but that someone else or something else is his god.

This is the matter of the Lordship of Christ. It is this Lordship, daily maintained in everything, that establishes a person as a prince of God and gives him authority before God in intercession and before the enemy in spiritual warfare. In a real sense, it is not just a matter of discipline. It is spiritual warfare. In a real sense, it is not just a matter of discipline. It is a matter of who is Lord and King. Maybe you ought to stop and sort this out.

For the real intercessor, four hours of intercession can become five, six, or seven hours of intercession. However, four hours earmarked for intercession must never be allowed to dwindle to three hours and forty-five minutes and then to three hours and thirty minutes. Such tendencies are manifestations of lack of discipline. They are also manifestations of a sick soul. If you are going to go far with God, four hours of intercession should mean a minimum *of four hours!*

Someone may ask, "Am I not to intercede until I am through with the burden that God has given me? When that burden has been discharged is the session not ended?" Well, to you we say, "It is true that intercession ends when the burden has been discharged. However, coming into God's presence to intercede can never be separated from coming into His presence to know Him and to minister to Him. Those who carry out the ministry of intercession to the satisfaction of His heart are those who have learned to know Him and to minister to His needs. Those who only come to make requests are 'exploiters' of God. They will not be fully blessed."

If you planned to intercede for four hours and after three hours you were through, you should thank the Lord that He has graciously given you one hour to spend in His presence. Begin to thank Him and to worship Him. That is a part of ministering unto Him. Thank Him for enabling you to discharge your own burden through intercession. Ask Him if He has some burden in His heart that He wants your intercession on. He will show you and what a privilege it is to intercede for the Lord on the burdens in His heart. There will be time when He tells you nothing in particular. Do not go away. He may be testing you to see if you love Him, for those who love Him always linger in His presence, finding it difficult to go away!

FOOD

Food is an enemy to intercession! The more one eats the less he is able to intercede. Anyone who is taking intercession seriously will also take discipline with regard to eating seriously. Although one may have a good feeling after a good meal, one needs only to withdraw into the prayer closet to find that there is no desire for God, no desire for intercession, rather the entire body yearns for sleep.

We say from hard-earned experience that all who will major in intercession should live constantly on a diet. They should eat in a most controlled way. It is advisable that those who intend to pray at night should not eat anything after the midday meal. Even the midday meal should be light for the effects of a heavy lunch on mar the body for prayer even up to nine hours afterward.

For the serious intercessor who has decided to buffet his body and put it under control, he will do the following.

1. If the time of intercession is scheduled for 3:00-6:00 A.M., then there should be abstention from supper so that the body is not drowsy at the hours of intercession.
2. If the time of intercession is 6:00-9:00 a.m., there should be no breakfast taken.

3. If the time of intercession is from 3:00-6:00 P.M., there should be no eating at lunch time.
4. If this time of intercession is from 6:00-9:00 P.M., supper is of necessity eliminated. A light lunch may be permitted but, for the one who wants the best communion with God, lunch should be given up as well.
5. If a person intends to intercede throughout the night, he should withdraw from food throughout the day.

We shall discuss the relationship between prayer and fasting in a subsequent chapter. All we want to say here is that there is much-needed discipline with regard to food, no progress will be made in the School of Intercession. Lovers of food are not lovers of intercession. Each one must make his choice. He cannot choose to eat generously and also intercede abundantly. Someone has said that the way to the heart of a man is through his stomach (i.e., through food); however, the way to the heart of God is not through food. If anything, it is through *not* eating.

1. Decide first of all that gluttony is as bad a sin as adultery, theft, or murder. Face this squarely. Repent for all past acts of gluttony that were taken lightly. Repent for all the times that you ruined someone's relationship with God by causing him to commit the sin of gluttony. You may actually find that you can do with half the quantity of food you are normally given to eating. If you are overweight, you do not need second thoughts about the matter. You are living in sin. Repent or perish. The soul that continues to sin will die. The soul that continues to commit the sin of gluttony will die. Repent and bear the fruit of repentance. Repent and never commit the sin of gluttony again.
2. *Decide that you will eat in order to do the most important business on earth, which is prayer. Because that is so, you must ask*

yourself before any meal, "Will eating this meal help me to do the most important business on earth, which is intercession? What is the minimum amount of food that my body needs in order to make progress in the School of Intercession? How many meals can I avoid and not do myself harm as I progress in intercession?"

As you honestly ask these questions and face the answers, decide that you will accept the discipline that is needed to apply them to your life. Decide to apply them at once. Buffet your body. Decide to transform your body into a servant. It will rebel at the beginning and complain, but its complaining will not kill you. After you have forced it to obey once, twice, ten, twenty, and perhaps one hundred times, it will accept the new pattern and be at home with it.

1. For people who intercede at night we recommend a complete suspension of supper until the Lord comes. It is sad to know that the crowning event of each day, which many people look forward to throughout the day, is not meeting the Lord in prayer but meeting food! How can such people who focus every day on food even possess the desire to meet the Lord? How can they ever burn after Him when they burn after food?
2. Decide that you will never eat anything that you do not really need. Put an end to that biscuit, fruit, piece of meat, piece of cake, glass of juice, and the like that is taken as a habit between meals. These things help the body to develop indulgent tendencies. Put them all away. You will not die if you wait to eat at mealtime. As you well realize, your desire for these snacks is just the result of wrong habits that were formed in the past, perhaps unconsciously. Break the habit. Do not allow anything to enslave you. The apostle Paul wrote, *"All things are lawful for me, but not all things are helpful. All*

things are lawful for me but I will not be enslaved by anything" (*1 Corinthians 6:12*).

3. Decide that you will not eat and then take strong coffee or large quantities of coffee to keep awake to pray. As you might realized or will soon realize, there is a point reached where regardless of how much coffee a glutton drinks after much eating, he will nevertheless sleep.
4. Even if you do not sleep, a heavy stomach does not help you to intercede. As you know too well, gluttony is a sin. The glutton is out of touch with God even if he is awake and desires to intercede. His gluttony has separated him from the Lord. Prayer sessions that follow gluttonous meals are dull and the presence of God distant.
5. It is good to maintain intimate fellowship with God even after the time of intercession. Make sure that what is built-up between the Lord and you is not destroyed by food soon after the intercession has ended. You have finished with formal intercession, but you are going to continue to intercede informally. God is interested in both. Be holy for both.

I believe that it is now obvious that discipline with regard to food is indispensable to a life of intercession. Go and be disciplined. Ask the Lord to help you to be disciplined. Work out a programme of discipline and give yourself to it. Even if you tried to be disciplined with regard to food in the past and failed, do not give up. Try again. Even if you try again and fail, keep trying and keep crying to God for help. This morning as I was reading the Word, the following verses from Psalm 107 struck me. They encouraged and they challenged and blessed me. May they do the same to you as you labour to be disciplined.

> *They cried to the Lord in their trouble and he delivered them from their distress, he led them by a straight way, till they reached a city to dwell in.*

They cried to the Lord in their trouble, and he delivered them from their distress; he brought them out of darkness and gloom, and broke their bonds asunder.

Then they cried to the Lord in their trouble, and he delivered them from their distress; he sent forth his word, and healed them and delivered them from destruction.

Then they cried to the Lord in their trouble, and he delivered them from their distress, he made the storm be still, and the waves of the sea were hushed (Psalms 107:6-29).

Cry out to the Lord in your war with indiscipline over food. Cry out to the Lord in your desire to buffet your body and bring it under control. Cry out today. The Lord will hear you and deliver you from your distress. He will bring you out of the darkness of indiscipline and break the bonds of food over you. He is able. He is willing. He will do it.

RELATIONSHIPS

Each relationship that anyone cultivates has its power over the ones involved in it. There can be no relationships built without real involvement. We suggest that all who plan to make progress in the School of Intercession concentrate on building their relationship with God. They should cut down on the number of human relationships that they are deeply involved in.

If they are to bear the burdens of God, they cannot carry too many burdens of man. It is possible for the heart to be overweighed with burdens in such a way that deep intercession is impossible. It is possible for the spirit of man to be crushed by too many burdens.

This means that the serious intercessor will protect his heart. He will not throw it away to too many people. He will weigh everyone who demands his attention. He will be careful about building even a casual relationship. Because of his ministry (intercession) he will judge every relationship by its impact on his life of intercession. He will deliberately judge every relationship by an unchanging standard. *"Will it help me to make progress as an intercessor? Will it help me to satisfy the heart of God?"* It is obvious that when such questions are asked and honest answers received and applied, many relationships will have to go. Many purposeless visits will have to be abandoned. There may have to be many partings with the accompanying heartaches, but there will be a new sense of attachment to God and attachment to intercessors that will enhance progress in the practice of intercesion .

Of necessity therefore, the intercessor will be united with the Lord and cling to Him. He may also be united with another intercessor and may loosely cling to him. He will certainly be a man apart. He will be separated from many earthly joys and many earthly activities. He will, by choice, be a man apart, a man set apart, a lonely man, a man unto God, a man of God. In that way, be undistracted and will make rapid progress.

6
THE INTERCESSOR AND HARD WORK

"Go to the ant, O sluggard; consider her ways and be wise. Without having any chief officer or ruler, she prepares her food in summer and gathers her sustenance in harvest. How long will you lie there, O sluggard? When will you arise from your sleep? A little sleep, a little slumber, a little folding of the hands to rest, and poverty will come upon you like a vagabond, and want like an armed man" (Proverbs 6:6-11).

"The soul of the sluggard craves, and gets nothing, while the soul of the diligent is richly supplied" (Proverbs 13:4).

"I passed by the field of a sluggard, by the vineyard of a man without sense, and lo, it was all overgrown with thorns; the ground, was covered with nettles, and its stone wall was broken down. Then I saw and considered it. I looked and received instruction. A little sleep a little slumber, a little folding of the hands to rest, and poverty will come upon you like an armed man" (Proverbs 24:30-34).

"Love not sleep lest you come to poverty; open your eyes, and you will have plenty of bread" (Proverbs 20:13).

"Slothfulness casts into a deep sleep, and an idle person will suffer hunger" (Proverbs 19:15).

"The sluggard does not plow in the autumn; he will seek at harvest and have nothing" (Proverbs 20:4).

"But by the grace of God I am what I am, and his grace toward me was not in vain. On the contrary, I worked harder than any of them, though it was not I but the grace of God which is with me" (1 Corinthians 15:10).

"Him we proclaim, warning every man and teaching every man in all wisdom, that we may present every man mature in Christ. For this I toil, striving with all the energy which he mightily inspires within me" (Colossians 1:28-29).

"Continue steadfastly in prayer, being watchful in it with thanksgiving; and pray for us also that God may open to us a door for the word to declare the mystery of Christ, on account of which I am in prison, that I may make it clear, as I ought to speak" (Colossians 4:2-4).

"For you remember our labour and toil, brethren; we worked night and day, that we might not burden any of you, while we preached to you the gospel of God. You are witnesses, and God also, how holy and righteous and blameless was our behaviour to you believers" (1 Thessalonians 2:9-10).

"Pray constantly" (I Thessalonians 5:17).

"In all toil there is profit, but mere talk tends only to want" (Proverbs 14:23).

"Wealth hastily gotten will dwindle, but he who gathers little by little will increase it" (Proverbs 13:11).

> *"So we laboured at the work, and half of them held the spears from the break of dawn till the stars came out ... so neither I nor my brethren nor my servants nor the men of the guard who followed me, none of us took off our clothes; each kept his weapon in his hand"* (Nehemiah 4:21-23).

The world belongs to those who work hard. Those who will govern in the world to come are those who have learned to work hard now. There is nothing that God can do for the lazy. Anyone who is lazy and continues to be lazy is permanently ruined.

Below are the marks of the lazy:

1. They do not know how to decide. They are filled with indecision. They may toss a simple decision in their minds for hours, days, and weeks. They do not want to decide because they fear that decision will lead to action. Because they do not want to act, they hide behind indecision. Because of the constant practice of this form of escape, they build a personality that avoids decisions and no longer know that it is rooted in laziness.
2. They easily start projects but never complete them. They are carried away by novelty. New ideas, thoughts, projects, and programmes easily sweep them off their feet. They can stay on a project for as long as there are no difficulties. When difficulties come, instead of labouring to overcome them, they fly off to something else. The result is that a string of unfinished projects mark their pathway.
3. They are easily bored. The lack of courage to see a project through and the unwillingness to work hard unceasingly, make them into people who are easily bored with things, people, places, and so on. They are ever looking for the new. This is clear evidence of laziness, for this search for the new and thrilling separates them from

the hard work that awaits all who want to have a project completed.
4. They easily give excuses. Some hide their laziness by saying that they are "conceivers" and not "accomplishers." We acknowledge the fact that some have to "conceive" and others "accomplish," but most people who say that theirs is to conceive - to get things initiated for others to accomplish - are just hiding their laziness in beautiful words. They know what they are running away from - hard work.
5. They lack any real sense of priorities. The lazy prefer to do the things of no consequence first. They prefer to converse with someone before they read the Bible. They prefer to cook before they pray. They prefer to keep the house clean before they intercede. All those are marks of laziness, for priority issues demand more time, energy, sacrifice, suffering, and the lazy do not have any real desire to pay the price needed. Laziness makes them settle for the lesser issues first and they hardly ever come to the major ones. They major in minors!
6. The lazy do not want to plan. They will do everything not to set any goals or draw up a timetable. They do not want to do any of these because they will show up what they are. There-is nothing as revealing as goals that are set, written down, and not accomplished. There is nothing that shows a man who he is, like a timetable worked out, written down, and ignored completely. The lazy cannot accept any system that makes them accountable. They prefer to go according to their fluctuating feelings.

No lazy person can ever really become an intercessor before he has broken loose from the fetters of laziness. Are you lazy? Do not give a quick answer. Look at the marks of the lazy that you have just read and see if they are applicable to you. If one or more of them are applicable to you then you are lazy. You are lazy yet you want to intercede! Is there any hope for you? There is hope, however. The hope is for those who will follow God's prescription and be cured of their laziness. If you want to be cured of your laziness, follow the instructions below:

1. To the extent that you know yourself to be lazy, acknowledge your sin of laziness before the Lord. Say to Him, "Lord, I am lazy. My laziness is manifested in the following ways." Then list them down.
2. Ask the Lord to reveal to you His own impression of your laziness and the consequences of it. (This is necessary so that the lazy person may see things from the divine perspective.)
3. Wait before the Lord in silence. Continue to wait before Him in silence. He will soon show you what your laziness means to Him and what its impact is on the kingdom.
4. When you see things from God's perspective, you may be brought to repentance immediately or you may be inwardly unmoved.
5. If you are still inwardly unmoved, pray to the Lord. Say to Him, "Lord, my heart is wrong. It is twisted. I know that I am lazy and that it is a sin before You. However, because of my hardened heart, hardened by all the laziness of the past, I know no contrition or sorrow for my sin. Lord, I beg You to give me the gift of repentance. Grant to me, in Your mercy, that I will have the sacrifices that a sinner must offer to You in order to be forgiven: a broken and a contrite heart. Lord, give me a broken and contrite heart over my sin of laziness. Grant me the grace to repent and to manifest the repentance by a complete turning away from the sin of laziness and a complete consecration to You, to love You, to work hard, and thus never return to laziness anymore." If you are sincere, the

Lord will hear you and grant you the gift of repentance. You will so hate the sin of laziness that nothing will convince you to be lazy in the future. You will become awake, enlightened and all will be different. You will not be able to understand how you could have been so lazy in the past.

6. Those who repent must bear fruit that befits repentance. You must bear fruit that befits repentance. Such fruit must come from deliberate planning. If you do not plan to work hard, you will go back into the yoke of laziness. I am talking about "planning" and not "feeling." I am talking about "acting" and not "hoping," or "wishing."

Take your pen and notebook. Pray to the Lord for guidance. Then make the following decisions before your God. Make them solemnly, knowing that they will be binding on you perhaps for the rest of your life.

1. I divorce with laziness and will put in time to complete the following uncompleted projects of my life. (List down projects.)
2. Project one shall be finished by (date) and project two by (date).
3. I separate myself from sleep. Before, I have been having seven or eight hours of sleep. I have been a lover of sleep. From now on, I cut off two hours and will now sleep for five or six hours. The two hours gained will be invested in intercession. I will give myself to two hours of intercession every day. I will intercede according to the following programme:

> ***Monday:*** *From_____to_____*
> ***Tuesday:*** *From_____to_____*
> ***Wednesday:*** *From _____to_____*

4. And others.

Now that you have separated yourself from laziness and committed yourself to hard work, we shall go on with the message on hard work and the intercessor.

WHAT IS HARD WORK?

Hard work is both the commitment and the capacity to put in all the force of spirit, soul, and body to ensure that what must be done is done correctly, on time and according to plan. To work hard is to put all of oneself into a task that must be done and to keep at it until it is done. It is a commitment not to be put off by obstacles but to press on until the job is done. Hard work is that desire, motivated by the fact that a job is being done for the Lord of glory, to give every ounce of energy until it is done. It is the labouring, pressing on, toiling, and striving with a divine commission, taking no rest, until the task is finished, so that His approval is obtained.

THE INTERCESSOR AND HARD WORK

We know that the Lord Jesus was so caught up with praying in Gethsemane that He did not only sweat, but His sweat was as drops of blood. To labour until one is sweating is hard work. The intercessor is so desperate to have the thing he is interceding for go through that he puts everything in his intercession. He prays and prays. He pleads and pleads. He supplicates. He gives his reasons to the Lord. He explains. He leaves no stone unturned. He takes for granted that God knows nothing except what he, the intercessor, tells Him. Therefore, he tells Him everything in detail. It takes time but there can be no shortcuts. God must be told everything. The intercessor knows that what he has not told God may not be acted upon. So he goes on and on.

He may talk to the Lord until he has lost his voice. He must go on. When the voice is lost he must continue to intercede with groans and sighs, doing what the Holy Spirit is doing. If he runs short of arguments to present he must intercede in tongues. The mind will be unfruitful, but the spirit will continue the ministry. The intercessor may find all his body trembling, carried away with the burden and perhaps with emotion for the cause at stake, but he must go on. He may feel that he will faint the next moment if he continues to intercede, but he must go on and if necessary faint in God's presence. God will lift him up.

An advancing intercessor may have to spend eight, twelve, eighteen or twenty-four hours in God's presence in toil and labour. He may have to continue at the same rhythm the next day without any rest. He may have to go on at that pace for forty days before he wins victory. The only thing that will matter to him is the fact that someone or some people or some cause is at stake, and that if he does not labour before God, disaster will come. Taken up so completely in that way, he would consider the pains and agonies endured of little consequence, provided the victory is won.

Moses spent forty days fasting on the mountain before God when he came back he found disaster in the camp of Israel. On the one hand, he was weak, very weak from his forty days of absolute fasting. On the other hand Israel was in such a mess that unless something was done, Israel would perish. What was he to do? He risked his health and immediately started another forty days of fasting while he laboured with God for them to be forgiven. He thus manifested what all true intercessors must manifest - a spirit of sacrifice. They are prepared to risk health, family, fortune, and all so that victory may be won through intercession. Had Moses been a man who was not used to hard work, he would not have taken the second fast of forty days to intercede for Israel. God did not call him to it. He decided to do it for his people. He lay prostrate before the Lord during all forty days! It was far from easy. It was far from comfortable. It was lonely. The only comfort and cheer that he knew was that which radiated from God's presence. Had he not been a man who had cultivated the art of being in God's presence, he would have failed, for how would he have survived being "locked up with Him" and with Him alone for forty days? Had he been a man who could not sustain a conversation with God for hours, the forty days would have been a nightmare. Had he not been a man who could endure pain and agony, he could not have borne the pain of maintaining the same posture before God for forty days.

One thing seems to come out clearly. The person who will go far with God in the ministry of intercession must be tough-minded and build a tough body. He must say a final good-bye to all that is called earthly comfort or comfort on earth. He must learn to buffet his body and to bring it under control. He must deliberately choose the harder and rougher way in each situation. He must never ask, "What will make me comfortable or what will put me at ease?" He must ask, "What will enable me to win the battle now? What will help me to prepare for the battles of tomorrow, next week, next year, the coming years?"

By asking the right questions and receiving the right answers and by rigorously applying oneself to hard work, the intercessor will find that the body is not an enemy but a servant to be used. The process of taming is often painful but when the pain is endured the body is converted into a servant that can cooperate with the spirit and the soul of man to do things that would ordinarily have been thought impossible.

We recommend that all would-be intercessors submit their bodies to austere discipline. We recommend that they put an end to all disease and all indulgence. We recommend that they buffet their bodies, appetites, likes and dislikes, and so build the bodies that will be useful in the intercessional battles of the future. We insist that now is the time to act. It will be impossible to continue in indulgence and then win when the battle is on.

We have already said something about cutting down on sleeping time. What we said was for the beginner. Some of us have been able to discipline our bodies to function properly for many years on three to four hours of sleep daily and we consider that we are still in the "School of Discipline" as far as sleep is concerned. We read of a worldly man who occupied the highest post in his nation and who was so caught up with the affairs of his nation that in two years he never slept more than two hours any day. We believe that that is an example to emulate. We consider that the one who recommends eight hours of sleep each night for would-be intercessors is preparing them for disaster. They will sleep while the enemy destroys the sheep. They will sleep while the anger of God consumes the people who have sinned.

It is said that the heights that great men reached and kept were not attained by sudden flight. It was while their companions slept that they kept toiling upward into the sky. The intercessor is one of those great men who keeps toiling upward into the sky while the non-intercessors sleep.

God has used people who were varied in gifts, natural endowments, temperaments, education, and the like. However, all whom God has used in a sustained way had two things in common. They loved God and they worked very hard. God can cause miracles to be performed through anyone for some time, but for sustained usefulness to God and man, hard work is indispensable.

The commitment to hard work causes a man who is faint to keep pursuing. It was said of Gideon, "And Gideon came to the Jordan and passed over, he and the three hundred men who were with him, faint yet pursuing" (Judges 8:4). They had battled the whole night. They were faint from hard work but as long as there was work to do, they kept pressing on even though they were tired. They were overcomers.

Everyone who has clearly been involved in intercession alone knows that a point is reached when all of one's being wants to give way under the burden. The cry of the entire body is, "stop and rest." Everyone who has ever truly warred in intercession also knows that to yield to the demands of the body and take the rest demanded, or even needed, is to tail, for things can no longer be the same after the break. What happens is that those moments when the body reacts as if it will break are crucial points in the battle. The forces of the enemy are attacking and they are attacking most furiously, in self-defence and to cause the intercessor to stop hitting hard. They are also most vulnerable then. If the intercessor presses on in intercession, not giving in to the demands of his tired body, he can inflict great harm on Satan and win a position before God. However, should he stop to rest, he will find afterward that upon returning to intercede things are no longer the same. The enemy took the break time to strengthen himself, receive reinforcement, and change the strategy for resistance so much that the battle may either be prolonged or lost completely. For this reason, once the battle has begun, the intercessor must press on to victory. He will be faint but he must continue to pursue. He must take no rest until the battle is won.

The other side of the matter is that God governs the universe on the basis of sacrifice. We see this demonstrated on the Cross. God chose a way to salvation that cost Him the very best that He had. God made a supreme sacrifice when He sent the Christ into the world. In dying on the Cross, the Lord Jesus made a supreme sacrifice of Himself. All that God did and does is at great cost. Because this is so, God honours those who are "faint yet pursuing." He blesses those who sacrifice; those who work hard; those who give their all. He passes by the lovers of ease and luxury. He will do no permanent work through those who hold back anything that they could put in.

Because intercession is the greatest work in the world and from the throne, those who intercede must work hard. They must put all of themselves and they must invest their energies into it. They must risk their lives, health, and all. They must run away from those whose cry is, "Take care of your health. Sleep enough. Do not become old in childhood." They must be prepared to be loners. They must be prepared to be misunderstood. They must desire God's best and they must press on at any cost, until He has given them His best.

This means that they must press on even when they are tired. They must press on even when they are weak. They must press on even when they are sleepy. They must overcome sleep by walking around while interceding. They must overcome sleep by going out of the house into the garden or yard and there interceding. They must overcome sleep by going out on a ten-kilometre intercession walk. They must overcome sleep by putting their feet in a basin of cold water and thereby continuing to intercede. They must do everything to keep awake. They must never say, "I will sleep first and then will intercede better." That is a formula for defeat. It is from the enemy. It will lead to failure because it places sleep ahead of intercession. It places self-pleasing ahead of the Lord's battles.

They must hearken to the Lord's injunction which says:

> *Upon your walls, O Jerusalem, I have set watchmen; all the day and all the night they shall never be silent. You who put the Lord in remembrance, take no rest, and give him no rest until he establishes Jerusalem and makes it a praise in the earth (Isaiah 62:6-7).*

An intercessor is a watchman. God commands you not to be silent the whole day and the whole night. He admonishes you to take no rest and to give Him no rest. He cannot go back on this admonition. It is for you to ask Him for a body that can go on night and day, taking no rest and giving Him no rest until the burden of intercession that He has laid on your heart has been discharged and until what He placed in your heart to ask has been done. God is prepared to make the natural supernatural. He did it for Moses. He had two forty-day fasts without food or water, without any recovery period between the two. God temporally made him supernatural. He can do this for you. He will do this for you if you ask and are willing to put in all that you have and all that you are, holding nothing back.

Begin now!

I recommend that you write down here, twenty things that you will do this moment to work hard in intercession. They could include:

1. I will spend three hours in intercession on Wednesday instead of watching television, visiting friends, or receiving visitors.
2. I will wake up every day at 3:00 a.m. in order to intercede for one hour before I have my morning encounter with God in meditation.
3. I will go on a ten-kilometre walk twice a week, and during that walk, which will be from___ to __ on Mondays and from _____ to ____ on Fridays, I will pray for the five hundred backsliders who are on my prayer list and also for the five hundred unsaved people who are on my list.

7
THE INTERCESSOR AND COURAGE

Intercessors must be courageous people. There are three areas in which they must manifest courage. They must have courage before God; they must have courage with regard to themselves, and they must have courage with regard to the object of intercession.

COURAGE GODWARDS

The intercessor will labour to live a holy life. He will deliberately and obviously separate himself from all sin. However, when he appears before God, he will still remember that he is a creature before the Creator. He is coming to ask God not to execute some course of action that is certainly right. For example, when a person, family, or nation sins and an intercessor has to plead for them to be forgiven, there is a sense in which it could seem to say that God is not considerate; that the intercessor is kinder than God and bears the people more on his heart than God bears them. When an intercessor has to cry out night and day for the salvation of some erring soul, it would seem as if he cares and God does not. Such thoughts could have very paralyzing effects on the intercessor. They could make him lose heart and to give up intercession. Nevertheless, he must not lose heart. He must press on. He must be very courageous.

The intercessor needs to remember that it is God Himself who instituted the ministry of intercession. He must remember that God has called him to intercede and that intercession, far from accusing God, glorifies Him. He must remember that intercession is an act of obedience and that those who love Him, obey Him and intercede. Every intercessor must bear in mind God has condescended to make him a co-labourer with Himself and that as a co-worker with God, God is graciously waiting to be given instructions, yea, commanded by man. It is, therefore, compulsory tor the intercessor to move ahead and command God so as to bring the waiting of God to an end.

The boldness of the intercessors of the Bible is astounding. Moses said to God,

"Turn from thy fierce wrath, and repent of this evil against thy people" (Exodus 32:12).

He again commanded the Lord, "Pardon the iniquity of this people, I pray thee, according to the greatness of thy steadfast love, and according as thou hast forgiven this people, from Egypt until now" (Numbers 14:19).

Moses was courageous and bold to ask God questions. It is as if he was taking God to task. He asked, "O Lord, why does thy wrath burn hot against thy people, whom thou has brought out of Egypt with great power and with a mighty hand?" (Exodus 32:11).

He gave God an ultimatum,

> "Alas, this people have sinned a great sin; they have made for themselves gods of gold. But now, if thou wilt forgive their sin, and if not, blot me, I pray thee, out of thy book which thou hast-written" (Exodus 32:31-32).

Each intercessor must come before God with boldness. He must be very courageous. He has nothing of his own to give him the merit. However, he must nevertheless come. God calls him to come. God calls him to draw near. God calls him to command Him. God waits to be commanded. God has asked him to ask and it will be given to him. God is desperate to have intercessors. He wants to save but there is a sense in which He cannot save without the cooperation of an intercessor. He wants to do great things but He cannot do them without the cooperation of the intercessor who asks Him to do them. God has unbound in heaven but heaven's unbinding is not enough. The intercessor must also bind on earth what God has bound in heaven but what He has bound will remain unbound in practice until the intercessor rises up and binds on earth. He has set people free, but they cannot enter into their freedom until the intercessor rise's up and proclaims what He has already brought to pass. When that is done, the effects will be seen. The intercessor has the holy duty to be bold. He must be very courageous.

He surely knows the God he is dealing with. He knows His greatness. However, he must rise and boldly do what God commands. In this way he will satisfy the heart of God.

My dear intercessor, do not be afraid. Cast away your fear.

God says, to you,

> "Ask of me, and I will make the nations your heritage, and the ends of the earth your possession" (Psalms 2:8).

The Lord Jesus complained,

> *"Hitherto you have asked nothing in my name; ask, and you will receive that your joy may be full"* (John 16:24).

It will certainly be said to the Lord about the intercessor,

> *"Thou hast given him his heart's desire, and has not withheld the request of his lips. For thou dost meet him with goodly blessings, thou dost set a crown of fine gold upon his head. He asked life of thee; thou gavest it to him, length of days for ever and ever. His glory is great through thy help, splendour and majesty thou dost bestow upon him, Yea, thou dost make him most blessed for ever; thou dost make him glad with the joy of thy presence"* (Psalms 21:2-6).

I know that you are aware of the exceeding greatness of God; however, come to Him, for you satisfy His heart by coming. It is His will; His burning desire that you come to Him and intercede. Do not delay. The Lord has encouraged people to move ahead and do great things for Him and for themselves. I believe that because intercession is the greatest work that anyone can do for God or for man, God does also encourage the intercessor. The Lord says to you today as Moses said to the spies,

> *"Be of good courage, and bring some of the fruit of the land"* (Numbers 13:20).

You, too, should be of good courage and bring some fruit of the Land of intercession for the glory of God and the blessing of His people.

The words of the Lord to Joshua are also addressed to you, intercessor. He was to take the land physically through physical warfare. You are to take the land and the people of the land through intercessional warfare. He needed courage. You, too, need courage. The Lord said to him and says to you,

THE INTERCESSOR AND COURAGE

> "Go over this Jordan, and all this people [fellow intercessors], into the land which I am giving to them, to the people of Israel. Every place that the sole of your foot will tread upon [in intercession] I have given you, as I promised to Moses. From the wilderness and this Lebanon as far as the great river, the river Euphrates, all the land of the Hittites to the great Sea toward the going down of the sun shall be your territory [from North pole to the South pole, where ever the curse is found, whenever there are people for whom My Son died]. No man shall be able to stand before you all the days of your life; as I was with Moses, so I will be with you [as I was with the Lord Jesus, so I will be with you]; I will not fail you or forsake you. Be strong and of good courage; for you will cause this people to inherit the land which I swore to their fathers to give them [for you will cause those for whom you intercede to inherit my salvation and the fullness which I gave them in Christ]. Only be strong and very courageous, being careful to do according to all the law, which Moses, my servant, commanded you [which Jesus My Son commanded you]; turn not from it to the right hand or to the left, that you may have good success [in intercession] wherever you go. This book of the law shall not depart out of your mouth, but you shall meditate on it day and night, that you may be careful to do according to all that is written in it; for then you shall make your way prosperous, and then you shall have good success [in intercession]. Have I not commanded you? Be strong and of good courage; be not frightened, neither be dismayed; for the Lord your God is with you wherever you go" (Joshua 1:2-9).

I find something interesting here. The Lord commands the intercessor to intercede. He commands him to be very courageous. He commands him not to fear (to ask for big things). He assures him that wherever the sole of his foot will tread, has already been given to him. God has done all and then commands. The intercessor is called in turn to command God to act. If the intercessor obeys the command of God, then he can be sure that when he commands God, God will obey him. To me this is a most wonderful thing - that the obedient intercessor will be obeyed by

God; that the intercessor who yields to God's command will in turn be yielded to by God!

COURAGE TOWARDS HIMSELF

As a person draws nearer to the Lord, he becomes increasingly aware of his unworthiness. This is clearly demonstrated in the life of the apostle Paul. Earlier on, he boastfully said,

> *"And those who were reputed to be something [what they were makes no difference to me; God shows no partiality], those, I say, who were of repute added nothing to me; but on the contrary, when they saw that I had been entrusted with the gospel to the uncircumcised, just as Peter had been entrusted with the gospel to the circumcised [for he who worked through Peter for the mission to the circumcised worked through me also for the Gentiles], and when they perceived the grace that was given to me, James and Cephas and John, who were reputed to be pillars, gave to me and Barnabas the right hand of fellowship, that we should go to the Gentiles and they to the circumcised"* (Galatians 2:6-10).

Later on he said,

> *"For I am the least of the apostles, unfit to be called an apostle, because I persecuted the church of God"* (1 Corinthians 15:9).

Later on he said,

> *"The saying is sure and worthy of full acceptance, that Christ Jesus came into the world to save sinners. And I am the foremost of sinners"* (1 Timothy 1:15-16).

Who could approach the glory of God and not cry out with Isaiah,

> *"Woe is me! For I am lost; for I am a man of unclean lips, and I dwell in the midst of a people of unclean lips; for my eyes have seen the King, the Lord of hosts!" (Isaiah 6:5).*

The intercessor cannot intercede from a distance. He must come into the very presence of God. He must tune in to God. He must be vitally united, welded, fused to God. It is only from such union that he can truly flow towards God. The question then arises, "How can someone who is the foremost of sinners ever intercede?" How can someone who knows a very deep sense of inner unworthiness ever come into the presence of God to plead for another?

The answer to this question is twofold. First of all, no intercessor dares to come on his own merit. He must come on the merit of another. God has graciously provided the merits of Another so that the intercessor can come. His Word says,

> *"He has appeared once for all at the end of the age to put away sin by the sacrifice of himself" (Hebrews 9:26).*
>
> *"For by a single offering he has perfected for all time those who are sanctified" (Hebrews 10:14).*

The word of the Lord continues to proclaim God's mind saying,

> *"And the Holy Spirit also bears witness to us," for after saying, "This is the covenant that I will make with them after those days, says the Lord; I will put my laws on their hearts, and write them on their minds," then he adds,*
>
> *"I will remember their sins and their misdeeds no more. Where there is forgiveness of these, there is no longer any offering for sin " (Hebrews 10:14-18).*

The Word of God continues to proclaim God's position and it invites you, the intercessor saying,

> *"Therefore, brethren, since we have confidence to enter the sanctuary by the blood of Jesus, by the new and living way which he opened for us through the curtain, that is, through his flesh, and since we have a great priest over the house of God, let us draw near with a true heart in full assurance of faith, with our hearts sprinkled Clean from an evil conscience and our bodies washed with pure water. Let us hold fast the confession of our hope without wavering, for he who promised is faithful"* (Hebrews 10:19-23).

You are certainly unworthy on your own. Another imparts to you His worthiness. Do not enter God's presence on your own merit. Stand in Christ; put on Christ and then come into His presence and you will be accepted. Confess to Him your lack of any personal merit. Accept the merit of the Lord Jesus and boldly come. Say to the Father, and to the accusing demons,

> *"I have no merit of my own. However, I have that of Jesus and with His merit I will enter God's presence and intercede. I will be as bold as Jesus. Putting on the merit of Jesus, I will approach the Father not as a sinner but as one who has been made worthy to stand in the gap. Because of the merit of Jesus, I am apart from the lost. I am apart from the saints who are failing. I can call on God on their behalf. Since I can, I will. Since I will, I begin now."*

When the devil accuses falsely, say to him, *"Depart from me you liar."* When he raises a point where you have actually failed, do not discuss it with him. Tell him, *"That is between my Father and myself. You have no part in it. Be gone."*

There are other grounds on which you as an intercessor can come to the Lord on behalf of others. One of these is that God has not called perfect people to intercede. He has called blameless people. As long as you are not knowingly living in sin, you are qualified. The Bible says of Elijah,

> *"Elijah was a man of like nature with ourselves and he prayed fervently that it might not rain, and for three years and six months it did not rain on the earth. Then he prayed again and the heaven gave rain, and the earth brought forth its fruit" (James 5:17-18).*

Elijah was not perfect. He could be discouraged and he was once discouraged. However, he obeyed God. He was courageous. He boldly challenged the prophets of Baal. He boldly asked water to be poured on the bull he was sacrificing. He courageously asked that a trench be dug around it and be filled with water. He boldly called on God and God answered him. Afterwards, he courageously gathered all the prophets of Baal and slew them! God calls you to be as Elijah.

The other reason why you should be courageous is that you are not a mere mortal. You are a god. The Bible says,

> *"You are the sons of the Lord your God" (Deuteronomy 14:1).*

> *"I say, Ye are gods, sons of the Most High, all of you" (Psalms 82:6).*

> *"What is man that thou art mindful of him, and son of man that thou care for him? Yet thou hast made him a little less than God, and dost crown him with glory and honour. Thou hast given him dominion over the works of thy hands; thou hast put all things under his feet" (Psalms 8:4-6).*

You are a god. Boldly come into the presence of God. You are a son of God. Boldly come into your Father's presence. You are a little less than God, come into the presence of your God.

You are accepted into His presence. Do not be put off by any sense of personal inadequacy. Do not confess your inadequacy when the Lord has made you adequate. In fact He has exalted you and made you a god. You are more than mortal. You are a god. Come now.

COURAGE TOWARDS THE OBJECT OF INTERCESSION

There will be situations in which the intercessor could ask,

> *"Is it right for me to ask God to pardon this person or this people? Is it right for me to ask God to bless this person or this people? Am I not asking God to thwart justice? Am I not asking God to cover sin with blessing?"*

Such questions may come up in the heart of the intercessor. I know them from my own experience. There are times when I have wondered whether it was not a sin to ask God to bless a nation that was given to hypocrisy. There have been times when I felt like crying out with the prophet Amos,

> *"Let justice roll down like water" (Amos 5:24).*

Three things have kept me back. First of all, I have known times in my own walk with God during which I have failed Him hopelessly. I deserved His worst yet I did not call for justice but pleaded for mercy. I can only do to others what I do to myself - plead for mercy even during the most desperate and deliberate rebellion from God. Secondly, to plead for a righteous people is not intercession. An intercessor really comes in when the situation is most hopeless. When people are walking with God and obeying Him from the heart, they do not need intercession. If one is to intercede, a people who have failed and deserve judgment provide room for the ministry. And lastly, the intercessors of the Bible pleaded for people who were given to erring from God. Moses interceded,

> *"If now I have found favour in thy sight, Lord, let the Lord, I pray thee, go in the midst of us, although it is a stiff-necked people; and pardon our iniquity and our sin and take us for thy inheritance"* (Exodus 34:9).

The people had sinned. They had not repented. They were still a stiff-necked people. Nevertheless Moses was pleading that God would go in the midst of them, take the stiff-necked people for His inheritance even though they had not ceased to be stiff-necked. He pleaded that God would pardon a stiff-necked people even though they had not yet repented and stopped their sinning.

There are a number of things that issue from here. First of all, the intercessor is inseparably bound up with the people for whom he is interceding. Their sin has become his sin and their destiny his destiny. Therefore, the matter of asking if he will intercede is out of the question. It is like asking if he will beg God to have mercy on him. If he has indeed become an intercessor for them, he will labour not only to save them, but also to save himself, for as their intercessor, he is one with them and if they perish, he, too, perishes. In the second place, every person who has ever walked with God knows that if He only forgives sins that were repented of, there will be no hope for anyone. There are so many sins that are forgiven by the Lord without the sinners repenting. It is only on that basis that anyone can have hope. God does forgive while He waits for repentance to follow. Am I being a heretic? I hope not. I only believe and I know that God has forgiven me many times and continued to walk and lead me long before He opened my eyes to the fact that I had sinned. I want to be very honest with you. There have been times when my sin was shown to me and I either lacked the power to put it away or I was unwilling to put it away immediately. I can only say that although, I deserved to have been abandoned from that point on, God nevertheless bore with me, forgave me, came along with me, spoke to me and through me, and wooed me to repentance. As His love conquered me, I was led to deep repentance and a forsaking of my sin. I know this too well in my own experience that somehow it makes sense to intercede that God should forgive a people who are not yet repentant. He does this so that as they experience His forgiveness, they will see the folly of their sin and run away from it.

This being the case, the intercessor can be very courageous before God. He can ask that the people be forgiven any sin that they have committed. He can insist. He can argue with God. He can command God. He can ask God if that is the only sin in the world. He can ask God if He has never forgiven people who have done such a thing. He can ask God if that particular sin was not covered by that single offering by which Christ perfected for all time those who are sanctified. He can ask God why He is looking at the sinner directly instead of looking at him through the finished work of Christ. Thus the intercessor can be very bold and very courageous.

The intercessor's courage and boldness do not only apply to pleading for mercy for those who have sinned. The intercessor is not only to stand in the gap so that God should not destroy. He is also to stand in the gap so that God should bless. The question then arises as to what extent the intercessor should ask God to bless a man, a family, a city, or a nation. The answer to that, we think, is twofold. First of all the intercessor should, in a general sense, ask all that the Word has promised for those concerned. Take for example the portion of the Bible that says,

> *"May the God of peace himself sanctify you wholly; and may your spirit and soul and body be kept sound and blameless at the coming of our Lord Jesus Christ. He who calls you is faithful, and he will do it"* (1 Thessalonians 5:23-24).

The intercessor can ask that the person be blameless in spirit, soul, and body. He can ask that the person never sin. He can ask that the person should love the Lord with all his heart. He could ask that he be in perfect physical health. He could ask that he be blessed materially. There is no limit to what the intercessor can ask for the one or the ones for whom he is interceding. He should not stop short of asking for God's best. For example, it would be quite in order to pray that everyone in a family be saved. There is nothing like asking too much. The intercessor who makes a list of the people in a city and labours in prayer for the salvation of each is being faithful. After all, who in that city was not included in the atonement? Who in that city will the Father reject when he repents? Because of the limitlessness of the atonement, there is intercession for all and all can be saved.

The second aspect as to how far an intercessor can ask God to bless a man, a family, a city, or a nation depends on the *rhema* of God. The intercessor will pray generally but he will also pray specifically. He will wait on God and have God reveal to him the needs of the person or persons that He (God) intends to meet. Having seen what God wants to do and what God will do, he will then labour in intercession so that God's will, will come to pass. There is a sense in which an intercessor is a person who has seen what God intends to do and unites his will with God's will to labour by prayer that what God has in mind might come to pass. He is a proclaimer, through prayer, of God's will. The eye of the intercessor then is fixed not primarily on the needs of man but on what God has in mind to do. The intercessor then is a co-labourer with God, labouring by prayer to ensure that God's will is brought to pass. This gives added grounds for boldness before God. Having seen the plans of God to bless a person, a people or a place, he then comes before the Lord and labours that it be done. We can clearly say that the greatest intercessors stem out of revelation.

What God wills to do for someone else revealed to a person → ← **God's will prayed back to Him for action**

Intercession

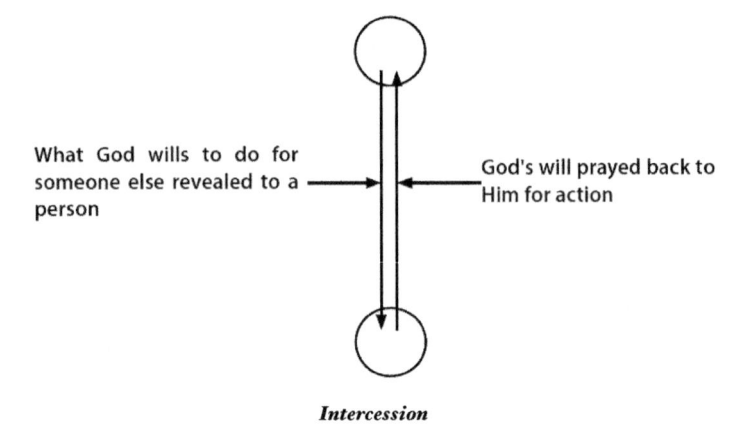

When a person has seen what God has purposed to do, how can he not be bold in prayer? Having seen what the Lord wants to do, how can he be vague? Having seen what God intends to do, how can he stop short of seeing it come to pass? We can say that revelation leads to intercession. God's will must be known and then prayed through with utter boldness.

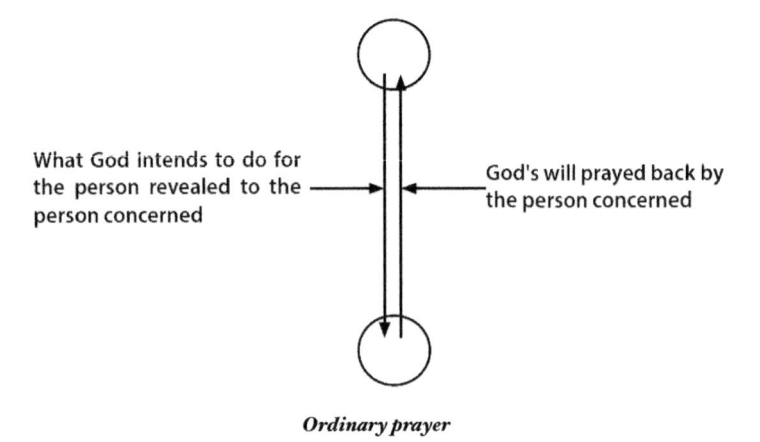

What God intends to do for the person revealed to the person concerned → ← **God's will prayed back by the person concerned**

Ordinary prayer

There will be times when intercession is not the fruit of revelation. However, all intercessors should labour to know God, live in His immediate presence, hear His voice, know His will, and pray it through to realization. Their boldness and courage will come out of this firm assurance that what they are asking is God's will and that He will do it. The intercessor is fully persuaded that God is so committed to His will that if he (the intercessor) only cooperates, that His will, will come to pass.

TWO EXAMPLES OF INTERCESSORS' COURAGE

Elijah and the Rain

"After many days the word of the Lord came to Elijah, in the third year, saying, 'Go, show yourself to Ahab, and I will send rain upon the earth.' So Elijah went to show himself to Ahab" (1 Kings 18:1-2).

"And Elijah said to Ahab, 'Go up, eat and drink; for there is a sound of the rushing of rain.' So Ahab went up to eat and to drink. And Elijah went up to the top of Carmel; and bowed himself down upon the earth, and put his face between his knees. And he said to his servant, 'Go up now, look toward the sea.' And he went up and looked, and said, 'There is nothing.' And he said, 'Go again seven times.' And at the seventh time he said, 'Behold, a little cloud like a man's hand is rising out of the sea.' And he said, 'Go up, say to Ahab, "Prepare your chariot and go down, lest the rain stop you."' And in a little while the heavens grew black with clouds and wind, and there was a great rain" (1 Kings 18:41-45).

God gave Elijah the revelation.

Elijah bowed himself in intercession.

Elijah continued in intercession until what God had revealed came to pass.

Praise the Lord!

David and the House

"Now when David dwelt in his house, David said to Nathan the prophet, Behold, I dwell in a house of cedar, but the ark of the covenant of the Lord is under a tent. And Nathan said to David, Do all that is in your heart, for God is with you. But that same night the word of the Lord came to Nathan, 'Go and tell my servant David, Thus says the Lord: You shall not build me a house to dwell in. For I have not dwelt in a house since the day I led up Israel to this day, but I have gone from tent to tent and from dwelling to dwelling. In all places where I have moved with Israel, did I speak a word with any of the judges of Israel, whom I commanded to shepherd my people, saying, Why have you not built me a house of cedar? Now therefore thus shall you say to my servant David, Thus says the Lord of hosts, I took you from the pasture, from following the sheep, that you should be prince over my people Israel; and I have been with you wherever you went, and have cut off all your enemies from before you; and I will make for you a name, like the name of the great ones of the earth. And I will appoint a place for my people Israel, and will plain them, that they may dwell in their own place, and be disturbed no more and violent men shall waste them no more, as formerly, from the time that I appointed judges over my people Israel; and I will subdue all your enemies, moreover, I declare to you that the Lord will build you a house. When your days are fulfilled to go to be with your fathers, I will raise up your offspring after you, one of your own sons, and I will establish his kingdom'" (1 Chronicles 17:1-11).

"Then King David went in and sat before the Lord, and said, Who am I, O Lord God, and what is my house, that thou hast brought me thus far? And this was a small thing in thy eyes, O God; thou has also spoken of thy servant's house for a great while to come, and hast shown me future generations, O Lord God! And what more can David say to thee for honouring thy servant? For thou knowest thy servant. For thy servant's

sake, O Lord, and according to thy heart, thou hast wrought all this greatness, in making known all these great things. There is none like thee,, O Lord, and there is no God besides thee, according to all that we have heard with our ears" (1 Chronicles 17:16—20).

"And now, O Lord, let the word which thou hast spoken concerning thy servant and concerning his house be established for ever, and do as thou has spoken; and thy name will be established, and magnified for ever, saying, The Lord of hosts, the God of Israel, is Israel's God, and the house of thy servant David will be established before thee. For thou my God has revealed to thy servant that thou wilt build a house for him; therefore thy servant has found courage to pray before thee. And now, O Lord, thou art God, and thou hast promised this good thing to thy servant; now therefore may it please thee to bless the house of thy servant, that it may continue for ever before thee; for what thou, O Lord, has blessed is blessed for ever" (1 Chronicles 17:23-27).

A number of things come out clearly here:

1. David wanted, on his own, to build a house for the Lord. This thought originated in him. It was human goodness. It was sacrificial, but it was not of God. The motive was good but it was not of God. The purpose was good but it did not originate in God. Real prayer and real intercession must have their origin in God. They must be God's will. All else is useless for God. The best that originates in man is useless before God.
2. God refused that which originated in David and instead revealed to David that He (the Lord) would build a house for him.
3. David on hearing this did not go away rejoicing. He went in and sat before the Lord, humbled himself before Him, praised and extolled His name and then laboured in prayer that all that God had promised would come to

pass. He could not pray clearly, but for the fact that "Thou hast wrought all this greatness, in making known these great things" (1 Chronicles 17:17). Prayer and intercession must begin where God has made things to be known.

4. David pleaded, "And now, O Lord, let the word which thou hast spoken concerning thy servant and concerning his house be established for ever, and do as thou hast spoken" (1 Chronicles 17:23). Prayer, intercession is a labour that the word *(rhema)* which God has spoken concerning a servant, a people, a place, should be established. It is insistence with God that He (the Lord) might do as He has spoken. It is as if God is under obligation to do what He has spoken, but only when there is an intercessor to "force" Him to do so!

5. David continued to plead, "For thou, my God, hast revealed to thy servant that thou wilt build a house for him; therefore thy servant has found courage to pray before thee" (1 Chronicles 17:25). Courage to pray and to intercede come mainly from the fact that the one praying or interceding has had God's will revealed to him and he is praying according to that will.

IN CONCLUSION

The intercessor then knowing God's will commits himself to labour until it is done. He will be courageous and pray even if the outward evidence shows that the person (or persons) is deteriorating as he intercedes. For example, a person may become apparently more resistant to God as the intercessor presses on. He must be courageous and not give up. He must press on even when God seems to have turned a deaf ear to his praying. He must press on even when he seems to see no hope. He must hope against hope and continue to intercede. He must continue even when people say to him, "Where is your God?" He must press on even when the devil tells him, "This is a hopeless situation." He must press on even when the flesh tells him, "This is a waste of time." He must press on even if he has laboured at it and grown grey in the process. He must press on until victory is won, for having heard God, having known His will, retreat is impossible. He must go on because victory must come! Praise the Lord!

THE INTERCESSOR AND THE DEVIL

Intercession would be a relatively easier job if we only had our heavenly Father to deal with. The reality is that we also have our deadly enemy to deal with. In fact, intercession is pleading with God for others and putting the enemy to nought as far as others are concerned. Anyone who does not ask God to avenge the enemy with regard to someone, some people, some places, is only doing a part of the job of intercession.

In the last chapter, we said that intercession was having a revelation of the will of God and praying that will through.

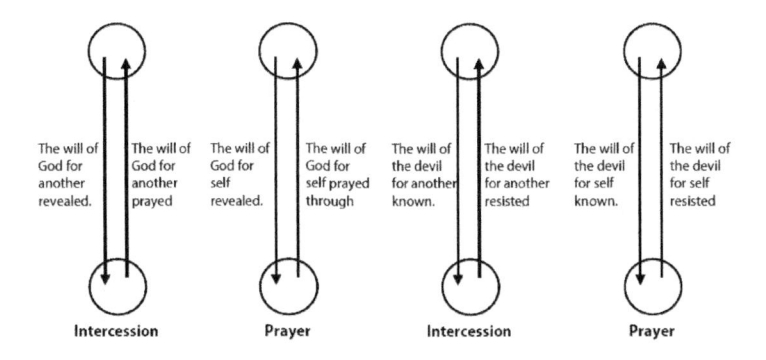

The will of God for another revealed.	The will of God for another prayed	The will of God for self revealed.	The will of God for self prayed through	The will of the devil for another known.	The will of the devil for another resisted	The will of the devil for self known.	The will of the devil for self resisted
Intercession		Prayer		Intercession		Prayer	

We add here that intercession is knowing the will or plans of the devil against another and labouring to resist those plans. Intercession is knowing what the devil plans to do and attacking him first he has time to attack.

I confess that I did not deal with the devil in prayer or intercession early in my prayer life. I grew up in spiritual circles where prayer and intercession dealt only with God. It is only in recent years that the Lord has begun to open my eyes to this fact. The truth is that since we have a heavenly Father, we also have a deadly enemy. There is the Father's will that must be known and prayed through to accomplishment. There is another will, the enemy's will, the devil's will, which he wants to impose on us and on others. If he is not opposed or attacked, he will bring that will to pass. Every believer has God's will for his life to seek and know. He also knows that there is the devil's will for his life which must be sought, known and resisted. The intercessor knows that there is God's will for the object of intercession and he labours with God in intercession that it might be brought to pass. He also knows that there is the enemy's will for the object of intercession which must be sought, known, and resisted.

The matter of the enemy's will is shown in the Lord's teaching. He said,

> "And there was a widow in that city who kept coming to him and saying, Vindicate me against my adversary" (Luke 18:3).

Yes, there was an enemy against whom she sought vindication.

AN IMPORTANT DIFFERENCE

The woman came to the judge and pleaded that she be vindicated. That was good for her. The Lord has not asked us to come to

Him and plead with Him to do something against the devil's will. Instead, He says to us what He said to the twelve:

> *"Behold, I have given you authority to tread upon serpents and scorpions, and over all the power of the enemy; and nothing shall hurt you"* (Luke 10:19).

The Bible admonishes us,

> *"Resist the devil and he will flee from you"* (James 4:7).

> *"Give no opportunity to the devil"* (Ephesians 4:27).

> *"Put on the whole armour of God, that you may be able to stand against the wiles of the devil. For we are not contending against flesh and blood, but against the principalities, against the powers, against the world rulers of this present darkness, against the spiritual hosts of wickedness in the heavenly places. Therefore, take the whole armour of God, that you may be able to withstand in the evil day, and having done all, to stand. Stand therefore, having put on the breastplate of righteousness, and having shod your feet with the equipment of the gospel of peace; besides all these, taking the shield of faith, with which you can quench all the flaming darts of the evil one. And take the helmet of salvation, and the sword of the Spirit, which is the word of God. Pray at all times in the Spirit, with all prayer and supplication. To that end keep alert with all perseverance, making supplication for all the saints, and also for me, that utterance may be given me in opening my mouth boldly to proclaim the mystery of the gospel"* (Ephesians 6:10-19).

The Lord has given us authority to tread over the enemy. He has given us authority (power) over all the power of the enemy. He has given us authority to resist the devil. He has given us authority to attack the enemy and bring him to nought. Part of the ministry of an intercessor is to be involved in this warfare with Satan on behalf of others.

The Lord has revealed what the host of the enemy is:

1. Principalities.
2. Powers.
3. World rulers of the present darkness.
4. Spiritual hosts of wickedness in the heavenly places.

This host aims at attacking the believer, other believers, unbelievers, God's projects, and everything that has its origin in God and is being done at the command of God, for the sole glory of God. Because the host of the enemy is arrayed against the believer, he must by prayer contend against them. He must put on the whole armour of God so as to be able to withstand.

When he has stood or is standing, he must be fully equipped to resist all further attacks of the enemy. The equipment is clearly spelled out and is available for all believers.

When the believer is standing, he must now contend for other believers and for unbelievers. He must contend for the will of God. He must contend for the projects of God; for all that God is doing.

We insist that it is not enough that the believer protects himself. It is not enough that he contends against the devil and his plan against him. He must not only resist the devil as far as he is concerned. He must contend, resist, and attack the devil on behalf of others. Unless he does this, the enemy will have an easy way with many. First of all there are many believers who cannot fully contend or resist the devil on their own. They need reinforcement. Unless they have the reinforcement, the enemy will penetrate. Secondly, there are other believers who by virtue of ministry are too exposed to the devil. They are perhaps doing great havoc against the enemy and his hosts are all arrayed against them. They need the additional protection of other believers so that they may continue to stand. And lastly, there are unbelievers who do not know how to resist the devil or to contend against him. Unless the believer contends for them, the enemy will do them great harm. The intercessor will come against the devil on the behalf of such. He will tell the Father to protect such and such a person against the attacks of the devil in a particular area. He will command the devil not to attack the person in that particular area. He will talk to the Father. He will ask the Father to put to nought what the enemy is building and he will confront the enemy and ask him in the name of the Lord Jesus to depart.

Do you wonder that unbelievers hear the word and it produces no impact in their lives or that its impact is short-lived? Part of the reason for this is that the word that is sown is not protected by a believer or believers and so the enemy has access to it and takes it away. The unbeliever cannot carry out spiritual warfare. Do you wonder why some who were hot for the Lord have become cold and have gone back to sin? Part of the answer is that the enemy saw their zeal and commitment and reasoned that if they continued that way, it would be bad for him. Realizing the fact that the young, zealous believer was still a novice in spiritual warfare, he attacked him violently and overcame him. Had an older, more experienced believer interceded for him, things would have been different. Had a more experienced believer commanded the enemy not to attack him, things would have been different. Had another believer attacked the devil before the devil could attack him, things would have been different. There have been times when someone has come under real conviction of sin and began to seek the Lord. All who know him felt certain that something was happening in his life and they began to expect and to await his spiritual rebirth. However, to the amazement of the watching and waiting believers he suddenly turned his back against the Lord and began to blaspheme. What had happened? I will try to explain what happened by telling you what happened in one of the city parks of Kampala (Uganda) in 1971. That Friday, I went to the park to witness. I saw three young men and asked them if I could talk to them about the Lord Jesus. Two refused while the third said that he was interested. The two of us then moved away from the two uninterested ones and sat somewhere where I began to talk to him about the Lord. He was very interested and open and the witnessing was progressing normally. After about thirty minutes I felt that he could be saved there and then. I then asked him if he wanted to turn from sin and turn to the Saviour immediately. He said yes, to my great joy. As he bowed his head in prayer, before we could begin to utter any words to the Lord, the other two young men who had said that they were not interested rushed swiftly towards us, lifted the one who was about to receive the Lord and carried him away by force. I stood there astonished, shocked, and angry. Two angels from hell had been sent to rescue that man from eternal life. I never saw him again but that lesson left an impact on my life about the reality of spiritual warfare and the need to protect all that is the Lord's in prayer. It left me knowing that the enemy is watching and will attack what is not protected. It left me realizing that I was at war and that if I did not attack the devil first, he will attack me and any project that God has entrusted into my hands. I now know that victory sometimes depends solely on whether I attack the devil or I let him attack me first.

ATTACKING THE DEVIL FIRST

It matters who attacks first. There is a sense in which, because of the triumph of the Lord Jesus over Satan or the Cross, the believers are principally to carry out defensive warfare. However the reality of the enemy: principalities, powers, world rulers of this present darkness, spiritual hosts of wickedness in the heavenly places; and the fact that we are warned,

> "*Be sober, be watchful. Your adversary the devil prowls around like a roaring lion, seeking someone to devour*" (1 Peter 5:8),

make it clear that the devil wants to attack. If all I do is to be watchful. I will of necessity have to keep my eyes constantly on him so that I will know how to resist him. This kind of warfare means that I will concentrate on Satan and keep my eyes on him and not only concentrate on Jesus and keep my eyes on Him. It also means that I am constantly exposed and at the mercy of the enemy. It gives him the upper hand.

There is a way out of that kind of situation. The answer is to attack the devil first. The believer should wait before the Lord, ask the Lord to reveal the plans that the devil is making to him. The Lord will reveal the devil's plans to the waiting, trusting child. Once the plans are revealed, they must be attacked at once. The devil's plans must be smashed before they mature. They must be smashed before they are executed. The devil's warships must be destroyed before they leave the harbour. His war planes must be destroyed while they are still under construction or at the latest, before they take off for attack. It is risky to wait and attack his war planes in the air. While his ships or planes are under construction or while they are still in the harbour or on the runway, it needs only a small force to destroy them. When they have taken off, it will need a larger force to destroy them.

The Lord Jesus did not start His ministry before He had given the devil a threefold knockout. He hit the devil so hard during the forty days fast that the enemy was compelled to leave Him for a while. We, too, must attack the devil and smash him. Then he will leave us for a while and when he comes again, we must hit him before he hits us. We must also watch on behalf of others. We must wait before God and ask Him to show us the plans of the devil against God's people, God's will, God's work, God's timing, God's provisions, and all else. As the Lord shows us the plans, we must destroy them before they mature and are executed. This aspect of waiting before the Lord, asking Him, receiving from Him the plans that Satan has against someone and then destroying them before they are executed, is a part of the ministry of intercession. Intercessors mature in building God's kingdom. They also mature in destroying Satan's kingdom. Amen.

BUILDING A HEDGE

The ruthless destroyer once told the Lord of Glory,

> *"Does Job fear God for naught? Hast thou not put a hedge about him and his house and all that he has on every side?" (Job 1:9-10)*.

God put a hedge about Job and about his house and about all that he had on every side. He did this in order to ensure that the devil had no access to Job, his house, or his property. God did it and thereby foiled the devil's attempts or plans to attack.

We notice that God did not just put a hedge around Job. He also put a hedge around Job's house, i.e., his wife and children. He did not stop there. He put a hedge around all that Job had. It is important to notice that a hedge was put around all that Job had. Nothing that he had was left unprotected. It is also significant that God put the hedge on every side. It was not a partial but a complete hedge. The devil would have loved to attack. He possibly tried to attack but the hedge made penetration impossible. Had God not put the hedge, the devil would have been in for a good time.

God did it for Job. He expects each believer to do four things:

1. Ask Him to put a hedge around himself, his house, and all that he has.
2. Actually put a hedge, in the name of Jesus, around himself, around his house, and around all that he has, on every side.
3. Ask the Lord to put a hedge around another person, that person's house, and all that that person has, on every side. He should also do this for a family, a city, a ministry, a nation, and so on.
4. Actually put a hedge, in the name of Jesus, around that person, that person's house and all that the person has, on every side.

The third and fourth aspects outlined above are a part of the ministry of intercession. They are the intercessor's responsibility.

God has left an example for all intercessors. He knows the devil and his desire to attack. He knows that the devil will attack all that he can attack. He knows that the devil is watchful, seeking for the slightest opening that is available. He knows that the devil could accomplish his purpose by attacking the man or the man's wife or the man's children or the man's relatives or the man's friends, or he could attack the man's house, car, water system, electricity supply, salary, drainage, job, and other things. Knowing this, God built the hedge around everything and ensured that the hedge was on every side. God also ensured that the hedge was always there so that the enemy was put off sixty seconds each minute, sixty minutes each hour, twenty-four hours each day, seven days each week, fifty-two weeks each year, and every year.

Those who stand in the gap for others should follow the Lord's example. It is not enough to pray, "Lord, protect him and his household and all that he has now and always." This will be equivalent to praying for a continent saying, "Lord, save everyone in Africa now and save all that will ever be born in Africa in the future, and ensure, Lord, that all who are saved mature to the full stature of Christ." If it were that simple, one person can pray for the whole world saying, "Lord, may Your will be done now and always in all the world," and that would make further praying unnecessary.

Intercessors will go into details. In building a hedge around the man's health, he will build it around his heart, lungs, liver, kidneys, spleen, his bladder, intestines, brain, his eyes, ears, nose, his mouth, tongue, neck, hands, his fingers, and other parts of the body. He will build a hedge around every part and he will leave none out since the enemy will attack wherever there is no hedge. He will do it for the man, his wife, each of his children, those living with him, and around all that concerns him. He knows that what is not protected is exposed. What is exposed can be attacked. What can be attacked will be attacked. What is attacked will be attacked with the one purpose of destroying it completely. Knowing this, he will act in intercession.

GOD WILL NOT BUILD THE HEDGE

There are some who say, "God will build the hedge around us and around ours." There is a sense in which that is true. There is also a sense in which that is the devil's lie. *God will not do that which we are able to do, which He has charged* us *to do.* If we do not build the hedge around ourselves and around the objects of our intercession, He will allow the devil to attack us, ours, those for whom we ought to intercede, and all that is theirs. He will allow the devil to do it because He has made us into co-workers—partners with Him. Partnership means that He will do what only He can do and we must do what He has charged us to do. He has charged us to intercede and expects us to do it. He has given us authority over all the power of the enemy and invited us to exercise that authority on our behalf and on the behalf of others. If we do not exercise it; if we are unbelieving; if we are lazy; if we are presumptuous; if we do not give intercession and prayer the importance and priority that they deserve, He will not step in to rescue us. He will let the devil attack and allow us and even His will to suffer defeat. We are to intercede, attack the devil, build hedges around ourselves, and build hedges around others as if it all depends on us. The truth is that God has decided to let it depend on us.

Fellow intercessor! Wake up and intercede. The destiny of one man, one family, a group of families, a city, or a nation depends on you. It could even be that the destiny of a continent and a planet depends on your intercession. God has taken you into great confidence. Respond as one who is worthy of the confidence that He has bestowed on you by allowing so much to depend on you!

Take no rest and give Him no rest. Storm Him with your intercession.

Take no rest and give the devil no rest. Pull down his plans; attack him unceasingly. Build a wall around all that he could attack. Stand in triumph and win a well-fought fight.

Amen.

THE INTERCESSOR AND BURDEN

When God wants to do something, He looks for a man after His own heart and reveals to him what He wants to do. As this person receives the revelation of what the Lord wants to do and meditates on it before the Lord, the revelation will become a burden on his heart to see that what God wants done becomes reality. If the burden is nourished by very intimate fellowship with the Lord and complete obedience in all things, it will grow. The person can begin to discharge the burden by praying to the Lord. If he does that, the burden will grow and as he prays, it will become bigger and bigger and heavier and heavier until it reaches a maximum. The intercessor will then be in a condition in which he is so weighed down that if he did not intercede he would collapse. At that point he will be compelled to intercede because he wants to see God's need met and because he wants to discharge the crushing burden on his heart. Such a person does not need to be encounged to intercede. We illustrate this below.

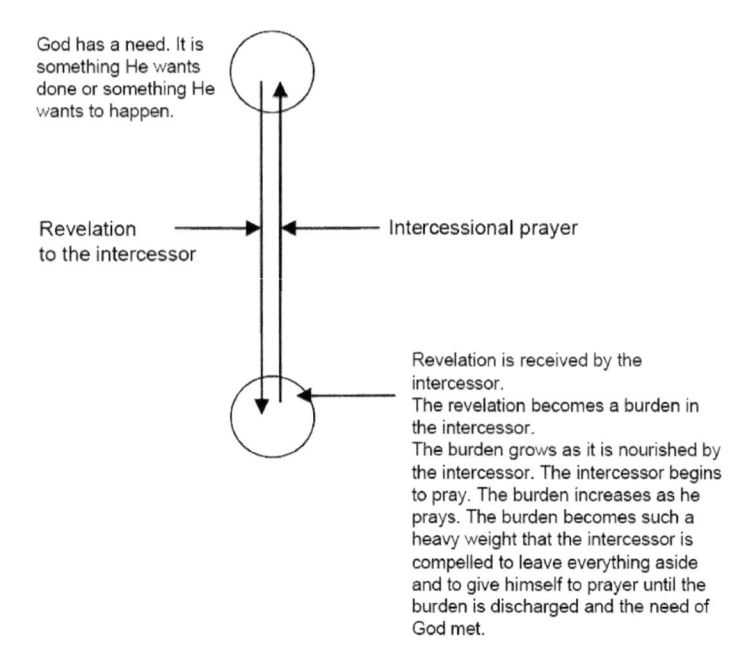

God has a need. It is something He wants done or something He wants to happen.

Revelation to the intercessor ⟶ ⟵ Intercessional prayer

Revelation is received by the intercessor.
The revelation becomes a burden in the intercessor.
The burden grows as it is nourished by the intercessor. The intercessor begins to pray. The burden increases as he prays. The burden becomes such a heavy weight that the intercessor is compelled to leave everything aside and to give himself to prayer until the burden is discharged and the need of God met.

We again see here the commitment of the Father to work with His children. God is able to go ahead and act in such a way that His need is met without the cooperation of the intercessor. However, out of love for His children, He has decided not to do that. If He did that, His children would become useless, for there would be nothing they could do for Him. Seeing it this way, intercession is a gift of love from the Father to His children. It is one of the greatest gifts that the Father has given to His own! May God open your eyes to see this! May God open my heart to grasp this and act accordingly.

Intercession is also one of the ways in which the Lord has chosen to humble Himself. He who is all powerful and can do all things has, by introducing the ministry of intercession, decided to limit His power and authority. He has so limited Himself that He is more or less "powerless" unless His children intercede. How great our God is!

As we have said, true intercession is the fruit of revelation that leads to burden. The shortage of intercessors is actually the shortage of people who have seen what the needs of God are. The most urgent need of the moment is, therefore, personal praying, that our eyes might be opened to truly see. A mental acknowledgement of the truth is not enough. There must be the imparting of divine light. That light received must be protected from being taken away by the devil. That light must be prayed through so that it is transformed into a burden. The burden must be helped to grow through prayer and through intercession until it has reached maximum intensity. All these require much time spent before God.

HOW TO RECEIVE REVELATION

The Lord reveals His needs to people after His own heart. He reveals them to His friends. Who would reveal his personal and intimate needs to everyone? The question then arises as to how a believer can become a man after God's own heart. I think that it is very simple, yet how few are such people in the Church! The Psalmist said, "The friendship of the Lord is for those who fear him, and he makes known to them his covenants" (Psalms 25:14). Those who fear the Lord obey Him in all things. They hate what He hates and they love what He loves. Such are close to Him. They enjoy His presence and so spend their time before Him. Because they are the Lord's friends, their preoccupation is to know the Lord's needs so as to ensure that they are met.

If you want to be a recipient of God's revelation, do the following:

1. Put away everything from your life that God does not

delight in. Do not leave anything that He barely permits because of the hardness of your heart.

2. Do everything that the Lord has told you to do for Him and for man. Do not do only those you love to do. Do all. Do not only do those that you think you can do. Do all, for His strength will be made perfect for you and in you as you go ahead to obey Him.

3. Delight in Him and spend increasing time in His presence. If you are always in His presence then He will reveal His needs to you as they come and how blessed you will be. However, if you are only occasionally present, you will miss many things. for He will not put those who are always in His presence aside and wait to reveal His needs to you when you come for your occasional appearances before Him.

4. Work hard. The Lord will first of all test you. He will reveal His need to you and then wait to see what you will do with it. If you work extremely hard and soon ensure that His need is met, you will qualify for further revelation. However, if you are sluggish, lazy or without a sense of priority, you will treat the thing that He has shown lightly. This will result in His need not being met. It will tell Him that you are not worthy of trust. This will mean that in the future He will ensure that His needs are not revealed to you. Because the Lord will only reveal His needs to those who were faithful with past revelations, there are many people today who will not receive further revelation from Him. They may be asking themselves, "Why does the Lord no longer speak to me?" The problem is sin. The sin of not having obeyed Him in the thing that was shown to you in the past. All this makes it quite obvious that no lazy person can become a friend of God. The apostle Paul received an abundance of revelation but he also worked very hard. He said, *"But by*

the grace of God I am what I am and his grace toward me was not in vain. On the contrary, I worked harder than any of them, though it was not I, but the grace of God which is with me" (*1 Corinthians 15:10*).

HOW TO CAUSE THE BURDEN TO GROW

Those who walk before God in holiness and total obedience will find that the revelation that they receive is just converted into a burden in their spirits. However, the burden often has to be nourished before it can grow to maturity. God's burden is very much alive. It will grow under favourable conditions and it will shrivel and even die under adverse conditions. Those who do not protect it will find that the enemy will come along and take it away. The following should be done in order to cause the burden to grow.

1. Walk very close to the Lord immediately the burden has been received. You will find that you need to walk in greater intimacy with the Lord after the burden was received than you did before. It is bad enough not to have received a burden. It is worse to lose it. A barren woman suffers for barrenness. However, a barren woman who becomes pregnant and then has an abortion is a very sorry sight, for great hopes have been built in her and now they are all dashed to the ground. Therefore, every pregnant woman is most careful with herself. She does not just do things. She does the things that will not harm the baby in her womb in any way.
2. Begin to pray about the burden you have received. Sometimes, it may be just a slight weight on your spirit and if you ignore it, it will disappear. However, as you begin to pray about it, asking the Lord to enlarge the vision and the burden, it will grow,
3. You need to fast, asking God to increase the burden that

He has given you.

4. You may have to apply yourself to receiving the type of information that will fill your mind with facts about the need in God's heart. If, for example, the Lord gives you revelation about His need to reach the Moslems with the Gospel of His grace, as you fast and pray, you may need to read books about Moslems in the world, their numbers, their resistance to the Gospel, the shortage of effective missionaries in their midst, and so forth. As you read those things, they will fill your mind and your mind will in turn aid your spirit to see the burden more clearly and to grow in it.

5. Begin to set special times aside to pray for the burden. Continue to do this and go on increasing the amount of time that you are putting into prayer. As you do this, two things will happen. First of all, the Lord will give you more revelation about the matter and this greater revelation will become a greater burden. Secondly, the initial burden you had will grow and possess you so that you become a "possessed" person. You will find no alternative to prayer and you will pray.

It is important that the burden on God's heart remain clear before you. Do not get so caught up with the burden that you no longer know what God wants done. It is good to write down what the Lord showed you was His need and not lose sight of it. If you do, your burden may become groans and sighs before God. You may be able to intercede with your spirit but you will not be able to intercede with your mind.

PROTECT THE VISION AND THE BURDEN FROM THE ENEMY

The Enemy hates vision and burden, for he knows the potential of people who have both. He will therefore do everything to confuse the revelation and cause it to become so blurred that it finally vanishes. He will also snatch away all burdens that are not protected especially when they are not-fully developed. He will try to mischannel the burden to secondary, tertiary, and quaternary issues. He will do all to ensure that the burden does not remain and grow as it was received. The intercessor, therefore, has the responsibility to protect the burden. He may do this by:

1. Prayer of protection and prayer for protection.
2. Attacking the devil before the devil attacks. By simple and repeated commands and confessions like, "Satan, I put to nought all the plans that you are making against the vision that God has given me and against the burden that has come from that vision and I want you to know that the vision will mature and be accomplished and the burden will grow to full maturity and be translated into unceasing intercession to the Lord, until that which He has in His heart has been accomplished. I, therefore, ask you to stop further plans and I give all the glory to God for your defeat on Calvary." Do far-reaching harm on the enemy and ensure that the vision and the burden are protected.
3. Believe that God will accomplish all His purposes including His purpose in giving you vision and burden. The Lord says, *"As I have planned, so shall it be, and as I have purposed, so shall it stand"* (Isaiah 14:24). *"For the Lord of Hosts has purposed, and who will annul it? His hand is stretched out, and who will turn it back?"* (Isaiah 14:27). *"My counsel shall stand, and I will accomplish all my purpose"* (Isaiah 46:10). You should confess with the Psalmist, *"The Lord will fulfil his purpose for me"* (Psalms 138:8).

10

THE INTERCESSOR AND FASTING

An intercessor is a person who is in such stress and under such a burden that he will pay any price in order to obtain the object of his intercession. Most intercessors of the Bible found that they needed to put aside food completely or partially as they laboured through to victory. We shall look at two examples.

MOSES

The Bible says,

> *"Even in Horeb you provoked the Lord to wrath, and the Lord was so angry with you that he was ready to destroy you" (Deuteronomy 9:8).*
>
> *"Then I lay prostrate before the Lord as before, forty days and forty nights; I neither ate bread nor drank water, because of all the sin which you had committed, in doing what was evil in the sight of God the Lord to provoke him to anger. For I was afraid of the anger and hot displeasure which the Lord bore against you, so that he was ready to destroy you" (Deuteronomy 9:18-19).*

"So I lay prostrate before the Lord for these forty days and forty nights, because the Lord had said he would destroy you. And I prayed to the Lord, O Lord God, destroy not thy people and thy heritage, whom thou hast redeemed through thy greatness, whom thou hast brought out of Egypt with a mighty hand. Remember thy servants, Abraham, Isaac, and Jacob; do not regard the stubbornness of this people, or their wickedness, or their sin, lest the land from which thou didst bring us say, Because the Lord was not able to bring them into the land which he promised them, and because he hated them, he has brought them out to slay them in the wilderness. For they are thy people and thy heritage, whom thou didst bring out by thy great power and by thy outstretched arm" (Deuteronomy 9:25-29).

"But the Lord hearkened to me that time also" (Deuteronomy 9:19).

NEHEMIAH

The Bible says of Nehemiah,

"I was in Suza the capital, that Hanani, one of my brethren, came with certain men out of Judah; and I asked them concerning the Jews that survived, who had escaped exile, and concerning Jerusalem. And they said to me, The survivors there in the province who escaped exile are in great trouble and shame; the wall of Jerusalem is broken down, and its gates are destroyed by fire.

"When I heard these words I sat down and wept and mourned for days; and I continued fasting and praying before the Lord of heaven. And I said, O Lord God of heaven, the great and terrible God who keeps covenant and steadfast love with those who love him and keep his commandments; let thy ear be attentive, and thy eyes open, to hear the prayer of thy servant which I now pray before thee day and night for the people of Israel thy servants, confessing the sins of the people of Israel,

which we have sinned against thee. Yea, I and my father's house have sinned. We have acted very corruptly against thee, and have not kept the commandments, the statutes, and the ordinances which thou didst command thy servant Moses. Remember the word which thou didst command thy servant Moses, saying, If you are unfaithful, I will scatter you among the peoples; but if you return to me and keep my commandments and do them, though your dispersed be under the farthest skies, I will gather them thence and bring them to the place which I have chosen, to make my name dwell there. They are thy servants and thy people, whom thou hast redeemed by thy great power and by thy strong hand. O Lord, let thy ear be attentive to the prayer of thy servant, and to the prayer of thy servants who delight to fear thy name; and give success to thy servant today, and grant him mercy in the sight of this man" (Nehemiah 1:1-11).

As can be easily seen, these mighty intercessors fasted and prayed. Moses fasted first and then prayed. That is, the first reaction was fasting and the second was prayer. The same was true of Nehemiah. He wept and mourned for days and continued fasting and praying. There was nothing mechanical about their fasting or about their praying. The situation before them touched their hearts at depth and the fasting and praying flowed out in response to the situation.

TWO POSSIBLE PATHWAYS

Those who walk close to God feel God's pain in a situation where His honour and glory have been dragged down. They will be so identified with Him that from the moment that they know the facts, they will not be able to resist mourning, weeping, fasting, and praying.

Those who walk with God and have their hearts welded to His purpose for man, will face situations where man has sinned and is in great danger of judgment, or where a man is in such desperate need that his heart will so go out to the person and identify so much with the person that he will not be able to do anything but mourn, weep, fast, and pray. We can call these spontaneous fasting, intercession, and they are wonderful. May God raise many more people in His Church whose hearts will be so welded to the Lord and to His people that they will immediately lose all desire for food and all else as they labour in intercession that God's glory be established and His people spared.

This is, however, not the only way to intercede. There will be sustained burdens that may take days, weeks, months and years to intercede for. What is the intercessor to do in such cases? Is he to fast without ceasing for years? First of all, we say that he may not be able to do this even if that was the desire of his heart. His body may give way. What he should do is to plan his intercession. He may decide to fast one day a week until the burden is discharged and God has answered. He may decide to fast one week a month or he may decide to fast one month each year as he intercedes for the particular issue at hand. How he decides to intercede will be something between him and the Lord but it is obvious that he will receive both the length and the duration of the fast from the Lord and, having received it, he will keep to it regardless of how difficult it may be to fast and pray.

No one can say that it was easy for Moses to lie prostrate before the Lord for forty-days, neither drinking nor eating food, to return only the next day to begin another forty days of lying prostrate before the Lord eating neither food nor drinking water, but interceding. May the lovers of ease read what God said to Ezekiel and rethink. The Lord said to him,

> *"And you, O son of man, take a brick and lay it before you and portray upon it a city, even Jerusalem; and put siegeworks against it and build a*

siege wall against it, and cast a mound against it, set camps also against it, and plant battering rams against it round about. And take an iron plate, and place it as an iron wall between you and the city; and set you your face toward it, and let it be a state of siege, and press the siege against it. This is a sign for the house of Israel.

"Then lie down upon your left side and I will lay the punishment of the house of Israel upon you, for the number of the days you lie upon it, you shall bear their punishment. For I assign to you a number of days, three hundred and ninety days, equal to the number of the years of their punishment; so long shall you bear the punishment of the house of Israel. And when you have completed these, you shall lie down a second time, but on your right side, and bear the punishment of the house of Judah; forty days I assign you, a day for each year" (Ezekiel 4:1-6).

"And you, take wheat and barley, beans and lentils, millet and spelt and put them into a single vessel, and make bread of them. During the number of days that you lie upon your side, three hundred and ninety days, you shall eat it. And the food which you eat shall be by weight, twenty shekels a day; once a day you shall eat it. And water you shall drink by measure, the sixth part of a hin; once a day you shall drink it. And you shall eat it as a barley cake, baking it in their sight on human dung" (Ezekiel 4:1-12).

Intercession is very serious business. Anyone who thinks that labouring in the spirit and seeing captives freed is 'an easy job, is very much mistaken. Great privileges go with great responsibilities. It was said to the blessed Mary,

"Behold this child is set for the fall and rising of many in Israel, and for a sign that is spoken against, [and a sword will pierce through your own soul also], that the thoughts out of many hearts may be revealed" (Luke 2:34-35).

If you are an intercessor indeed, a sword may have to pierce through your own soul, body, eating habits, and love of ease so that the purpose of God may be accomplished.

Are you ready for that? Part of it is fasting, serious fasting!

11

THE INTERCESSOR AND PERSONAL HOLINESS

"Feebleness of living reflects its debility and languor in the prayer hours. We simply cannot talk to God, strongly, intimately, and confidently unless we are living for Him, faithfully and truly. The prayer-closet cannot become sanctified unto God, when life is alien to His precepts and purpose. We must learn this lesson well - that righteous character and Christlike conduct give us a particular and preferential standing in prayer before God. His holy Word gives special emphasis to the part conduct has in imparting value to our praying when it declares: 'Then shall thou call and the Lord shall answer; thou shall cry, and He shall say, Here I am, if thou take from the midst of thee the yoke, the putting forth of the finger, and speaking vanity'

— E. M. BOUNDS, THE NECESSITY OF PRAYER
[GRAND RAPIDS: BAKER BOOK HOUSE, 1984]

The intercessor must be holy. He cannot afford to knowingly commit any sin for:

- Sin is a tragedy.
- Sinning is utter self-destruction.

- Sinning is an attempt to overthrow God.
- Sinning is a desire that Satan might be given the throne of the universe and that he might reign in the place of the Lord God of Hosts.
- Every act of deliberate sin is a heart-cry to Satan, "Satan, I love you and I desire your lordship, kingdom, and glory."
- Every act of deliberate sin is spitting on God's face.
- Sin, however small, is a determined effort to forfeit God's best.
- Sinning is the most useless thing any believer can ever be involved in, for it brings him neither real blessings in this life nor in the life to come.
- Each sin that a man commits eventually turns into lashes and thrashes him.
- There is no sin committed in motive, thought, word, and deed that will not be exposed someday.
- There is no sin that brings glory to God.
- There is no sin that actually helps to advance the interests of the kingdom of God.
- Every sin and every act of sin is a problem to God.
- The quickest way to lose one's place in the heart of God is to sin deliberately.
- Only a fool deceives himself by saying that he can sin deliberately and be the same in his relationship with God.
- Sin destroys a man's spirit.
- Sin destroys a man's soul.
- Sin destroys a man's body.
- There comes a time in the life of a person who has deliberately practised sin and resisted the Holy Spirit that repentance is impossible, for the Spirit of God will not strive with man endlessly.
- There comes a time when a man who has indulged

- persistently in the practice of some sin finds out that he cannot hate the sin even though he wants to.
- There comes a time in the life of a person who has practised sin persistently that his conscience begins to approve the sin so much that he even sees the sin as a holy duty. The Lord Jesus said, "They will put you out of the synagogues; indeed, the hour is coming when whoever kills you will think he is offering service to God" (John 10:2).
- There comes a time when God will even allow the stubborn-hearted to continue in sin.
- Because of the harm that sin causes in a person's total being and in his relationship with God one of the prior duties of an intercessor or would-be intercessor is to ensure that he has been delivered from sin and is living a holy life. The Psalmist said, "If I had cherished iniquity in my heart, the Lord would not have listened" (Psalms 66:18). God may sometimes answer the prayers of a believer who still deliberately practises sin in one area or the other of his life, but one thing is sure, there will be some prayers of his to which God turns a deaf ear. Such prayers can only be answered when they come from hearts that are pure.
- Sin ensures that the burden on God's heart is not received in the spirit of a man who is practising it. It also ensures that the cry of such a one does not reach God.

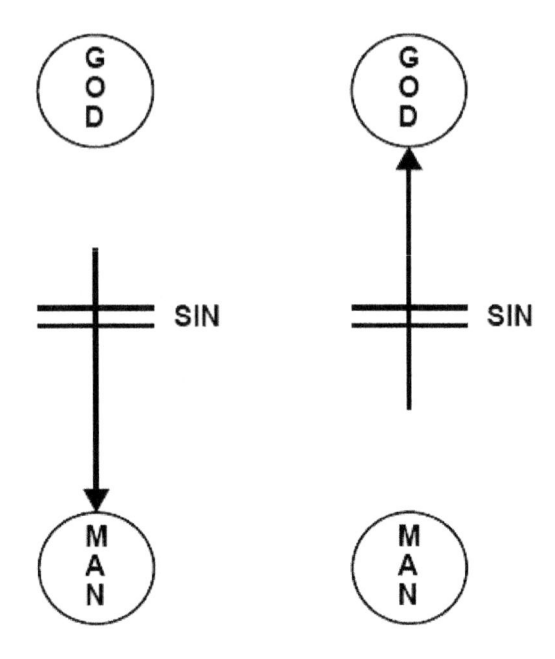

- God hides his face from those who pray with sin in their lives. The Bible says, "When you come to appear before me, who requires of you this trampling of my courts? Bring no more vain offerings; incense is an abomination to me. New moon and Sabbath and the calling of assemblies - I cannot endure iniquity and solemn assembly. Your new moons' and your appointed feasts my soul hates: they have become a burden to me, I am weary of bearing them. *When you spread forth your hands, I will hide my eyes from you: even though you make* many prayers, I will not listen; your hands are full of blood. Wash yourselves; make yourselves clean; remove the evil of your doings from before my eyes; cease to do evil" (Isaiah 1:12-16).
- It is self-deception for anyone to mutter a few words of

"repentance" to God for a sin committed, without a full determination to stop the sin now but to go back in the future and then begin to make noise before God in the name of intercession. This is of course self-deception. Fellowship with God has not been restored. The burden on God's heart will not be communicated to such a one and the cries of his heart may not be heard by the Lord. When sin is committed, until there is genuine repentance and a genuine and complete putting off of the sin in a complete way and with no desire to come back to it in the future, there can be no real intercession,

- The following sins put a person out of fellowship with God and therefore disqualify him from intercession or weaken his cries to God: lying, exaggeration, hypocrisy, falsehood, pretence, anger, pride, gossip, jealousy, impure motives, impure thoughts, wicked thoughts, impure words, impure acts and touches, embraces, kisses, gluttony, dishonesty, robbing God, love of vanity, love of the world, love of the things of the world, greed, selfishness, covetousness, envy, bitterness, an unforgiving spirit, a judgmental spirit, and the like. If a person commits one or more of these sins, he is not qualified to intercede. He is desperately in need. How can he carry the needs of another to God in prayer?

- The prerequisite for anyone to come to God and intercede, is self-examination before Him. The person comes before the Lord and honestly asks the Lord to show him what his heart is like. Before he can even ask God to do that, he must repent for any sin that he knows he has committed. He must confess the sin and put it away forever. Secondly, he must examine himself before God. The apostle exhorts, "Let a man examine himself, and so eat of the bread and drink of the cup. For any one who eats and drinks without discerning the body eats and drinks judgment upon himself. That is why many of you are weak and ill, and some have died. But if we judge ourselves truly, we should not be judged" (1 Corinthians 11:28-31).

Before interceding a man should take some time of quiet before God and ask himself the following questions:

1. Have I spoken ill of any one? After asking the question, he should think back to the conversations he has had. If he discovers that he spoke ill of a person who was absent he should repent at once and carry out restitution before he can intercede .
2. Have I been covetous in any way? He should again examine himself and if he sees areas in which covetousness has been manifested in his life, he should repent at once and carry out restitution before he sets out to intercede.
3. Have I lied, exaggerated, pretended, or practised any form of falsehood in my speech, acts, or impressions? As things are seen, they should be repented of, confessed, forsaken, and restitution carried out.
4. Have I practised any immorality in my thoughts, words, or actions? Have I touched anyone I should not have touched? Have I touched anyone in a way that I ought not to have touched? Have I thought of anyone in a way that I ought not to have thought? Did I desire anyone that I should not have desired? Have I given myself to loving anyone I know I should not love in the way I am loving her? Do I have misplaced affections? As light comes on each of these issues, there must be repentance before God, a total putting away of that which is evil and a total commitment from the heart not to go back that way, and restitution if need be, before intercession can be

honest. Anyone who dares to intercede without examining himself and putting things right in his life is only deceiving himself and adding to his sin.

When a person has finished examining himself before the Lord and has put right all that needs to be put right, he can intercede but his intercession is not from the best standpoint. The best standpoint is reached by the person who, after he has examined himself before God, realizes that there may be many things wrong in his life that he is not aware of. He, therefore, desires God to show him things as He sees them. Such a person will, after examining himself, go before the Lord and ask, "Lord, I have examined myself and put things right. I am anxious to be in the best condition before I can intercede. I pray you to show me the things that are wrong in my heart and life that I do not know." The Psalmist prayed,

"Search me, O God, and know my heart! Try me and know my thoughts! And see if there be any wicked way in me, and lead me in the way everlasting!" (Psalms 139:23-24).

"Prove me, O Lord, and try me, test my heart and my mind" (Psalms 20:2).

When a person asks the Lord to show him if there is any wicked way or things in his heart, he must wait before the Lord. He should not ask and then go away. He must ask and wait and the Lord will show him things that he thought were right but are wrong and things that he was not conscious of that are not acceptable to Him. He will repent of these, confess them, put them away completely, and carry out any restitution that is necessary. He is then prepared to intercede. He can then come boldly to the throne of grace because his conscience has been cleansed. He can come boldly to the throne of grace because there is fellowship between him and the Lord. He can come because he is sure that the Lord will hear him.

We can illustrate the three levels of intercession of the one with unconfessed and unforsaken sin; the one who has examined himself and put things right with God and man, and the one who has in addition subjected himself to the examination of God and as a result has put things right with God and man, as shown below.

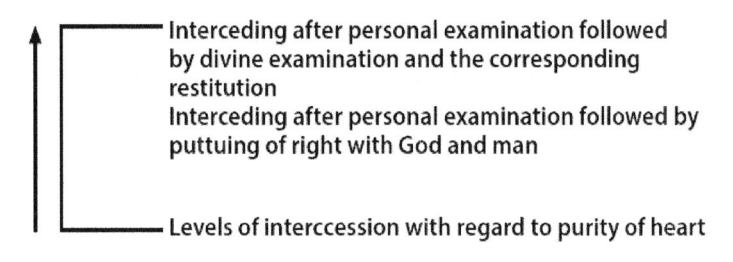

- Interceding after personal examination followed by divine examination and the corresponding restitution
- Interceding after personal examination followed by puttuing of right with God and man
- Levels of interccession with regard to purity of heart

Many years of intercession could be wasted

Normally, fasting has spiritual effects. However, there was a time when the children of Israel fasted but it was to no avail. They actually fasted for many years, but God did not receive or consider their fast. The Bible says:

> *"Now the people of Bethel had sent Sharezer and Regemmelech and their men, to entreat the favour of the Lord, and to ask the priests of the house of the Lord of hosts and the prophets, Should I mourn and fast in the fifth month, as I have done for so many years? Then the word of the Lord of hosts came to me, Say to all the people of the land and the priests, When you fasted and mourned in the fifth month and in the seventh, for these seventy years, was it for me that you fasted? And when you eat and when you drink, do you not eat for yourselves and drink for yourselves? When Jerusalem was inhabited and in prosperity, with her cities round about her, and the South and the lowland were inhabited, were not these the*

words which the Lord proclaimed by the former prophets?" (Zechariah 7:2-6).

"And the word of the Lord came to Zechariah saying, Thus says the Lord of hosts, Render true judgments, show kindness and mercy each to his brother, do not oppress the widow, the fatherless, the sojourner, or the poor; and let none of you devise evil against his brother in your heart. But they refused to hearken, and turned a stubborn shoulder, and stopped their ears that they might not hear. They made their hearts like adamant lest they should hear the law and the words which the Lord of hosts had sent by his Spirit through the former prophets. Therefore great wrath came from the Lord of hosts. As I called, and they would not hear, so they called, and I would not hear, says the Lord of hosts, And I scattered them with a whirlwind among all the nations which they had not known. Thus the land they left was desolate, so that no one went to and fro, and the pleasant land was made desolate" (Zechariah 7:2-14).

What happened to the fasting people could happen to an interceding person or people. If there is sin in the life of a person that is known to him, he must terminate it at once. If he does not, he can continue to intercede for even ten hours each day for seventy years but that intercession will be to no avail. A lifetime may thus be invested and thus become a wasted lifetime!

There is something more to it. The one who knows that there is sin in his life but would not radically terminate the sin, but rather goes on to intercede, will not only waste his time. He will be punished. The Lord will send great wrath upon such a one. He will scatter him with a whirlwind among the nations that he has not known. The Lord may scatter his family, his abilities, and so forth. This is a most solemn matter. It means that anyone who attempts to intercede while hiding his sin is bringing judgment upon himself. His words of intercession become cries to God that say, "Lord, here I am. I am mocking You by my prayers of intercession. Do to me as You have promised. Send Your wrath upon me."

Will the Lord hearken to such a plea? The Bible says that He will. That being so, the first prerequisite of a life that wants to intercede is the separation from all sin. This can never be negotiated. This means that each one is asked to choose between the pleasure that is derived from sin and the blessings that will come on another because of intercession. None can have both.

SEPARATION UNTO GOD

The intercessor will not only be separated from sin. He will be separated from many other things, which although innocent in themselves may yet hinder him from making the most progress in the school of intercession. For example, there are certain careers that he may not get into because they may not leave him with enough time for his ministry. He may have to give up mariage because he may not have enough time to intercede and yet take care of a wife and probably children. He will be a man apart - separated from man, separated from men, separated from things, and separated unto God. He will seek God, seek God increasingly, and be lost in Him and from His immediate presence. He will intercede. Amen.

Such a person will wield spiritual power so much that regardless of what others around him may be doing, he will intercede, be heard by the Lord and in that way bring deep and lasting answers to the situation.

12

THE INTERCESSOR AND GOALS

There is some place in the ministry of intercession in which a person can become a general intercessor. By a general intercessor I mean one who is open to intercede for the diverse needs of an endless number of people. Such an intercessor will receive topics like the following:

1. "My body is paining. I need prayers." The intercessor will intercede for his healing but he will not dwell on interceding for the person until he is well. He will soon pass to the next request, which may be what is in numbers two, three, and four.
2. "I need to succeed in my examination. Please pray for me."
3. "My son is a problem at home and at school. Please pray for him."
4. "My husband is difficult. Please pray for him."

Praying for such topics is intercession. At this level, everyone can intercede. No special revelation is needed nor is any special burden needed. The intercessor may pray once and pass on to other issues, or he may pray many times at leisure until the need is met. There are people who make it their preoccupation to receive such topics and pray for them. Often the majority of them have to do with physical health, family life, or jobs. Very few of them refer to purely spiritual matters of a relationship with God.

There is another level of intercession. At that level, God lays one burden on a person's heart and only one burden. He carries it with him day and night and labours at it all day long and all night long. All other things and other ministries have no place in his heart. He closes himself to everything else except that one. He is possessed by that one burden to see some particular purpose of God accomplished.

It is of such that the Lord said,

> *"Upon your walls, O Jerusalem, I have set watchmen, all the day and all the night they shall never be silent. You who put the Lord in remembrance, take no rest and give him no rest until he establishes Jerusalem and makes it a praise in the earth"* (Isaiah 62:6-7).

As is obvious, these watchmen were interceding night and day. In fact they were interceding all the day and all the night. They took no rest. They gave God no rest. They had a goal. They had to labour that way until God established Jerusalem and made it a praise in the earth. So from the beginning their goal was clear. It was so clear that they could know for sure when it was accomplished. Because their goal was clear, they kept at it and they sacrificed everything for it. It was of such critical importance to them that God established Jerusalem and made it a praise in the earth that they were willing to invest all of themselves into it. In a special sense they knew that if they gave God rest He would not do it. However, if they gave Him no rest, He would do it. They found that the only way for them to give God no rest was for them to take no rest. Therefore, they took no rest.

The question may arise as to what goals there are that could "possess" an intercessor and thus enable him to put his all into the *one* business of praying for *one* thing. We shall suggest a few but each person has to deal with God about this matter.

1. The restoration of a backslider.
2. The salvation of an individual, family, village, tribe, city, nation.
3. The penetration of some place with the gospel.
4. The raising up of a spiritual man.
5. The restoration of a fallen minister.
6. The protection of a man of God.
7. The protection of a ministry.
8. The raising up of funds for some God-commanded task.
9. The protection of a city, nation or political leader.
10. The outpouring of the Holy Spirit on a person, assembly, groups of assemblies, and so on.

As can be seen from the topics suggested, it is clear that when God answers, the intercessor will know that God has answered. It is also obvious that for someone interceding for the protection of a certain man of God or a certain ministry, he may have to intercede until God calls the man of God home or that ministry has satisfied God's heart and therefore been brought to an end. This may mean investing five, ten, twenty, or fifty years into praying for one person, but it is worth it when seen from an eternal perspective. Real spiritual men are rare to come by. The few who are there at the moment can only make real progress if some lives are invested 100 percent to intercede for them and for God's call on their lives. In this way there will be fewer scandals and the Lord's purpose will be better accomplished.

The intercessor may hide behind the scene and never be seen or known, praying eight, ten, twelve, or fifteen hours a day, that another who is daily in public, may succeed. What will be his reward? For that we must wait for the return of the Lord. On that day it may be surprising to find that the intercessor is given a greater reward by the Lord than that which will be given to the man, who received the acclaim from man, for whom he interceded. All must seek their calling from the Lord and, having received it, be faithful in it. The rest is the Lord's affair and He is just. Amen.

13
THE INTERCESSOR AND URGENCY

There are some things in this life that can be postponed without serious consequences. For example, a man can postpone his marriage by one, two, five, or ten years without great harm either to himself or to the kingdom of God. However, there is one thing that cannot be postponed without great losses. That one thing is intercession! Consider the following situations:

> *A young man is walking along life's way, wondering if he should experiment with sex and find out what pleasure might be found in it. The Lord sees the impending danger and lays a burden on the heart of someone to stand in the gap for this young man so that he should not go the way of sin, shame, and disgrace that is occasioned by sexual immorality. The intercessor receives the burden but would not do anything about it at once. All he says is, "I will pray about it this evening." In the evening he is busy with other things and says, "I will pray about it in the morning." In the morning people come to see him and he says to himself, "I ought to intercede but because these people have come, I will meet their needs first." He ministers to them and by the evening he is too tired and says, "I will intercede when I go on the week-end, since my days are too charged and I do not want to intercede superficially." The week-end is again full of*

activities and he says, "I know what I will do. I will wait for my vacation time. During that time there will be nothing on my hands and I will truly take time and settle this matter with God because it is very important."

However, before vacation time the young man falls into sexual immorality, a child is conceived and later born into the world outside the perfect will of God. In addition, that initial sexual act set the young man aflame so much that from then on, he goes from one girl to another, causing untold harm and ending up with AIDS. Soon he is on his dying bed and all this because an intercessor received God's call to intercede, postponed it, and failed completely.

Take another situation.

A man of God with an important ministry of national and international importance to God is driving on the highway. The devil has been looking for possible ways to destroy him but could not. He tried to use women but failed. He then tried to use the love of money but it did not work. Then he tried to use the love of fame but it did not work either. Finally, he decided to destroy his life completely. So as the man of God is driving along the highway to go and minister to the people of God, the devil says to himself; This is my one opportunity. I must act at once. He finds a truck driver who loves alcoholic drinks ready to drive the opposite way. He encourages him to take the first bottle of beer. Then he moves him to take the second and the third bottles. As the truck driver is about to move to his truck, the devil immediately sends an old friend to him who says to him, "I have not seen you for a long time. Much has happened to me and since I do not know when we shall next meet, I want to tell you all at once. Can we talk over a glass of beer?" The two enter a pub; the conversation lasts three hours, during which six bottles of beer are "polished off by the two of them, the truck driver drinking five and his friend one. At the end of the conversation, the truck driver enters his truck and in his drunken condition begins to drive at top speed. He is driving on the right lane on the same road on which the man of God is driving on the other lane in the opposite direction. As his truck comes within distance of the car of the man of God, he suddenly gets excited, turns left and crashes into the car of the man of God and kills him. Six hours before the man of God was killed, the Lord saw what the devil was planning and laid a burden on a sister to pray very specifically for the man of God. She knows him and has often ministered to him through intercession and through other practical ways. When the burden was put on her, she became restless and her spirit told her to go at once and pray for him. On the other hand she reasoned with herself and said, I must finish the work that I have planned to do today. When I go on my six-hour prayer retreat tomorrow, I will pray for him and cover him under the blood of the Lord Jesus. I have this burden and I am sure others have it. I believe that someone who is not as busy as I am now is responding to the burden and praying now. I will take my turn tomorrow and everything will fit in orderly and perfectly. Before tomorrow, she received the message of the man's death. It was too late to intercede for him. God had placed the burden to intercede for him on no other heart but hers, and since she did not respond, the devil had his way!

This woman made a number of mistakes. She decided that it was better to stick to programmes and timetables made by herself than to respond to God's timetable that demanded that she should leave her own timetable and intercede at once. She also convinced herself that the burden that God had placed on her heart to intercede at that moment had also been placed by the Lord on other hearts to intercede then. This again was an error. There is no guarantee that God lays one burden on many hearts at the same time. It is safest that anyone who has received a burden from the Lord should consider himself the sole recipient of that burden and consequently the only person on whom intercession depends. He should then act accordingly. Her third error was that she decided that others who received the burden would not have their timetables to follow and leave things for the next day as she was doing. Because she postponed things, the man of

God was killed and that was the end of his ministry, nationally and internationally. God had waited for fifty years for a man of his spiritual calibre to rise up on the spiritual horizons in His body. He might have to wait for another fifty, one hundred, and even five hundred years before He can find another vessel that He can use in the same way! How sad and how far-reaching was that decision taken to postpone intercession that day!

The one thing in this life that a believer should not postpone is the call to intercede. The one thing for which all timetables should be put aside (in order that it is done) is intercession. The only thing that cannot be left for tomorrow is intercession. Sudden burdens are God's emergency calls upon His people to act with Him in an emergency. Not to respond at once is great folly. Such burdens are the calls of God to special duty. Because of Who He is, His calls take precedence over all other calls even if the other calls are from an earthly ruler. Those who know authority know that the authority that must be obeyed first in every situation is the highest. God is the highest authority and when He calls to a task, all other things and all other calls must be allowed to wait. Not to put this into practice is to fail and to fail in intercession is to fail utterly.

May we learn from the intercessors of Jerusalem. Of them the Lord says,

> *"Upon your walls, O Jerusalem, I have set watchmen, all the day and all the night they shall never be silent. You who put the Lord in remembrance, take no rest, and give him no rest until he establishes Jerusalem and makes it a praise in the earth"* (Isaiah 62:6-7).

They were to take no rest, and they were to give God no rest. It was most urgent. They laboured at it in the day and they laboured at it in the night. All else was suspended; their normal activities were suspended; sleep was suspended, and everything was put into the work of pleading with God.

The intercessors of this day must see the urgency with which they must carry out their duties. The intercessor for an individual, a family, a city, a nation, a continent must know that one day or an hour of delay could be fatal. There are decisions being made by individuals, by families, for cities, for nations, for continents, for planet Earth that could be altered by the intercessor. There are laws being thought about that could be altered by him if he acts at once through intercession. If he acts after the laws have been passed or wrong decisions taken, he has lost the battle. He must act at once! He must act today! He must act now!

Every intercessor needs to know that there are many situations that cannot wait. He cannot just passively wait for the good pleasure of God. He is not only dealing with God. He is also dealing with the devil. The devil is urgent and when the intercessor decides to postpone things the devil always decides to act at once. We know that often in warfare the one who acts first wins.

Decide today that you will act at once and then act! Be urgent when it is convenient and be urgent when it is inconvenient. Intercede when you feel like interceding. Intercede when all of your being rebels against intercession. Intercede according to your programme. Intercede when your programme does not permit it. By all means intercede. Amen.

14

THE INTERCESSOR AND HIS BIBLE

We shall look briefly at some intercessors of the Bible as we approach the whole matter of the intercessor and his Bible.

MOSES

Moses said to the Lord,

> *"Remember Abraham, Isaac, and Israel, thy servants, to whom thou didst swear by thine own self, and did say to them, I will multiply your descendants as the stars of heaven, and all this land that I have promised I will give to your descendants, and they shall inherit it for ever. And the Lord repented of the evil which he thought to do to his people"* (Exodus 32:13-14).

Moses knew the following:

1. God had sworn to Abraham, Isaac, and Jacob by His own self.
2. God had told them He would multiply their descendants as the stars of heaven.

3. God had promised that He would give their descendants land to inherit for ever.

Knowing all these things that God had promised and even sworn, Moses then pleaded with God to forgive the people, for not to do so would have meant that He would be breaking His Word. The result of this was that God changed His mind and spared the people. Without a knowledge of the oath that God had taken and the promises that He had made, Moses would have had no arguments with which to intercede. Having the knowledge, Moses was more or less saying, "My God, it is absolutely necessary for the sake of Your own integrity that You forgive these people."

Moses did not only know the promise of God. He knew Bible history. He said to the Lord,

> "O Lord, why does thy wrath burn hot against thy people, whom thou hast brought forth out of the land of Egypt with great power and with a mighty hand? Why should the Egyptians say, With evil intent did he bring them forth, to slay them in the mountains, and to consume them from the face of the earth? Turn from thy fierce wrath, and repent of this evil against thy people" (Exodus 32:11-12).

Moses knew the following:

The people of Israel were God's people. He knew that God had said,

> "Now therefore, if you will obey my voice and keep my covenants, you shall be my own possession among all the people; for all the earth is mine, and you shall be to me a kingdom of priests and a holy nation" (Exodus 19:5-6).

He knew that God had not yet disowned them and therefore they were His people.

The Lord had brought the people of Israel out of Egypt with great power and great might.

The Egyptians would speak evil of the Lord if the people perished in the wilderness.

Using the facts, Moses was more or less saying, "Lord, it is to the best interest of Your all glorious name that You pardon these people."

Without a knowledge of the events that had taken place and the promises of God, Moses would not have been able to intercede successfully. But as we can see, he knew them, used them, and won the battle.

Another important thing comes clearly. Moses approached the matter of having the children of Israel forgiven from two angles. He approached it from the self-commitment of God and he approached it from what the Egyptians would say. From both angles, he insisted that God should change His mind. An intercessor must work out all the possible ways in which he would tackle the issue with God. The more the ways, the better. In addition, the intercessor must try as possibly as he can to argue that it is necessary for God's glory that the intercession is granted. It is only when this fails absolutely that some other approach is needed.

NEHEMIAH

Nehemiah in interceding said to God,

> "Remember the word which thou didst command thy servant Moses, saying, If you are unfaithful, I will scatter you among the peoples; but if you return to me and keep my commandments and do them, though your dispersed be under the farthest skies, I will gather them thence and bring them to the place which I have chosen, to make my name dwell there.

They are thy servants and thy people, whom thou hast redeemed by thy great power and thy strong hand" (Nehemiah 1:8—10).

Nehemiah knew the following:

1. God had given His command to Moses.
2. He knew the contents of the command. He knew that the command said that if the people sinned, they would be scattered. If in exile they returned to Him and kept His commandments, He would bring them to their land.
3. He knew that the function of an intercessor was to stand in the gap on behalf of the people. He knew that all the people had not repented and returned to the Lord. However, he had and therefore, as one for the whole, he demanded that God do that which He had promised He would do if the people repented.

In the practice of intercession, one represents all. One argues with God on behalf of all, one repents and gets right with God and after doing that argues with God that the people have repented and gotten right with God. This is a fundamental principle in intercession. It is also a principle that is widely applied in God's dealings with man. We see this in the fact that Adam sinned and all men sinned in him and Christ died and rose again and multitudes die to sin and self and rise up in Him. The high priest said, "You know nothing at all, you do not understand that it is expedient for you that one man should die for the people, and that the whole nation should not perish." He did not say this of his own accord, but being high priest that year he prophesied that Jesus should die for the nation, and not for the nation only, but to gather into one the children of God who are scattered abroad (John 11:49-52).

You, as an intercessor, represent the person, the persons, the city, the nation, and the continent you are interceding for. When you have gotten right with God then they have gotten right. This, however, means that unless you are absolutely right with God you cannot plead for another. All who are living in sin in one area or the other in their lives are excluded from intercession. They may make noise but it will surely be to no avail.

Nehemiah knew the Word and acted upon it! God answered!!

DANIEL

The Bible says,

> "In the first year of Darius the son of Ahasuerus, by birth a Mede, who became king over the realm of the Chaldeans - in the first year of his reign, I, Daniel, perceived in the books the number of years which, according to the word of the Lord to Jeremiah the prophet, must pass before the end of the desolations of Jerusalem, namely, seventy years.
>
> "Then I turned my face to the Lord God, seeking him by prayer and supplications with fasting and sackcloth and ashes. I prayed to the Lord my God and made confession, saying, O Lord, the great and terrible God, who keepest covenant and steadfast love with those who love him and keep his commandments. . . Now therefore, O our God, hearken to the prayer of thy servant and to his supplication, and for thy own sake, O Lord, cause thy face to shine upon thy sanctuary, which is desolate. O my God, incline thy ear and hear; open thy eyes and behold our desolations, and the only city which is called by thy name; for we do not present our supplications before thee on the grounds of our righteousness, but on the ground of thy great mercy. O Lord, hear; O Lord, forgive, O Lord give heed and act; delay not, for thy own sake, O my God, because thy city and thy people are called by thy name" (Daniel 9:1-19).

Daniel walked with God. He was a student of the Word. Had he *not* studied the Word, he would not have perceived in the books that the number of years, which, according to the word of God to Jeremiah the prophet, must pass before the end of the desolations of Jerusalem had indeed ended. Because he saw this, he did three things:

1. He turned his face to the Lord and put aside all else.
2. He sought the Lord by praying and supplication.
3. His prayer and supplication were with fasting, sackcloth and ashes.
4. He was desperate to succeed. He *did not say,* "God promised in Jeremiah chapter twenty-five verses eleven and twelve saying, "This whole land shall become a ruin and a waste, and these nations shall serve the king of Babylon seventy years. Then after seventy years are completed, I will punish the king of Babylon and that nation, the land of the Chaldeans, for their iniquity, says the Lord," and therefore He is compelled to do it.

Every intercessor knows that there is a sense in which God is compelled to do nothing until He finds those who will cooperate with Him in prayer. Knowing this, and knowing that the time was fulfilled, Daniel turned his face to the Lord, sought Him by prayer and supplications with fasting, sackcloth and ashes and pleaded that God should act.

Daniel interceded that God should act for His own sake. There were the two aspects—the need of the people to be liberated and the need of God to fulfil His word.

The final note of Daniel's intercession was that the Lord should give heed, act, and not delay:

1. For *thy* own name's sake.

2. Because of *thy* city.
3. Because of *thy* people.
4. Because *thy* people are called by *thy* name.

Again we see that although all the people had not yet repented, Daniel's repentance and holy walk with God was used as an argument that the people had repented. He used *we,* considering that his repentance and holy walk were representative. We praise the Lord that He established this principle and honours it and because of that, the salvation of the lost and intercession are possible.

Did He not say,

> *"Run to and fro through the streets of Jerusalem, look and take note! Search her squares to see if you can find a man, one who does justice and seeks truth; that I may pardon her" (Jeremiah 5:1).*

One man would have been enough for all to be spared. Let us rise, get absolutely right with God, and intercede. Many will be spared. Many will be blessed.

THE INTERCESSOR OF TODAY AND HIS BIBLE

The intercessor of today will need to be a student of God's Word. He will read and reread it and read it again. He will read it so that it may help him to know God and draw close to Him. He will read it so as to know the promises of God, the conditions under which God has promised He would do certain things. He will read it in order to know what man must do in order to have God do some things. He will read and he will study it in order to know the history therein, on the basis of which God often acts. He will read and study it in order to know the timing of God. For example, had Daniel not known the timing of God, he might have been pressing on God not to delay, twenty years ahead of the promised date!

The intercessor will read the Bible in general and know it. Then he will read the prayers of the Bible and study them in detail. Furthermore, he will study the praying men and women of the Bible. He will learn the secret of moving the hand of God, of being a co-worker with Him and realizing that God delights in fulfilling His Word. He will make sure that he prays according to the promises of God. Then he will succeed. Failure in a knowledge of the Bible can prove fatal to an intercessor. He may have a burden and groan but he will not have the right words to express his burden to God. He will be like a man who is faced with a snake to kill, is zealous, strong, and willing to kill it but lacks a stick with which to bring the enemy reptile's life to an end. God bless you as you take the Word more seriously.

15

THE INTERCESSOR AND PERSONAL REVELATION

As an intercessor makes progress in the School of Intercession, he will need to know the mind of God on a number of issues that are related to the object of intercession or to God's purpose that cannot be obtained directly from the Bible. Take for example the fact that the Lord may be angry against a nation and plans to punish it. How will the intercessor know so that he may stand in the gap on behalf of that nation? The only answer is that the intercessor must be someone to whom God can speak at a personal level; someone to whom God is compelled to reveal the thoughts in His heart before they happen.

Abraham was one such man and of him God says,

> *"The Lord said, Shall I hide from Abraham what I am about to do, seeing that Abraham shall become a great and mighty nation, and all the nations of the earth shall bless themselves by him?" (Genesis 18:-17-18).*

There were reasons why God felt "compelled" to tell Abraham what He was about to do. Had God not revealed to Abraham what He was about to do, Abraham would not have known and had Abraham not known, he would not have interceded.

Moses was another man of the same kind. Had God hid His intentions to destroy the children of Israel from him, he would not have known and therefore, he would not have interceded. However, God revealed what He was about to do to him. The Bible says,

> *"And the Lord said to Moses, I have seen this people, and behold, it is a stiff-necked people, now therefore let me alone, that my wrath may burn hot against them and I may consume them, but of you I will make a great nation"* (Exodus 32:9—10).

When Moses heard this he set out to intercede.

To a modern-day intercessor the Lord said, "Judgment is coining on this nation. You can do something to delay it by prayer but it must surely come. It cannot be averted completely without national repentance. It cannot be averted unless hundreds of thousands turn to Me in deep repentance and humble themselves. Those who walk the way of truth are in short supply. Truth is lacking. Lying and hypocrisy are the national way of life. Even the lips of My people are not free from lying and many hearts are false that say they belong to Me. Judgment is coming. When it comes, it will be swift and fast and many will be taken by surprise."

When the Lord spoke that way, the intercessor in question and others who were labouring with him, continued to intercede and plead. Judgment did come upon that land but after two years the Lord again spoke saying, "I will bless your nation. I will bless your nation. I will bless her not because of her righteousness but because I have chosen to bless her. I will bless her and anyone who stands in My way I will take out of the way. Pray that My blessing will flow forth unhindered." The message gave a fresh impetus to our prayer.

The question is, "How can one receive revelation from the Lord?" The answer is that there are no techniques involved. The Bible says,

> *"The friendship of the Lord is for those who fear him, and he makes known to them his covenants"* (Psalms 25:14).

> *"He made known his ways to Moses, his acts to the people of Israel"* (Psalms 103:7).

If a man's heart is pure towards the Lord and he fears the Lord, God will show him the things in His heart.

The other thing is that God answers the prayers of those whose hearts are right towards Him. An intercessor can ask for special revelation. Moses prayed for such a revelation when he asked,

> *"Now therefore I pray thee, if I have found favour in thy sight, show me now thy ways, that I may know thee and find favour in thy sight. Consider too that this nation is thy people" And he said, "My presence will go with you, and I will give you rest"* (Exodus 33:14).

God answered the prayer of Moses for revelation. He will answer yours if you are rightly related to Him. It will require that you be one who waits before Him in silence even as the Psalmist confessed,

> *"For God alone my soul waits in silence; from him comes my salvation"* (Psalms 62:1).

Those who wait in silence hear His voice. Those who make prayer a dialogue hear His voice.

Those who make prayer a monologue do not hear His voice. He wants to speak but because they would not give Him an opportunity to speak, He is compelled to keep silent.

An intercessor who does not hear God is finally of little consequence to the King and to the kingdom. May the Lord grant that you never become such a one.

16

THE INTERCESSOR AND SECRECY

One of the problems that the King of heaven has in our day is a shortage of people who can keep a secret. The people who indeed hear the Lord's real voice in our day are few, very few. Fewer still are those who can, after hearing God's voice, keep their mouths shut. The desire to receive the praise that comes from man has eaten so deep into the fibres of the Church in our day that it is almost impossible to find a man who is not doing one thing or the other to advertise himself. The apostle Paul was given revelations by the Lord, some of which he kept to himself for twelve years. On many occasions, when the Lord Jesus performed miracles, He told the recipients of the miracles to tell no one. He did not want the praise of men.

For anyone to reach high levels in the School of Intercession, he must know how to keep a secret. God will show him things to come so that he may be able to intercede intelligently. He ought to consider what the Lord has told him as a sacred trust and not tell anyone about it, rather, to give himself to intense intercession that the promise of God might be fulfilled or that promised judgment would be averted. This means that there will be burdens that the intercessor will bear alone. They will weigh on his heart and come close to crushing him but he would have to keep his mouth shut.

Unless a person is prepared for burden-bearing in that way, only sharing what the Lord commands him to share, he will not be allowed to progress beyond some point in the School of Intercession. This is because the processes through which God produces mature intercessors includes the following:

1. The bearing of heavy burdens alone.
2. Pressures.
3. Loneliness.
4. Misunderstandings where a word of explanation would have brought relief.
5. Rejection."

So the one who would make progress must accept these as part of the price to be paid for the ministry of intercession. These are useful instruments against the self-life and the intercessor is only too aware that apart from the devil, his other potent enemy is himself or the self in him.

In the pathway of secrecy, the intercessor will experience some of what the apostle Paul experienced when he wrote,

> *"We are afflicted in every way, but not crushed, perplexed, but not driven to despair; persecuted, but not forsaken; struck down, but not destroyed; always carrying in the body the death of Jesus, so that the life of Jesus may also be manifested in our bodies. For while we live we are always being given up to death for Jesus' sake so that the life of Jesus may be manifested in our mortal flesh. So death is at work in us, but life in you"* (2 Corinthians 4:8-12).

I have asked myself why I rush to tell people what God has told me in secret. Although it is possible to give many useful reasons, I have to admit that the real reason has its roots in the self-life. Somehow, I want people to know that God has spoken to me. I want people to know that I am interceding. I want people to know, when what the Lord has said would come to pass has come to pass, that I was correct in hearing Him. To put it plainly, I must admit that something inside me still wants the praises of men.

> *"Lord, have mercy on me. Deliver me from the love of myself so that I will not frustrate Your purpose by putting a limit to the progress that You have ordained for me to make in the School of Intercession. Lord, deliver me from the self-life in other areas of my service for You so that I may grow into a vessel that is useful in Your hands. Lord, I ask this in the name of the Lord Jesus Christ. Amen."*

Does that prayer also express the desire of your heart? If it does, pray it to the Father in the name of the Lord Jesus. Continue to pray along those lines until God does something to increase your freedom from the self-life.

The intercessor must not only pray. He must take practical steps to keep the things that God has told him to himself. There is no substitute for that. Amen.

THE INTERCESSOR AND A KNOWLEDGE OF FACTS

As we have already shown, there are some facts about a person, persons, and places that only God knows. For anyone to have that knowledge, God has to reveal these to him. However, there are many facts that can be found out by human effort. Let us look at some examples of such.

An intercessor for a minister needs to know the following and more and could easily find out:

1. His working hours.
2. The quality of his relationship with his wife.
3. The quality of his relationship with his children.
4. The quality of his relationship with unbelievers.
5. What he is doing at all hours of the day each day or on a day-to-day basis.
6. What his health problems are.
7. What health problems he is inclined to by genetic inheritance.
8. What his character strengths are.
9. What his character weaknesses are.

10. Where his basic weakness is: Is it the love of money, women, or fame?
11. Is he given to food?
12. What is his vision?
13. Has it gripped him in such a way that nothing can separate him from it?
14. Is he paying all the price that he should pay?
15. Does he read the Word?
16. Doe he pray? If he does, is it with real intensity?
17. What is he counting on as the source of his power?
18. How does he want success in his ministry to be manifested?
19. Does he fast?
20. Does he withdraw to seek God often?
21. Does he listen to God?
22. Is he very susceptible to public opinion?
23. Does he have the strength of his convictions?
24. What is the level of his basic education?
25. Does he have a superiority or inferiority complex about his education?
26. Does he have a superiority or inferiority complex about his physical appearance?
27. Does he have a friend?
28. Does he have friends?
29. Does he listen to others?
30. Is he able to build a team?
31. Is he building a team?
32. Is he at home with his superiors and inferiors?
33. Is he deeply interested in people?
34. Does he hurt when people hurt?
35. What are his future plans about himself?
36. What are his future plans about the ministry?
37. Is he ministering out of the desire to earn a living or out of burden?

38. What problems preoccupy him?
39. What hurts him easily?
40. What hurts is he carrying from childhood?
41. In what areas of his personality does he need inner healing?
42. What is his specific gift for ministry?
43. What is his motivational gift?
44. And so many other things.

By carefully listening, by asking questions, by fellowshipping with the man, by listening to what his friends say, by listening to what his enemies say, you should have the answers to these important questions that will help you intercede for the man as you ought to.

An intercessor for a city ought to find out the following facts by talking to people, by reading books, by interviewing people, by reading the newspapers, by listening to what is happening and by many other methods that are open to him.

1. The size of the city.
2. The population.
3. The sins committed there in the past.
4. The spiritual history of the city: Has God once moved there in might; was the gospel ever preached there? Was there a move by her leaders for or against the gospel? Did the gospel ever go from there to other parts of the nation or world? Does it seem to have some significant spiritual importance?
5. The special sin or sins of the city.
6. The religious system that predominates there.
7. The natural disasters that have occurred there.
8. The natural disasters that are likely to occur there, e.g., is it in a belt where earthquakes are likely?

9. The different tribal groups represented in her and the attitude of each to the Lord and the gospel.
10. The different nationalities represented there and the attitude of each to the Lord and the gospel.
11. The economic system.
12. The availability of food.
13. The political system.
14. Who the leaders are.
15. What the lawmaking system is like.
16. The commitment of the leaders and the people to keeping the law.
17. The greatest fear of the political leaders.
18. The greatest strength of the government in power.
19. The greatest influence on the Head of State.
20. The power struggle in the government.
21. The educational system.
22. The employment opportunities.
23. The attitude of the youths to God.
24. The attitude of the youths to life as a whole.
25. The family structure.
26. The divorce rate.
27. The suicide rate.
28. The extent of the spread of the gospel among the people.
29. Was the gospel preached by people who were students in the school of prayer, holiness, fasting. ... Or was it preached by religious showmen?
30. The presence or absence of a team or teams that are given to the one task of praying for God's move in the city.
31. The presence or absence of a chain or chains of people who will give God no rest and are taking no rest until He has risen, moved in power, and blessed the city.
32. The presence or absence of local assemblies where the

Lord is being worshipped in spirit and truth and separation from sin and the world is being emphasized.
33. The presence or absence of a man or men of God of true spiritual weight.
34. Any prophecies that have stated God's mind for the city, for better or for worse.
35. The extent to which one, some, or all of these have come to pass.
36. The state of maturation of the saints in the city.
37. The presence or absence of Bibles and good Christian litenature .
38. The heresies present in the churches.
39. The quality of spiritual leadership.
40. The commitment of the assemblies to minister to children and so on.

As we have said, these facts can be found out and they should be found out and used in intercession. They may even be instrumental in showing the direction in which the intercessor must proceed. For example, a man who is interceding for a city that has heard the gospel clearly and then turned its back to God will not continue on the same basis with another intercessor who is interceding for a city where the gospel has never been preached. A person interceding for a city that is under the grip of a false kind of Christianity has a different type of problem from that of another man who is interceding for a city with men of God who walk close to Him and are, through the instrumentalities of prayer, sacrifice, radical obedience to Jesus Christ, holiness and fasting, resisting the devil constantly. A person interceding for a city from which the gospel is going out to many nations has a different task from that of a person interceding for a city filled with many believers who are given to comfort, ease and self-preservation and have no vision beyond themselves. Because these details are important, the intercessor should seek and have them.

The intercessor will be a man of alertness. He will listen to what is going on in the government, banks, business, schools, and he will gather facts, analyse them, and then know how to pray. He will find out what are the popular books, films, concerts, and the like that are attracting crowds and then he will analyse these and know what to bind in prayer and what to release in prayer. He will weigh every law that is passed as to how it affects the kingdom of God. He will weigh every comment, joke, project, and so forth in the same light. He knows that the ultimate purpose of his intercession is the glory of the Lord Jesus being established in that city and from that he never departs. That is his job.

The Lord God said,

> *"My people are destroyed for lack of knowledge"* (Hosea 4:6).

May it not be true of any intercessor that he failed in intercession because he was too lazy to obtain the knowledge that he ought to have obtained by disciplined search and by disciplined recording of events as they happened.

Praise the Lord!

THE INTERCESSOR AND WORLD CONQUEST FOR CHRIST

The Bible says of the Lord Jesus that,

> "When he saw the crowds, he had compassion for them because they were harassed and helpless, like sheep without a shepherd. Then he said to his disciples, The harvest is plentiful, but the labourers are few; pray therefore the Lord of the harvest to send out labourers into his harvest.
>
> "And he called to him his twelve disciples and gave them authority over unclean spirits to cast them out, and to heal every disease and every infirmity. The names of the twelve apostles are these: first Simon, who is called Peter, and Andrew his brother; James the son of Zebedee, and John his brother; Philip and Bartholomew; Thomas and Matthew the tax collector; James the son of Alphaeus, and Thaddaeus; Simon the Cananaean, and Judas Iscariot, who betrayed him.
>
> "...These twelve Jesus sent out, charging them, "Go nowhere among the Gentiles, and enter no town of the Samaritans, but go rather to the lost sheep of the house of Israel. And preach as you go, saying, The kingdom of heaven is at hand. Heal the sick, raise the dead, cleanse lepers, cast out demons. You received without paying, give without pay. Take no gold, nor

silver, nor copper in your belts, no bag for your journey, nor two tunics, nor sandals, nor a staff; for the labourer deserves his food" (Matthew 9:36-10:1-10).

When the Lord saw the crowds, he had compassion for them because they were harassed and helpless, like sheep without a shepherd. He did not do what many have done over the years:

1. Form a missionary organization.
2. Work out a method of recruiting candidates.
3. Work out a method of funding.
4. Decide what fields they wanted to go to.
5. Decide the dates for the departure of the first group of misionaries .
6. Work out the details of the laws and by-laws that will bind them, and so on.

The Lord instead gave God's verdict for world conquest for Christ. He gave God's verdict on how to handle the ripe and perhaps the overripe harvests of the world. He gave God's point of view, which is timeless, about the issue. The Lord Jesus understood that the harvest was God's and not man's. Today people compete for regions and publish false figures about the extent of their success. This is horrible! They went their own way, to do a work of their own initiative, in a place of their own choosing, at the time of their own choosing, by methods that are essentially worldly.

The Lord's verdict was that those who had seen the ripe harvest and the few labourers, were to pray to the Lord of the harvest to send out labourers into His harvest. The harvest is God's. It does not belong to this mission or the other. It does not belong to this denomination or that other one. The harvest is God's and it could be that the "harvest" of many denominations or missions is not

God's. Those whose eyes have been opened *see*. They *see* and they know that the harvest is God's. They also know that only God can send out labourers into His harvest. He knows that all the labourers who are sent out at man's initiative, will in the long run, ruin the harvest.

Because the Lord commanded that man's real part in world conquest was to pray to the Father of the harvest to send out labourers into His harvest, we can safely say that the harvest "belongs to the Lord and the intercessors." God's principal co-workers in the task of conquering the world for Christ are intercessors. Whether there will be labourers in the Lord's harvest fields the world over, will depend on whether or not there are intercessors who, night and day, will take no rest and give God no rest until He arises and sends forth labourers into His harvest.

Such intercessors must see what the Lord has seen. They must not only be familiar with the number of people who are on Planet Earth and how many people are dying without Christ, but they like Christ, would *see* the crowds. The "crowds" that a real intercessor sees may be one person, ten people, one thousand people, or one billion people. The Lord will work in such a way that once the "crowd" has been "seen" the Holy Spirit will give the burden that will make the person to intercede and intercede until the Lord has raised people for His harvest. Yes, the intercessor would see the people harassed and helpless, like sheep without a shepherd. He would, on seeing them, have compassion for them. The compassion will become a burden that weighs heavily on the intercessor's heart and he would be compelled to do something about it not because of the manipulations of skilful men using figures and pictures to create a temporary impact, but in response to the inner movement of the Holy Spirit. Thus touched by the Lord, he would pour himself out at any cost to himself, interceding until the Lord has raised up labourers for His harvest.

The greatest need of the moment in order that the gospel may be proclaimed to the whole world is not funds as many think. The greatest need is not people who are willing to go out into the harvest of the Lord. The greatest need is *for* intercessors who will plead with God, "O Lord, O my Lord, look at these perishing people. Look at them rushing on to perdition. Lord, look at them being harassed by false doctrines, look at them swimming slowly to the lake of fire. Lord, look at them giving themselves so wholeheartedly to a religion that has no cross and no Saviour. Lord, would You not do something about it? Would You not act quickly? Won't You, O Lord, move at once and save some? …"

Such men and women will not only pray that the Lord should send out labourers into His harvest. They will intercede that God send out the labourers who are labourers indeed. They will intercede against labourers sent out by mere men or merely by human organizations. They would plead, "Lord, protect Your harvest from the hirelings that are being recruited by this organization or the other one. Lord, do not allow that man or that woman to go out. Lord, You know that You are not sending them. Lord, You know that if they go, they will preach a distorted message and the people will eventually be disappointed and may never turn to the Lord. Lord, in Your might prevent false labourers, hirelings, the disobedient, the lovers of the world, the lovers of fame . . . from going into the harvest and spoiling it. Lord, do it now, O Lord. Lord, O Lord, move in for the sake of the One who died on the cross."

When intercessors pray, God will do the following:

1. He will pick out people who love the Lord Jesus.
2. He will lay a burden for the lost on them.
3. He will further train them in the Jesus' School of Missions. In this school, the principal subjects will be: a)

how to love the Lord with all your spirit, soul and body; b) how to hate sin with a deep hatred; c) how to possess and maintain a broken and contrite heart; d) how to fast and pray; e) how to put on the character of Christ; f) humility; g) believing in God; h) burden for the lost; and i) how to walk by faith.
4. He will raise more men to pray for them.
5. He will decide the where, when, with whom, and so on of their ministry.
6. He will send them out into His harvest.
7. He will give them authority to overcome all the powers of the wicked one.
8. He will ensure that they bear fruit and that their fruit abide to the glory of God.

The Lord Jesus demonstrated this soon after He told the disciples the secret of world conquest. He did the following:

- He called to Himself the twelve whom He had trained in the school where knowing Him, walking with Him, and serving Him were the principal subjects.
- He gave them authority.
- He sent them out.
- He sent them to very specific places.
- He gave them the message which they were to proclaim.
- He gave them clear instructions about money and other material possessions.
- They went away and were a success.

The methods of God always work. His method for world conquest for Christ is prayer first. It is turning to God to do the one thing that only He can do: send out labourers into His harvest! It is intercession!

May the Lord move in our hearts and transform them into hearts that labour at intercession!

THE INTERCESSOR AND HIS NEEDS

There is a fundamental need for the intercessor to grow in spiritual depth and in the knowledge of the Lord Jesus. There is also great need that he should grow in spiritual experience. Without this, he will find it difficult to discharge his ministry.

Take for an example, an intercessor for a man who is called by the Lord to the overthrow of principalities and powers. If that intercessor is to be effective he has to have Biblical and practical knowledge of what is involved in the overthrow of principalities and powers. If his knowledge is superficial, he will intercede superficially. But if his knowledge is profound, he will intercede profoundly. Therefore there is a fundamental need for an intercessor to experience what the one he is interceding for is going through. An intercessor who has no knowledge of principalities and powers and the wrestling that must take place in the spiritual realm can, at best, just throw some words at God. He cannot agonize. A young believer who wants to intercede for a mature warrior will not be able to do it satisfactorily. He may learn the correct vocabulary of what is involved but his lack of experience will show up. Deep issues call for deep people. Deep issues can only be interceded for by deep people. Mighty warriors can only be interceded for by mighty intercessors.

This means that an honest intercessor will ask himself some questions like the following:

1. Do I understand, intellectually, what this person is going through?
2. Do I understand, spiritually, what he is going through?
3. Am I able to stand with him in this battle?
4. Am I able to stand against the forces that are against him?

If upon asking these questions he finds that he is not equal to the task, two pathways are open to him. One is for him to leave the matter entirely and confess that the issue demands someone of greater and deeper spiritual experience than himself and move to the issues within his competence and there fulfil his ministry. The other possibility is to ask God to reveal to him what he does not know and to enlarge his heart so that he is able to handle the situation. The Lord will answer such a prayer and enable the person to satisfy the heart of God in the situation by interceding accordingly.

The fact that God is able and will step into an emergency and cause an intercessor to have sudden spiritual expansion is a miracle. God will allow such to happen occasionally but He will not allow an intercessor to continuously live beyond his spiritual depth. The way out is that the intercessor must grow.

If an intercessor intends to invest his whole life interceding for one who is called upon by the Lord to overthrow principalities and powers, he should labour to grow and attain the spiritual heights that the person he is interceding for has attained. He will need to know where he (the intercessor) is spiritually. He will also need to know where the one called to war against principalities and powers is spiritually. He will now set out to ensure that the Lord does something to promote him to the spiritual level of the one for whom he has to intercede. He will have to pray and to actively seek to grow. My suggestion is that he should go 'on a spiritual retreat and there ask God to show him the spiritual difference between him and the one for whom he wants to intercede. This is necessary because too often we think that we are at a certain level spiritually, whereas the reality is that we are below it. The other thing is that we are often so blinded by our own sense of self-importance that we do not fully see that some of God's frontline soldiers have made so much spiritual progress in a very short time that they have entered "the glory of God." Time taken on retreat during which we ask God to show us the two positions will be useful and indeed indispensable.

When the revelation of the spiritual gap between the intercessor and the person for whom he wants to intercede has been received, the intercessor will labour to grow rapidly in order to bridge the gap. He may pray the Lord to meet his needs as follows:

1. Lord, thank You for opening my eyes to see my need of spiritual growth, growth that is indispensable for me to pray for ....
2. Lord, enable me to study Your word more seriously in order to grow and bridge the gap.
3. Lord, enable me to receive revelation as I read Your word so as to grow faster.
4. Lord, enable me to grow in the other areas of prayer: Thanksgiving, praise, adoration, and so on.
5. Lord, enable me to grow in obeying You in all things, small and big, so that I may find favour with You and give You an opportunity to reveal Yourself increasingly to me.

6. Lord, cause me to hate sin increasingly so that my communion with You will deepen.
7. Lord, enable me to give more sacrificially to Your service.
8. Lord, open my eyes to see anything in my life that does not please You and give me grace to put it away.
9. Lord, You are able to restore past years that were wasted. I plead that You restore to me the years that I wasted in sin, folly, and purposelessness so that I may use them to make spiritual progress.
10. Lord, one day before You is like a thousand years and there is nothing too hard for You. I pray, Lord, that You will perform a miracle so that I will learn the lessons that I ought to have learned in a thousand years in one day and therefore be one thousand years ahead. This will make me to know what I need in order to pray for as I ought.
11. Lord, open my eyes to see what You have enabled Your servant for whom I am interceding to see, so that I will be an able intercessor for him.
12. Lord, put on my heart the burden that You have put on his heart so that together we may accomplish that which needs to be accomplished: he by the method You have given him to war with, and I, by interceding for him.

It becomes obvious that the intercessor has to grow not only in the ministry of intercession, but in other aspects of the Christian life knowledge of God; giving to the Lord, Christian character, walking in the Spirit, and so on. Without this growth, he will be hindered in his ministry.

This is probably why many, intercessors of the Bible interceded and carried out other activities in life. They either set fixed times of each day for intercession or they set aside seasons for intercession. This enabled them to grow as believers and also as intercessors.

It, therefore, follows that an intercessor will spend a good portion of his prayer time praying for himself and thereby contributing to the building of his ministry as an intercessor. No one should become so preoccupied with praying for another that he allows his spiritual life to become barren. If anyone does that he will soon find that the obvious evidence of neglecting his spiritual life would be the loss of the burden to intercede.

A wise intercessor will also prayerfully control the other areas of his life, for they will affect his ministry. He must control his health, finances, job, family, and every aspect of his life. He will labour in prayer to ensure that the Lord is reigning in each of these areas and thereby increase his chances of fighting the good fight of faith through intercession.

20

THE INTERCESSOR AND THE SOVEREIGN WILL OF GOD

We have said that the Lord does exalt the intercessor to a place of such authority with Him that He will do anything that the intercessor asks Him to do. Although this is true, it must be remembered that the intercessor remains man, "a god, a little less than God" and not God the Almighty. The final decisions must be left with God. No intercessor can ever take God to task and ask Him (God) to explain why He did not do as he (the intercessor) had asked.

There are a number of reasons why an intercessor may not succeed:

1. The intercessor may not have fulfilled the conditions of holiness required to intercede at the level at which he was interceding. He was handling an issue that was too big for him and that required someone of greater spiritual weight, authority, holiness, and experience. Sure enough, he was very sincere, but sincerity is not all. Take for example, a young and zealous believer who tried to carry a nation or a continent through a major issue, and

therefore fasted and prayed for two, three, four, or six weeks. His prayers were well worded. His fasts were sacrificial, but he was not just the man for the job. Prayer and fasts are good, but before God looks at the quality of the fast he looks at the man who is fasting. When such a one fails, he should not give up to discouragement, but rather say to the Lord, "I did the best I could. I accept your verdict. You are absolutely correct. Praise, honour, and glory be to Your name."

2. The conditions for the intervention of God may be such that a single intercessor is not equal to the task. Take the matter of Sodom and Gomorrah, for example. It was settled by God and Abraham that these cities would be spared if ten righteous people were found in them. Ten righteous people were not found there and therefore God destroyed them. He had been faithful to Himself and to the intercessor. In fact He had been faithful to these cities for *"the outcry against Sodom and Gomorrah is great and their sin is very grave" (Genesis 18:20 ESV)*. He had spared them for long. He had *"Endured with much patience the vessel of wrath made for destruction" (Romans, 9:22)*, and the day of wrath had finally come.

3. The person, persons, city, nation for which intercession is being made might have crossed the fatal line. We know that there is a point that no one knows, but the Lord, that may be reached in a man's rejection of God, that return is impossible. Pharaoh hardened his heart against God many times but there was a point reached where God gave him up and began to harden his heart. From that point on, Pharaoh was hardening his heart against God and God was hardening Pharaoh's heart against Himself. Intercession would have been useless then. It was too late.

The Lord Jesus gave Judas Iscariot three and a half years to repent. He studied under the best Teacher and received the best ministry, but hardened his heart and remained a thief for the entire length of time. Towards the end, he refused the Lord's final appeal of love. From that moment Satan entered into him and it was too late. Before, Satan acted from outside. From then on, he acted from inside. When that point was reached, the Lord stopped interceding for him. He instead cursed him! Intercession would have been useless.

The Lord Jesus in talking to some of the cities where the most of His mighty deeds had been done, said,

> "Woe to you, Chorazin! Woe to you Bethsaida! For if the mighty words done in you had been done in Tyre and Sidon, they would have repented long ago in sackcloth and ashes. But I tell you, it shall be more tolerable on the Day of Judgment for Tyre and Sidon than for you. And you, Capernaum, will you be exalted to heaven? You shall be brought down to Hades. For if the mighty works done in you had been done in Sodom, it would have remained until this day. But I tell you that it shall be more tolerable on the Day of Judgment for the land of Sodom than for you" (Matthew 11:21-24).

It was too late for intercession. Even the Lord, the King of intercessors gave them up and even cursed them. Tears, prayers, cries, and fasts for such places are wasted.

The Lord, continuing to emphasize the fact that a point may be reached where intercession is useless said,

> "Though Moses and Samuel stood before me, yet my heart would not turn toward this people. Send them out of my sight and let them go! And when they ask you, Where shall we go? you shall say to them, Thus says the Lord: Those who are for pestilence, to pestilence, and those who are for the

> *sword, to the sword, those who are for famine, to famine, and those who are for captivity, to captivity.*
>
> *"I will appoint over them four kinds of destroyers, says the Lord: the sword to slay, the dogs to tear, and the birds of the air and the beasts of the earth to devour and to destroy" (Jeremiah 15:1-3).*

The Bible continues to proclaim, through the prophet Ezekiel, saying,

> *"Son of man, when a land sins against Me by acting faithlessly, and I stretch out my hand against it, and break its staff of bread and send famine upon it, and cut off from it man and beast, even if these three men, Noah, Daniel and Job, were in it, they would deliver their own lives by their righteousness, says the Lord God. If I cause wild beasts to pass through the land, and they ravage it, and it be made desolate, so that no man may pass through because of the beasts; even if these three men were in it, as I live, says the Lord God, they would deliver neither sons nor daughters; they alone would be delivered, but the land would be desolate. Or if I bring a sword upon the land, and say, Let a sword go through the land, and I cut off from it man and beast; though these men were in it, as I live, says the Lord God, they would deliver neither sons nor daughters, but they alone would be delivered. Or if I send a pestilence into that land, and pour mil my wrath upon it with blood, to cut off from it man and beast; even if Noah, Daniel, and Job were in it, as I live, says the Lord God, they would deliver neither son nor daughter; they would deliver but their own lives by their righteousness.*
>
> *'For thus says the Lord God: How much more when I send upon Jerusalem my four sore acts of judgment, sword, famine, evil beasts, and pestilence, to cut off from it man and beast!" (Ezekiel 14:13-21).*

In these cases it would be too late to intercede. Earlier, it would have been possible but the point of no return was reached. The apostle John taught, saying,

> *"If anyone sees his brother committing what is not a mortal sin, he will ask, and God will give him life for those whose sin is not mortal. There is sin which is mortal; I do not say that one is to pray for that. All wrongdoing is sin, but there is sin which is not mortal"* (1 John 5:16 - 18).

The clear teaching of Scripture is that intercession for one who has committed a mortal sin (a sin that is unto death) is forbidden. A person can waste his entire life interceding for such a person, but it will all be in vain. The question arises as to how to know if a person has committed a sin that is mortal. We know that Ananias and Sapphira committed a mortal sin by lying and died for it. We also know that Moses committed a mortal sin by not honouring God at the waters of Meribah and died for it, even though he asked to be allowed to go over and see the land. We know that Achan committed a mortal sin when he

> *"...saw among the spoil a beautiful mantle from Shinar, and two hundred shekels of silver, and a bar of gold weighing fifty shekels, then I coveted them, and took them; and behold, they are hidden in the earth inside my tent, with the silver underneath"* (Joshua 7:21)

We know that Korah, Dathan, Abiram, and On committed a mortal sin when they rebelled against Moses and despised his authority and the ground opened up and swallowed them. We also know that the priests Nadab and Abihu committed a mortal sin when they offered up strange fires to the Lord such as He had not commanded and were killed instantly by the Lord. We also know that Uzzah, out of a sincere but mistaken zeal to save the ark of the Lord from falling to the ground, committed a mortal sin of touching the ark and died immediately.

The Bible says,

"And when they came to the threshing floor of Nacon, Uzzah put out his hand to the ark of God and took hold of it, for the oxen stumbled. And the anger of the Lord was kindled against Uzzah; and God smote him there because he put forth his hand to the ark, and he died there beside the ark of God" (2 Samuel 6:6-7).

From these examples, it is obvious that what is a mortal sin for one person may not be a mortal sin for another person. It also shows that only a fool commits sin, even a small sin. That which he commits may be the sin unto death for him. He may die on the spot. He may die in an accident. He may die by one of many ways. God has a way of executing His judgments even now. There are people who die after a brief illness and people wonder what happened. There is surely a reason for it. It might have been God's way of dealing with the people because of a mortal sin that they committed!

All mortal sin does not result in immediate death. Moses committed a mortal sin but did not die on the spot. There are people who commit mortal sins but go on for years. There are people whom God has given up spiritually even though He allows them to go on physically for long. However, when God has given up a man who has reached the point of no return, no amount of intercession can change anything.

HOW IS THE INTERCESSOR TO KNOW?

From what we have said, it is possible to waste a lifetime of intercession pleading in a situation in which God will never answer. For such sincere but ignorant work, there will never be any reward. The life that has been spent in such activity is wasted, and what a tragic waste! Sacrificed but wasted! Disciplined but wasted!

It is imperative that the intercessor receives his ministry from the Lord both in general terms and in detail. When that is done there can be no problem of wasting a life, for the Lord will lead the intercessor to intercede where there is hope.

Lastly, as far as salvation and restoration is concerned, the best thing is for the intercessor to intercede generally until God tells him to stop. The intercessor who desires to pray for a backslider should go on praying until the backslider is restored or until God tells him that the backslider has committed a sin that is unto death.

FINALLY

All intercessors must intercede. They must work at it night and day, yet having done all, they must yield to the sovereign will of the God who cannot err. They dare not question God. They dare not be angry with Him. They yield to Him in loving submission even when what they interceded for did not happen as they wanted. They know that God's plans are the best and that the pathway chosen by the Lord will, from eternity's viewpoint, be seen as the best for the glory of God - and that is all that really matters to the intercessor. Is it not?

21

THE INTERCESSOR AND INTERCESSORS

The Bible says,

> "*Then came Amalek and fought with Israel at Rephidim. As Moses said to Joshua, Choose for us men, and go out, fight with Amalek; tomorrow I will stand on the hill with the rod of God in my hand. So Joshua did as Moses told him, and fought with Amalek; and Moses, Aaron, and Hur went up to the top of the hill. Whenever Moses held up his hand, Israel prevailed, and whenever he lowered his hand, Amalek prevailed. But Moses' hands grew weary; so they took a stone and put it under him and he sat upon it, and Aaron and Hur held up his hands, one on one side, and the other on the other side; so his hands were steady until the going down of the sun. And Joshua mowed down Amalek and his people with the edge of the sword*" (Exodus 17:8-13).

There is an interesting lesson here about intercession and prayer. We shall mention them in passing. First of all it is obvious that God's ways are not man's ways. According to human thinking, since the enemy was in the plain, what happened in the plain would be decisive. However, the reality was that the events on the plain were governed by what happened on the hill where apparently no warfare was taking place. The natural man would find it hard to associate Moses' actions on the hill with the success or failure of the battle that raged in the plain. Naturally minded people are caught up with what can be seen, touched, smelled, and all that can be perceived by the five senses. Spiritually minded people know that there is the world of spiritual reality and that the physical can really be controlled by the spiritual. To put it more plainly, God controls the affairs of men, and victory in human relationships is determined by relationship with God.

Secondly, it is obvious that God has decided that man must cooperate with Him in order that many of His designs for man can come to fruition. This is clearly seen in the fact that *"Whenever Moses held up his hands Israel prevailed, and whenever he lowered his hand Amalek prevailed."* Although the Lord was the one who asked Moses to go to war, and although Joshua was fully installed on the battleground and was putting in all that he could put in, God did not just say, "They are doing their best. I will take sides with them and let them win." God did not say, "Moses has seen the importance of prayer. He has gone on the hill and he is praying. I know that he is human. I know that it is not possible for a human being to lift up his hands tirelessly. I will look at the intentions of his heart and I will bless on the basis that he has done all that he could. I will receive the intercession when he is able and my grace will cover up for the period when he is no longer able because of sheer tiredness." God looked at Moses in strength, with hands lifted up and let Israel have victory. Then God looked at Moses, weak, exhausted with drooping hands, and He let Amalek have victory for that moment. In fact, He let Amalek continue to have victory until Moses' hands were up again. Immediately Moses' hands were up again, the victory passed from the hands of Amalek into the hands of Israel. Victory was decided by the position of Moses' hands because Moses represented the intercessor.

We say vehemently that victory is decided by whether or not the intercessor is interceding. If he is tired but willing, the battle is nevertheless lost. If he has stopped interceding when the battle is still raging, it will still be lost even though there was real victory at the moment he was actually interceding.

Lastly, God will temporarily allow a cause that has its origin in Him and in which He is most fully committed, to suffer loss if there is no intercessor, or if the intercessor does not press on to total victory. God will not take over and intercede in anyone's place. He will not fill in the gap left because an interceding man was tired, sick, or was taken up with other issues. God has raised us up to such a position of partnership with Him in the rulership of the universe through intercession that it has become almost like a company in which two people must sign the cheque for it to be cashed. God has already signed the cheque and He always signs the cheque, but the cheque cannot be cashed until the second signature, that of the intercessor, is signed through intercession. That is why even though God wanted Israel to win and had all that He had to do to cause Israel to win, whenever Moses stopped "signing the cheque" by lifting up his hands, Amalek prevailed. This is a most serious issue, for it explains much of the unaccomplished spiritual projects of today. It is also serious because it shows us how much faith God has in His children and how much good or evil they could cause by cooperating or not cooperating with Him.

THE NEED FOR UNCEASING INTERCESSION

The Bible says,

> *"Pray constantly"* (1 Thessalonians 5:17).

Because battles are decided by what happens in prayer instead of what happens on the physical front, unceasing prevailing of God's purpose demands unceasingly prevailing in prayer. Those who intercede for an individual, family, local assembly, ministry, city, nation, or continent must do so without ceasing. Each intercessor should know that while the issue in which he is battling remains unsettled, he cannot stop interceding. If he stops, much will be lost. This is the basis for prayer chains to which we shall come in a later portion of this book.

There are some issues that can be handled through occasional praying. However, there are situations in which the only way of victory is through unceasing intercession. In such situations, like the one of the battle against Amalek, the intercession had to be unceasing. The prophet Isaiah describes intercessors as people who will,

> *"Take no rest and give him no rest until he establishes Jerusalem and makes it a praise in the earth" (Isaiah 62:6-7).*

Intercessors are not just out to show people that they are serious. No! They are dead serious. They are so involved with the battle that

> *"All the day and all the night they shall never be silent" (Isaiah 62:6).*

Yes, they intercede all the day and all the night. If the need continues to exist, they will intercede all the day and all the night for an unlimited number of weeks, months, or even years.

That is what happened to Anna, the prophetess. There was a need for intercession. She gave herself wholeheartedly to it for a period of nearly sixty years. The Bible says,

"And there was a prophetess, Anna, the daughter of Phanuel, of the tribe of Asher; she was of a great age, having lived with her husband seven years from her virginity, and as a widow till she was eighty-four. She did not depart from the temple, worshipping with fasting and prayer night and day" (Luke 2:36-37).

Her intercession was unceasing, night and day, for about sixty years. I cannot but ask what would have happened had she not given herself to such unceasing intercession for so many years. One thing I believe: something significant that happened because she interceded would not have happened and the loss would have been terrible. Was it because of her intercession that the Lord Jesus was able to come for the first time? If that is so, then it would mean that if she had not interceded He would not have come! I tremble as I think about it. Plainly looking at things, it would suggest that perhaps without her intercession, He would not have come. There would have been no atonement and our sins would still be upon us! If that is the case, we can only thank God that she paid the harsh price that went with her unceasing intercession. Seen from that light, her life was immense gain and not a waste. Seen from that perspective, every pain and anguish that she felt during the sixty years of unceasing fasting and prayer, was worth it.

THE INTERCESSOR AND INTERCESSORS

There might have been a period during which Aaron and Hur watched Moses raise his hands and Israel prevailed and as he got tired and lowered his hands, Amalek prevailed. They came to appreciate the fact that the important thing was the position of the hands of Moses. Perhaps, they might have initially thought that what mattered was that some hands were raised up. Like Aaron and Miriam they could have said,

> *"Has the Lord indeed spoken only through Moses? Has he not spoken through us also?" (Numbers 12:2).*

If they thought that way, they might have said, "Moses would lift up his hands and when he is tired Aaron would take over and lift up his hands and when he gets tired, Hur would take over and lift up his hands. By this division of labour, there will always be some hands up and things would go on well." If they had thought and acted that way, they would have discovered that the question was not that of just having any hands up but that of having the hands of Moses up! Only Moses was qualified, by God's appointment, to stand in the gap in the particular issue at hand. When they discovered that, they arranged for Moses to sit down and Aaron and Hur held up his hands, one on either side.

We have said that God did not just want any hands up. He wanted the hands of Moses to be raised. God is the Director of all His enterprises. He calls men, commissions them, and determines the spheres of their services according to His good pleasure. Sometimes it is obvious why He choses one person and not another. At other times the reasons are beyond human understanding. All who co-work with Him must yield absolutely to Him and say,

> *"His dominion is an everlasting dominion, and his kingdom endures from generation to generation: all the inhabitants of the earth are counted as nothing; and he does according to his will in the host of heaven and among the inhabitants of the earth; and none can stay his hand or say to him. What doest thou? (Daniel 4:34-35).*

Aaron and Hur understood this and gave themselves not to the task of raising their own hands, but to the task of ensuring that the hands of Moses were raised. They forgot their own importance and gave themselves to the one task of ensuring that

Israel prevailed and that one task was accomplished by raising the hands of Moses.

There are a number of situations where God needs only one person of the right kind for His cause to prevail. For example, he said,

> "Run to and fro through the streets of Jerusalem, look and take note! Search her squares to see if you can find a man, one who does justice and seeks truth, that I may pardon her" (Jeremiah 5:1).

> "The people of the land have practised extortion and committed robbery; they have oppressed the poor and needy and have extorted from the sojourner without redress. And I sought for a man among them who would build the wall and stand in the breach before me for the land that I should not destroy it; bin I found none" (Ezekiel 22:29-30).

In these situations, one person would have been enough. The problem today is that in a similar situation, there may be one person who meets God's requirements and consequently is standing in the gap. What may be needed is not another person to join him in standing in the gap but to help him, through interceding for him, to better stand in the gap. That principal person with the full qualifications required by God, can then carry the burden of interceding for a nation or for a continent while many "lesser" intercessors intercede for him and by their prayers raise up his hands until the victory is won.

The question is, "Are there people in the Body of Christ today who are honest enough to say, This burden of intercession is beyond my spiritual capacity. I will look for the one who has the weight before God, that can carry it, and give myself to interceding for him?" If there are such people, they will make themselves intercessors for the intercessor and leave the matter of who gets the reward from man aside. Such people may invest their entire lives interceding for the intercessor and win a full reward at the end, in addition to contributing to satisfying the heart of God!

O Lord, raise some such persons in the Body of Your Son in our day!

22
THE INTERCESSOR AND PRAYER RETREATS

Intercessors must learn to withdraw and seek the Lord. They must learn to withdraw and intercede. The far-reaching importance of intercession demands that the intercessor sometimes leaves all else aside and withdraw to intercede. Moses withdrew to intercede for forty days when Israel sinned. He said,

> *"So I lay prostrate before the Lord for these forty days and forty nights, because the Lord had said he would destroy you. And I prayed to the Lord"* (Deuteronomy 9:25-26).

Anna was permanently on a fasting-prayer retreat for about sixty years, shut up in the temple. Because they withdrew and interceded, great things happened. God heard their cries of intercession and there were mighty deliverances.

The intercessor of today must also learn to go on prayer retreats. It is possible to have a very short retreat of fifteen minutes. This has its place. It is also possible to have longer retreats, three days, one week, one month, one year. Below are some suggestions that an intercessor could follow as he retreats in order in make spiritual progress:

FIFTEEN-MINUTE RETREAT - A

- **First minute:** a) Confession of any sin committed but not yet confessed and forsaken. b) Receive the filling of the Holy Spirit.
- **Second minute:** Thank the Lord for some of His goodness to you.
- **Third minute:** Pray for your local assembly.
- **Fourth minute:** Pray for the spiritual life of your spiritual leader.
- **Fifth minute:** Pray for five people who have not yet believed in the Lord Jesus.
- **Sixth minute:** Pray for another five people who have not yet believed in the Lord Jesus.
- **Seventh minute:** Pray for five believers that they might grow in the Lord.
- **Eighth minute**: Pray for five backsliders that they might be restored to the Lord.
- **Ninth minute:** Pray for a ministry serving God's interest in your country or in any part of the world.
- **Tenth minute:** Pray for the ministry that you are a part of physically and/or financially.
- **Eleventh minute:** Continue to pray for the ministry that you are a part of.
- **Twelfth minute:** Pray for the leader of the ministry of which you are a part.
- **Thirteenth minute**: Pray for an unevangelized area of your country or the world.
- **Fourteenth minute:** Pray for the political leaders of your nation.

- **Fifteenth minute:** a) Thank the Lord for the privilege of praying. b) Sing a song unto the Lord.

FIFTEEN-MINUTE RETREAT - B

- **First minute:** Confess any sin committed in thought, word and deed and receive forgiveness and restoration from the Lord.
- **Second minute:** Pray for the prayer life of someone.
- **Third minute:** Pray for any outstanding needs in the direction of the spiritual growth of someone.
- **Fourth minute:** Continue to pray for outstanding needs in the direction of the spiritual growth of another person.
- **Fifth minute:** Pray for a ministry of Bible translation and production that you know.
- **Sixth minute:** Pray for the advance of the gospel in a Communist country.
- **Seventh minute:** Pray for the advance of the gospel in a Moslem country you know of.
- **Eighth minute:** Pray for the advance of the gospel in China.
- **Ninth minute:** Pray for the penetration of one unreached tribe.
- **Tenth minute:** Pray for some minister who is suffering persecution because of his refusal to compromise the standards of Christian conduct.
- **Eleventh minute:** Pray for the preparation of the Bride of Christ in the area of holiness.
- **Twelfth minute:** Pray for the preparation of the Bride of Christ in the area of service.
- **Thirteenth minute:** Pray for the preparation of the Bride of Christ in the area of maintaining the first love.

- **Fourteenth minute:** Pray for the preparation of the Bride of Christ in the area of mature Christian character.
- **Fifteenth minute:** Thank the Lord for the time of prayer.

THIRTY-MINUTE RETREAT

A thirty-minute prayer retreat can be considered as:

- 30 periods of one minute each.
- 15 periods of two minutes each
- 10 periods of three minutes each.
- 6 periods of five minutes each.
- 5 periods of six minutes each.
- 2 periods of fifteen minutes each.

These divisions may be suitable for different occasions, depending on what you want to pray for. For example, I sometimes pray for myself in thirty minutes as follows:

- **First minute:** Thanksgiving to the Lord for His goodness to me and for calling me to serve Him.
- Second minute: Thanksgiving to the Lord for those aspects of the ministry that have already been completed.
- Third minute: Praying for my spirit, conscience, intuition and communion.
- Fourth minute: Praying for my soul, the will, the mind, and the emotions.
- Fifth minute: Praying for my body, physical and mental health.
- Sixth minute: Praying for my growth in knowing the Lord.
- Seventh minute: Praying for my growth in loving the Lord.

- Eighth minute: Praying for my growth in obeying the Lord.
- Ninth minute: Praying for my deliverance from all traces of the self-life.
- Tenth minute: Praying for my growth in Christian character.
- Eleventh minute: Praying for my growth in denying myself, taking up my cross, and following Him
- Twelfth minute: Praying for the vision the Lord has given me: its clarity, growth, and protection.
- Thirteenth minute: Praying for my growth in spiritual power and authority.
- Fourteenth minute: Praying for my time.
- Fifteenth minute: Praying for my ministry as a disciple-maker.
- Sixteenth minute: Praying for my ministry to those who do not yet know the Lord.
- Seventeenth minute: Praying for my ministry to those who are weak in the Lord.
- Eighteenth minute: Praying for my ministry to those who are strong in the Lord.
- Nineteenth minute: Praying for my life as a writer for the Lord and His Body.
- Twentieth minute: Praying for my fasting life.
- Twenty-first minute: Praying for my prayer life.
- Twenty-second minute: Praying for my co-workers.
- Twenty-third minute: Praying for my wife.
- Twenty-fourth minute: Praying for my children
- Twenty-fifth minute: Praying for my ministry as a husband.
- Twenty-sixth minute: Praying for my ministry as a father.
- Twenty-seventh minute: Praying for my job as a university teacher.

- Twenty-eighth minute: Praying for my job as a research scientist.
- Twenty-ninth minute: Praying for my finances.
- Thirtieth minute: Thanksgiving to the Lord for the prayer time.

ONE-HOUR PRAYER RETREAT

Again it is possible to divide a one-hour retreat into sixty retreats of one minute each or two retreats of thirty minutes or four retreats of fifteen minutes, and so on. We recommend that as much as possible the periods be kept short. This will enhance concentration and reduce the possibility of the mind wandering. We recommend the following one-hour retreat for God's move in the continent of Africa. It could be that one aspect is chosen and prayed for different countries as the Lord leads through His Spirit.

Minute —> How used in prayer

1 -> Thanksgiving for God's goodness to Africa.

2 -> Thanksgiving for God's past and present moves in Africa.

3 -> Thanksgiving for God's future plans for Africa

4 -> Intercession for British Indian Ocean Territory.

East Africa

5 -> Intercession for Burundi

6 -> Intercession for Comoros

7 -> Intercession for Djibouti

8 -> Intercession for Ethiopia

9 -> Intercession for Kenya

10 -> Intercession for Madagascar

11 -> Intercession for Malawi

12 -> Intercession for Mauritius

13 -> Intercession for Mozambique

14 -> Intercession for Reunion

15 -> Intercession for Rwanda

16 -> Intercession for Seychelles

17 -> Intercession for Somalia

18 -> Intercession for Tanzania

19 -> Intercession for Uganda

20 -> Intercession for Zambia

21 -> Intercession for Zimbabwe

22 -> Intercession for Angola

Central Africa

23 -> Intercession for Cameroon

24 -> Intercession for Central African Republic

25 -> Intercession for Chad

26 -> Intercession for CongoCentral Africa

27 -> Intercession for Equatorial Guinea

28 -> Intercession for Gabon

29 -> Intercession for Sao Tome and Principe

30 -> Intercession for Zaire

Northern Africa

31 -> Intercession for Algeria

32 -> Intercession for Egypt

33 -> Intercession for Libya

34 -> Intercession for MoroccoNorthern Africa

35 -> Intercession for Sudan

36 -> Intercession for Tunisia

37 -> Intercession for Western Sahara

Southern Africa

38 -> Intercession for Botswana

39 -> Intercession for Lesotho

40 -> Intercession for NamibiaSouthern Africa

41 -> Intercession for South Africa

42 -> Intercession for Swaziland

Western Africa

43 -> Intercession for Benin

44 -> Intercession for Burkina Faso

45 -> Intercession for Cape Verde

46 -> Intercession for Ivory Coast

47 -> Intercession for Gambia

48 -> Intercession for Ghana

49 -> Intercession for Guinea

50 -> Intercession for Guinea Bissau

51 -> Intercession for LiberiaWestern Africa

52 -> Intercession for Mali

53 -> Intercession for Mauritania

54 -> Intercession for Niger

55 -> Intercession for Nigeria

56 -> Intercession for St. Helena

57 -> Intercession for Senegal

58 -> Intercession for Sierra Leone

59 -> Intercession for Togo

60 -> Thanksgiving for the period of praying and for the many answers that will come from the throne.

WEEK-END PRAYER RETREAT

In many countries, there is no official work on Saturdays and Sundays. This is a great blessing. The world has transformed the week-end into times of debauchery and sin. The sad thing is that even believers use the week-end to commit the sin of indulgence and idleness.

The Lord has enabled me to use my week-ends effectively. In the following pages are the ways in which I use three types of week-ends that characterize my month. One is for prayer, another is for writing, and the third is for ministering the Word to the saints in house retreats. You may want to adapt them to your own situation.

It should be observed that a retreat is a serious event and as much time as possible has to be invested into the goal of the retreat. In addition to this, is the need to make the most of the time. Finally, eating and hard work are sometimes mutually exclusive as most people soon feel sleepy after a good meal. The serious person on retreat will either fast completely or partially or else eat sparingly.

TIMETABLE FOR A WRITING WEEK- END

Friday

3:00-4:00 -> Prayer - 1

4:00-5:00 -> Writing - 1

5:00-6:00 -> Writing - 2

6:00-7:00 -> Writing - 3

7:00-8:00 -> Prayer - 2

8:00-8:30 -> Supper

8:45-11:45 -> Sleep

Saturday

12:00-1:00 -> Bible Reading— 1

1:00-2: 00 -> Bible meditation

2:00-3:00 -> Prayer — 3

3:00-4:00 -> Writing — 4

4:00-5:00 -> Writing — 5

5:00-6:00 -> Writing — 6

6:00-7:00 -> Writing — 7

7:00-7:30 -> Bible Reading — 2

7:45-8:45 -> Rest

9:00-10:00 -> Writing — 8

10:00-11:00 -> Writing — 9

11:00-12:00 -> Writing — 10

12:00-1:00 -> Prayer — 4

1:00-1:30 -> Bible Reading — 3

1:30-2:30 -> Siesta

2:45-3:45 -> Writing — 11

3:45-4:45 -> Writing — 12

4:45-5:45 -> Writing- 13

5:45-6:45 -> Writing-14

6:45-7:45 -> Prayer — 5

8:00-8:30 -> Supper

8:45-11:45 -> Sleep

Sunday

12:00-1:00 -> Bible Reading — 4

1:00-2:00 -> Bible meditation

2:00-3:00 -> Prayer — 6

3:00-4:00 -> Writing — 15

4:00-5:00 -> Writing — 16

5:00-6:00 -> Writing — 17

7:00-7:30 -> Bible Reading — 5

7:30-8:45 -> Rest

9:00-10:00 -> Writing — 19

10:00-11:00 -> Writing — 20

11:00-12:00 -> Writing — 21

12:00-1:00 -> Writing — 22

1:00-1:30 -> Bible Reading — 6

1:30-2:30 -> Siesta

2:45-3:45 -> Writing — 23

3:45-4:45 -> Writing — 24

4:45-5:45 -> Prayer — 7

6:00 -> End of the week-end

PROGRAMME FOR A MINISTRY WEEK-END

Friday

Arrival -> 6:00 - 6:30 P.M.

Preparation -> 6:30 - 7:30 P.M.

Supper -> 8:00 - 9:00 P.M.

First Message -> 9:00 - 10:00 P.M.

Second Message -> 10:30 - 11:00 P.M.

Sleep

Saturday

2:00-1:00 -> Writing

1:00-2:00 -> Writing

2:00-3:00 -> Writing

3:00-4:00 -> Writing

4:00-5:00 -> DDEWG

5:00-6:00 -> DDEWG

6:00-6:30 -> Rest

6:30-7:00 -> Preparation

7:00-8:00 -> Third Message

8:00-9:00 -> Fourth Message

9:00-9:30 -> Breakfast

9:30-10:00 -> Rest, counselling

10:00-11:00 -> Fifth Message

11:00-12:00 -> Sixth Message

12:00-1:00 -> Counselling

1:00-1:30 -> Lunch

1:45-2:45 -> Siesta

3:00-4:00 -> Seventh Message

4:00-5:00 -> Eighth Message

5:00-6:00 -> Ninth Message

6:00-7:00 -> Tenth Message

7:00-7:30 -> Supper

7:30-8:00 -> Rest

8:00-9:00 -> Eleventh Message

9:00-10:00 -> Twelfth Message

10:00-12:00 -> Sleep

Sunday

12:00-1:00 -> Writing

1:00-2:00 -> Writing

2:00-3:00 -> Writing

3:00-4:00 -> Writing

4:00-5:00 -> DDEWG

5:00-6:00 -> DDEWG

6:00-6:30 -> Rest

6:30-7:00 -> Preparation

7:00- 8:00 -> Thirteenth Message

8:00-9:00 -> Fourteenth Message

9:00-10:00 -> Fifteen Message

10:00-11:00 -> Sixteenth Message

11:00-12:00 -> Breaking of Bread

12:00-1:00 -> Lunch and departure

TIMETABLE FOR A PRAYER WEEK-END

Friday

3:00 - 4:00 -> Preparation

4:00 - 5:00 -> Prayer - 1

5:00 - 6:00 -> Prayer - 2

6:00 - 7:00 -> Prayer - 3

7:00 - 8:00 -> Prayer - 4

8:00 - 8:30 -> Supper

8:45 - 11:45 -> Sleep

Saturday

12:00-1:00 -> Bible Reading— 1

1:00-2:00 -> DDEWG

2:00-3:00 -> Prayer — 5

3:00-4:00 -> Prayer — 6

4:00-5:00 -> Prayer — 7

5:00-6:00 -> Prayer — 8

6:00-7:00 -> Prayer— 9

7:00-7:30 -> Breakfast

7:45-8:45 -> Rest

9:00-10:00 -> Prayer— 10

10:00-11:00 -> Prayer — 11

11:00-12:00 -> Prayer — 12

12:00-1:00 -> Prayer — 13

1:00-1:30 -> Lunch

1:30-2:30 -> Siesta

2:45-3:45 -> Prayer — 14

3:45-4:45 -> Prayer — 15

4:45-5:45 -> Prayer — 16

5:45-6:45 -> Prayer — 17

6:45-7:45 -> Bible Reading — 2

8:00-8:30 -> Supper

8:45-11:45 -> Sleep

Sunday

00-1:00 -> Bible Reading — 3

1:00-2:00 -> DDEWG

2:00-3:00 -> Prayer — 18

3:00-4:00 -> Prayer — 19

4:00-5:00 -> Prayer — 20

5:00-6:00 -> Prayer — 21

6:00-7:00 -> Prayer-22

7:00-7:30 -> Breakfast

7:45-8:45 -> Rest

9:00-10:00 -> Prayer-23

10:00-11:00 -> Prayer-24

11:00-12:00 -> Prayer-25

12:00-1:00 -> Prayer— 26

1:00-1:30 -> Lunch

1:30-2:30 -> Siesta

2:45-3:45 -> Prayer — 27

3:45-4:45 -> Prayer — 28

4:45-5:45 -> Prayer— 29

6:00 -> End of weekend

23

THE INTERCESSOR AND GRATITUDE

One of the sins that is very often committed by the people of God is ingratitude. The Lord Jesus healed ten lepers and only one returned to give thanks. The Lord was surprised and asked,

> *"Were not ten cleansed? Where are the nine? Was not one found to return and give praise to God except this foreigner? And he said to him, Rise and go your way; your faith has made you well"* (Luke 17:17-19).

Ten were healed physically. Nine were ungrateful and went away with their physical healing. One came back to show and express gratitude. That one received a bonus. He received spiritual healing in addition. The ungrateful will receive what they ask of the Lord but they may not receive the Lord's bonuses. These are specially reserved for the grateful, and the grateful come back to the Lord to give Him praise for what He has done.

It is easy to pray when one is carrying a burden. In fact, the intercessor with a burden has no choice but to pray. However, after the burden has been discharged and the answer received, only mature people come back into the presence of God to worship and give praises and thanks. Why is that so? It is so because even among those who make requests of God there are few who have become so caught up with the needs of God, to the extent that they see not only what God wants, but God Himself. Intercession is often tied to what God wants to do. Praise and thanksgiving are often tied to the very Person of God. Those intercessors who come back to give thanks have gone beyond doing things *for* God to doing things *on* God.

Gratitude can be expressed by giving all the praise for what has been accomplished to the Lord instead of taking the praise for themselves. This is second-class gratitude. First class gratitude is to come to the Lord and spend time in thanksgiving and praise before Him. This is good and commendable.

When I set out to write this book, I wrote two hundred prayer topics that were taken up by those who intercede for me. They have interceded for me in the course of the eight months that it has taken to write the book. This is the last chapter of the book. We have arranged a thanksgiving service where the saints who have been involved with the book shall meet to thank the Lord for causing the book to be written. I shall write another two hundred topics of thanksgiving and distribute them to my prayer partners so that we may not be people who take God for granted. We fasted and prayed for the book as it was being conceived and as it was being written.

We shall also dedicate a thanksgiving fast to give thanks to the Lord. That fast shall be a

> "... *season of joy and gladness*" *(Zechariah 8.18)*

to the Lord for His goodness in enabling the book to be written. After the season of praise, we shall again intercede for the production, distribution, and impact of the book.

We recommend that each ministry of intercession should be viewed as having three phases:

PHASE ONE:

Waiting before God in order to receive the object of intercession, the direction of intercession and the burden for intercession.

PHASE TWO:

Carrying out the art of intercession.

PHASE THREE:

Praise and thanksgiving for God's answers to the issues over which intercession was carried out.

We recommend that phase two should immediately be followed by phase three or else the Enemy who was defeated during intercession may say, "They outclassed me during intercession. Let me see if I can have some part of the victory by preventing them from giving praise and thanksgiving to my Enemy, the God of heaven who gave them victory. I will cause them to postpone the session of praise and thanksgiving and soon they will become so caught up with something else that they will forget praise and thanksgiving altogether."

Knowing his methods so clearly, we must make sure that he does not have his way at all. We must work things out so that each victory is followed by a season of praise and thanksgiving.

When the Lord defeated Pharaoh and his horsemen and chariots in the Red Sea, there were two immediate reactions from the camp of Israel. First of all, Moses and the people sang this song to the Lord saying,

> *"I will sing to the Lord, for he has triumphed; the horse and his rider he has thrown into the sea ..." (Exodus 15:1 - 18).*

Secondly, Miriam, the prophetess, the sister of Aaron, took a timbrel in her hand, and all the women went out after her with timbrels and dancing. And Miriam sang to them,

> *"Sing to the Lord, for he has triumphed gloriously; the horse and the rider he has thrown into the sea" (Exodus 15:20 - 21).*

Such praise must be heard again in our day and it must flow forth in thanksgiving to the Lord of hosts. The "Moseses" who lead the battles of God must lead the people in thanksgiving and praise and the "Miriams" must lead the women of God to thanksgiving for mighty answers to intercession. God's heart will be satisfied and the intercessors and all the people of God blessed. Praise the Lord! Amen.

PART 3

LEVELS OF INTERCESSION

God has called all people to intercede but all believers cannot intercede at the same level. A believer who has just come to know the Lord today and a believer of many years' standing who has been through experiences with the Lord and has been deeply wounded and thoroughly broken by the Lord, cannot pray at the same level. A person who has a fresh burden from the Lord, but a burden that has not become an integral part of him so that it eats itself into the very centre of his being, and a man who has borne a burden for many years, prayed it through and by an increasing knowledge of the Lord has had the burden deepened and purified, are intercessors at two different levels. We can illustrate the levels as shown below.

We cannot go into the matter of discussing the differences between figure one and figure two here.

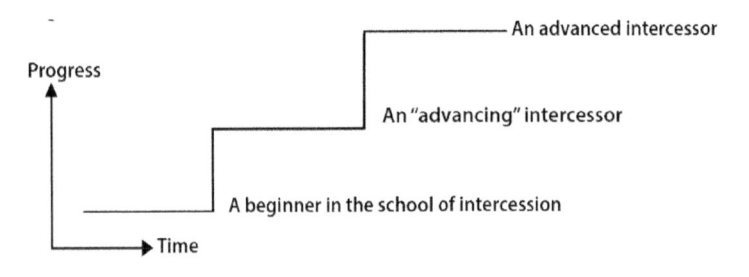

```
Progress
   ▲
   │                    ┌──────── An advanced intercessor
   │                    │
   │                    │   An "advancing" intercessor
   │          ┌─────────┘
   │          │  A beginner in the school of intercession
   │──────────┘
   └──────────► Time
```

Levels of Intercession

The change from one level to the other may be through a less sharp crisis and therefore can be shown below.

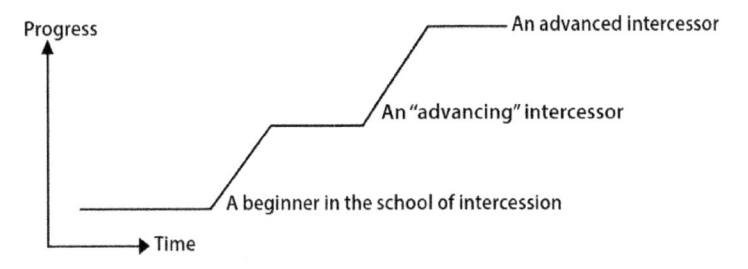

```
Progress
   ▲
   │                      ╱──────── An advanced intercessor
   │                     ╱
   │                    ╱  An "advancing" intercessor
   │          ─────────╱
   │         ╱  A beginner in the school of intercession
   │────────╱
   └──────────► Time
```

Levels of Intercession

We can only say that there are some believers who receive a lot of light in one go and respond to it totally in one go and experience a sharp crisis that moves them from one plane of intercession to another. They may be given a fresh, sudden revelation of the Lord Jesus to which their total being responds. They are therefore so caught up with the One they now know better, that they can no longer intercede for His cause and interests as before. Others may be given a sudden, fresh revelation of the Father to which they respond. They are now caught up with Him in an entirely new way. They can no longer pray as they did before. It is as if before, they prayed from the outside and now, they have been admitted into the inside, they see Him and it is all different! There is no more need for shouting, there is place only for whispers. There is no place for doubts. There is a gaze at His face and then there is immediate certainty as to whether or not He approves a particular project.

Some may be given a revelation of hell and from that moment their intercession for the lost becomes a supreme passion that does not fade. They are immediately carried away into another plane of intercession.

Others may be given a revelation of the holiness of God and the Judgment Seat of Christ. From that moment, they can never be the same. Night and day they will burn for God and burn for the saints in intercession. No one will be able to discourage them. No one will be able to distract them. They have "seen" and they can no longer pray as those who have not seen.

Others may be given a revelation of the fact that the world: its monarchs, its systems, it agents have been judged and that there is absolutely no future for it. Such then will intercede that there will be no further investments in the world. They will labour with deepest passion that those who have investments in the world will take them out of the world system and invest them in the kingdom of God. They will obey the injunction of the Lord Jesus,

> *"Do not lay up for yourselves treasures on earth where moth and rust consume and where thieves break in and steal, but lay up for yourselves treasures in heaven, where neither moth nor rust consumes and where thieves do not break in and steal. For where your treasure is, there will your heart be also" (Matthew 6:19-21).*

They will not rest but pray that all those who know the Lord Jesus Christ will do likewise. Their burden and urgency will be like that of a man who sees people taking large sums of money to invest in a bank that is absolutely bankrupt.

So, these are some of the things that may lead to a crisis and a move from a lower to a higher level of intercession. It will always involve some fresh revelation and an immediate response to it, or some sudden response to some aspect of the truth that was known but not obeyed.

There are people who receive light rather gradually and responded to it slowly. This is one of the reasons for the more gradual crisis

There is a third possibility in the matter of making progress in the School of Intercession and levels of intercession. There are some people who entered the School of Intercession after years of walking in holiness and consecration. They already have received a lot of light from the Lord. They may not have many crises. They will begin to intercede, learn to intercede, and advance in intercession as they intercede. There are others whose difference will not come because of some crisis in spiritual experience but simply because the Lord has called them to prayer and by spending more time in prayer, progress is made and levels of intercession are changed. We can represent these two figures.

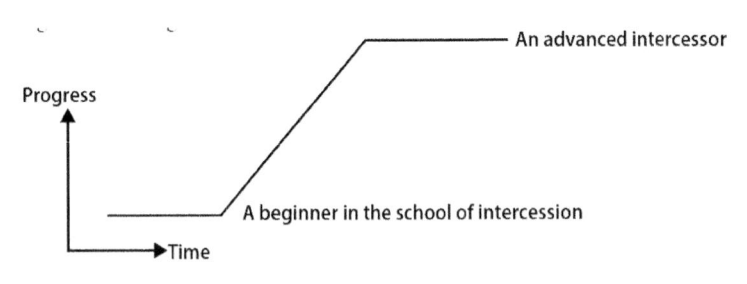

A fast but move, without crisis, from a beginner to an advanced intercessor

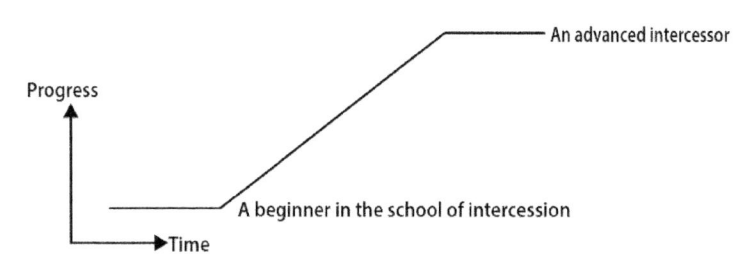

A slower but steady growth without crisis, from a beginner to an advanced intercessor

YEARS WITHOUT PROGRESS

It is important to pray for many hours each day and the more hours are spent in prayer, the better. Normally, the person who spent more time in praying ought to have made more progress. Although it ought to be the case, it is not always so. We know that there are physical dwarfs, whose sizes are not related proportionally to their ages. They stopped growing. They may be seventy years of age but they reason and act like children. They have years behind them but no growth. A problem developed somewhere and it was not dealt with as it should have been.

In the spiritual realm, the same thing can happen. I once met a man who had known the Lord for forty years who told me that he had wasted the first forty years of his life in the Lord in purposelessness. Because of this, even though he was forty-four years old in the Lord, his growth was at the point where someone who had been born again four years ago and grown properly should be. This is enough to warn us that a person can pray for eight hours every day for twenty year's without making progress. If there is sin in a person's life, known but not confessed and forsaken, he is wasting his hours and years in prayer. No progress can be made until the sin is repented of, confessed and forsaken. Not to deal clearly and thoroughly with a particular area of sin or disobedience is to court disaster. It will come!

The curve for an intercessor who keeps his sins, hardens his conscience, and continues to make noise before the Lord is shown below.

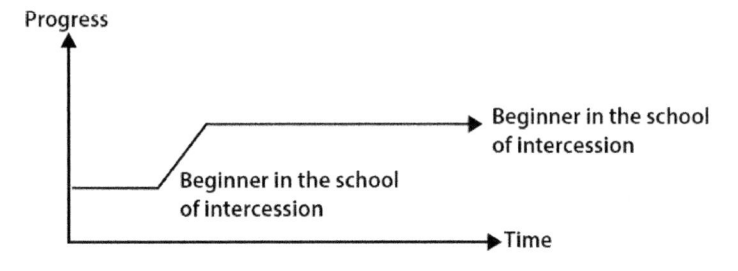

Time spent in intercession without progress

A BEGINNER IN THE SCHOOL OF INTERCESSION

WHO MAY ENROL IN THE SCHOOL OF INTERCESSION?

Not every human being can enrol in the School of Intercession. It is only those who possess the entry qualifications into that School who may. Below are the entry requirements:

1. A deep encounter with the Lord Jesus who said, *"I am the way, the truth and the life. No one comes to the Father but by me"* (*John 14:6*).
2. A practical commitment that is being worked out daily to obey the Lord Jesus in everything He commands.
3. A practical commitment to be separated from every known sin in thought, word, and deed, which is being worked out on a daily basis.
4. A practical commitment to the known will of God, with a heart that yields to obey the other aspects of the will of God that may be revealed in the future.
5. Personal faith that God hears and answers prayers.
6. Personal conviction that having authority with God is

more important than having authority with anyone else on earth.
7. Personal conviction that God can hear him and do great things in response to his prayers.
8. A commitment to pay any price that God may demand so that his prayers may be answered.
9. Some real commitment, however small, that God's will be done on earth as in heaven. (This commitment generally grows in the School of intercession until it becomes a consuming pasion).
10. Some real commitment, however, small, that the lost should be brought to a saving knowledge of the Lord Jesus.
11. Some real commitment, however small, that the Church which is the Bride of the Lord Jesus should grow into the perfection of the Father in all things: without spot, without wrinkle, and without blemish.
12. A determination to be a student indeed and to remain in the School all his life.
13. Conviction that he does not know how to pray and needs to learn.

Any one with these qualifications can enrol in the School of Intercession. All believers do pray but enrolment in the School of Intercession is something else. It is a commitment to make intercession a serious issue. It is a commitment to intervene. It is a commitment to be a man who makes it impossible for God to say,

"The people of the land have practised extortion and committed robbery; they have oppressed the poor and needy, and have extorted from the sojourner without redress. And I sought for a man among them who should build up the wall and stand in the breach before me for the land, that I should not destroy it; but I found none. Therefore I have poured out

my indignation upon them; I have consumed them with the fire of my wrath; their ways have I requited upon their heads, says the Lord God" (Ezekiel 22:29 - 31).

Intercession is the commitment to stand in the gap so that God will not be able to do what He intended. God said in His Word,

"Run to and fro through the streets of Jerusalem, look and take note! Search her squares to see if you can find a man, one who does justice and seeks truth; that I may pardon her"(Jeremiah 5:1).

The intercessor says,

"Because I am there, God will pardon this city, nation, or continent. I will do all that is necessary to be established as an intercessor before God."

Enrolment in the School of Intercession is not equivalent to being an intercessor. A student who enrols in a medical school does not become a doctor on enrolment. Some fail to pay the price and drop out of the school, never becoming a doctor! So do not begin to call yourself an intercessor. Learn to intercede but keep away from titles and names. They soon get into people's heads, madden them, and put them out of fellowship with God and out of the real ministry of intercession.

THINGS A BEGINNER MUST NOT DO

1. Do not carry a badge or accept the title "intercessor."
2. Do not imitate the way you heard someone pray. He might have been impressive without being an intercessor. He might have been pouring out thoughts from his head and not from his heart. He might have been speaking to

man and not to God. He might have been speaking in public when in private he cannot pray because he dares not confront God alone. He is out of touch. This being a possibility, to imitate such a man will be to move into the pathway of falsehood from the beginning. Another reason why you must not imitate another person: his words, the way he puts them to God, the way he addresses God ... is that the person may indeed be interceding in truth out of deep experience with God. He knows God. God knows him. He has known God. He, out of a prolonged relationship with God, can say some things to God, just as two friends can address each other. However, you do not know God that deeply and you have not known Him for that length of time. If you spoke like him you will be totally out of place. Here is an example: I call my wife Linda. That was her play name in school twenty-three years ago. The name speaks of a relationship that has existed between us since I was nineteen. If any of our children should decide to call her "Linda," he will be being absolutely rude! So do not imitate others. Decide on this and stick to it. There will be temptations to imitate. Do not yield to temptation for yielding is sin.

3. Do not attempt to pray for things you do not understand. You will not intercede intelligently. Do not say, "Although I do not understand this, I will just throw the words and God will sort them out." That is not God's job. He will not sort them for you. He has given you a mind. Think the things through and intercede intelligently. I know that there will be times when there is a burden placed on the heart of the intercessor that is beyond his mind and vocabulary, and this will only flow back to God through prayer in unknown tongues, groans, sighs, and the like. However, this is not in the day-to-day life of intercession

The intercessor should use his mind to think and to intercede and when the Lord intervenes to bring in burdens that can best be discharged in other ways, He must be allowed to do what He wants.
4. Do not attempt to intercede if there is some sin in your life, however small, of which you have not repented, forsaken, sought the forgiveness of God, and received His restoration. If things are not right with Him, do not intercede. You will be spitting on His face.
5. Do not seek to exalt yourself. Remain humble.
6. Do not think that you already know much about prayer and are just applying it to intercession. You do not know much. As you grow in intercession, you will understand more clearly how to offer up praise, thanksgiving, and adoration to God. You will know in an increasing way how to make your own needs known. Come as a learner. You are a learner. Accept that you are one. You may be the leader of a denomination, ministry, or some Christian affair for many years. You might have believed over ten, twenty, or thirty years ago and therefore assumed that you know how to pray. Be careful! Do you really know? Could it be that what you need to do is to acknowledge, "I have never learnt to pray. I do not know how to intercede. I want to learn. I must learn?"

THINGS A BEGINNER MUST DO

There are some things that a beginner must do in order to make rapid progress in the School of Intercession. We shall outline a few of them below but leave him in the hands of the Lord.

1. He should decide that the only person from whom he wants to gain honour is the God who answers prayers. He must decide never to seek the praise of men. This will

save him from the following pitfalls: a) Exaggerating prayer hours in order to impress people; b) Lying that he prayed when he did not; c) Divulging secrets received from God in prayer to receive praise, d) Carrying out publicity about personal contribution in prayer when the answer comes.
2. He should make a timetable for his week and fit the hours for intercession on it.
3. He should ensure that he intercedes during the allotted times and refuse to be moved from them. He should consider his times of intercession as the top priority. He should consider that, intercession being in audience with the King of kings, means that all other things and all other people can wait and must wait.
4. He should learn to pray on even if his entire being does not want him to pray.
5. He should keep a list of those for whom he is interceding so that he may not intercede once or twice and forget.
6. He should seek the companionship and the counsel of an intercessor.
7. He should receive all the help he can from the human intercessor.
8. He should read books on prayer, supplication, and above all intercession.
9. He should study the intercessors of the Bible.
10. He should ask the Lord to teach him how to intercede.
11. He should apply what he has been taught by the human intercessor, the authors of the books, and the heavenly intercessors, to his life of intercession.
12. He should ask God to bless him increasingly and give him increasing burden and revelation.
13. He should learn to wait on God in order to hear God's voice and direction.
14. He should be zealous.

15. He should continue to grow in holiness and in Christian character.

WHEN DO I CEASE BEING A BEGINNER?

There is a sense in which every intercessor must remain a beginner. This is in the sense that he does not presume to know what he does not know. He should always be a beginner in asking the Lord to teach him. However, there is also the matter of growth. The Lord expects us to grow. The Bible says,

> *"And his gifts were that some should be apostles, some evangelists, some pastors and teachers, to equip the saints for the work of ministry, for building up the body of Christ, until we all attain to the unity of the faith and of the knowledge of the Son of God, to mature manhood, to the measure of the stature of the fulness of Christ; so that we may no longer be children, tossed to and fro and carried about with every wind of doctrine by the cunning of men, by their craftiness in deceitful wiles" (Ephesians 4:11-14).*

God expects the one who has enrolled in the School of Intercession to make progress and one day become an Advanced Intercessor. If the beginner does not make progress, he will become a burden to God. Believers who did not make progress were burdens to the writers of the Bible. One of them wrote,

> *"For though by this time you ought to be teachers, you need some one to teach you again the first principles of God's word. You need milk, not solid food; for every one who lives on milk is unskilled in the word of righteousness, for he is a child. But solid food is for the mature, for those who have their faculties trained by practice to distinguish good from evil" (Hebrews 5:12-14).*

The beginner will know that he is no longer a beginner. His relationship with God will change. A desire to know God will burn in his heart. Many things that satisfied in the past will lose their power. The change may come gradually or it may come through a crisis. One thing we know: it will come!

26
MAKING PROGRESS IN THE SCHOOL OF INTERCESSION

We have just written about a beginner in the School of Intercession. We shall afterwards write about the advanced intercessor. Between the beginner and the advanced intercessor is the "advancing intercessor" or the person making progress in the School of Intercession.

What does it take to make progress in the School of Intercession? We have answered this question in various chapters in this book. We want to summarize these factors here so that the beginner will clearly see in one go the way ahead.

The first thing that will be needed to make progress is a deep and increasing knowledge of God and a knowledge of His ways, His methods, and His will. Without this knowledge progress will be impossible.

The next thing is a radical commitment to obey every aspect of the known will of God. Those who do not obey the will of God will find it impossible to make progress in the School of Intercession. So the one who would make progress has settled it forever that obedience to the will of God - total, immediate, and complete - is the only way open to him and that he will obey regardless of what it will cost him.

The third thing is a radical commitment to the sanctified life. Every intercessor knows that sin is a tragedy and that to sin and intercede is a waste of time. The advancing intercessor knows that he cannot make progress beyond the extent to which he is prepared to walk in holiness and as such he makes holiness his aim.

The fourth thing that is necessary for progress in the School of Intercession is faith. The intercessor must believe God. He must believe God even when he has to hope against hope. He must believe the Word of God and the promise of God regardless of what he sees around. He will be called to intercede in near-hopeless situations and, at such times, only unshakeable faith in God will see him through. He will grow in faith not only in the aspect of intercession but in his whole life.

The fifth thing that is necessary for making progress in the School of Intercession is discipline. Progress is the lot of those who will press on and keep pressing on even when others have given up. They will discipline themselves to pray and pray and they will labour to pray increasingly more and more. Like Moses of old, they would refuse to go away from the place of intercession. They will linger in God's presence pleading, interceding, and supplicating until they receive an answer. They are incapable of receiving a "no," for they have so bound themselves to the object of intercession that for them to let go would be to be utterly ruined.

The sixth thing that is necessary for making progress in the School of Intercession is a commitment to the musts of life. The Lord Jesus was moved by the musts of His life. He had time for these and gave time to nothing else. He put this in the following way:

1. "I must be in my Father's house" (Luke 2:49).
2. "We must work the works of Him who sent me" (John 9:4).
3. "I must preach the good news of the kingdom of God to other cities also, for I was sent for that purpose" (Luke 4:43).
4. "I have other sheep, that are not of this fold; I must bring them also" (John 10:16).
5. "I must stay at your house today" (Luke 19:5).
6. "Nevertheless I must go on my way today and tomorrow and the day following" (Luke 17:33).
7. "The Son of man must suffer many things" (Luke 9:22).
8. "Jesus began to show His disciples that He must go to Jerusalem" (Matthew 16:21).
9. "The Son of man must be delivered into the hands of sinful men" (Luke 24:7).
10. "Everything written about Me in the law of Moses and the prophets and the Psalms must be fulfilled" (Luke 24:44).
11. "As Moses lifted up the serpent in the wilderness, so must the Son of man be lifted up" (John 3:14-15).

The Lord Jesus was a total success because He was given to the musts of His life. The one who would make progress would also be given to very clear musts in his life. For example such a person will have the following as some of the musts in his life:

1. He must intercede.
2. He must pray or perish.
3. He must worship the Lord.
4. He must give thanks in everything.

5. He must supplicate.
6. He must be holy.
7. He must hate all sin.
8. He must be separated from the common.
9. He must seek the Lord.
10. He must know God.
11. He must know the will of God.
12. He must do the will of God.
13. He must do the will of God at any cost.
14. He must continue, press on, in prayer until the answer comes.
15. He must eat only the quantity of food that will help him to keep awake and intercede.
16. He must sleep only for the length of time that will allow him to be awake while praying.
17. He must not love the world nor the things of the world.
18. He must protect the vision God has given him.
19. He must pray until the vision grows and until his heart is enlarged to contain all of the vision.
20. He must make friends with intercessors.
21. He must separate himself from prayerless people.
22. He must read books on prayer.
23. He must study the biographies of the men who changed the course of history through prayer.
24. He must read and read and reread the Bible.
25. He must make timetables with seasons of prayer and keep to them.
26. He must become a man who satisfies God's heart by praying without ceasing.

The one who establishes such musts for his life and works ceaselessly at them will make progress in the School of Intercession. As he presses on along this way day after day, week after week, month after month and year after year, he will make the progress that will transform him from an "advancing" to an "advanced" intercessor. Along that way the cross will deal regularly and sharply with the self in him so that he will become not only a man who talks to God but also a man who has nothing in him that will stand in the way of God. Such people are not only intercessors. They are blessed people.

Glory be to God.

27

THE ADVANCED INTERCESSOR

The advanced intercessor is the person who, out of a long history of walking with God in purity and holiness, truly knows God. He has had many transactions with God and out of that relationship, he knows how best to present each issue to God.

The men of the Bible who interceded were not all advanced intercessors. Moses was particularly advanced. He had so much intimate knowledge of God. He spoke to God and God spoke to him most intimately. The Lord said of him,

> *"Hear my words: if there is a prophet among you, I the Lord make myself known to him in a vision, I speak with him in a dream. Not so with my servant Moses; he is entrusted with all my house. With him I speak mouth to mouth, clearly, and not in dark speech; and he beholds the form of the Lord..." (Numbers 12:6-8).*

Moses spent two forty-day periods on the mountain with God, lying prostrate before Him. He had seen so much of the power and the glory of God that there was a most intimate relationship between them. He had been given the unusual opportunity to have all the "goodness" of God pass before him; the Lord had even passed before Moses, proclaiming His own name Himself. So deep and so intimate was the relationship that most of the time Moses remained in the presence of God. Because of the intimate union between Moses and the Lord, the glory of the Lord would rest so much on Moses as he left God's presence and came to the people of Israel that

> *"Moses did not know that the skin of his face shone because he had been talking with God. And when Aaron and all the people of Israel saw Moses, behold, the skin of his face shone, and they were afraid to come to him. But Moses called to them; and Aaron and all the leaders of the congregation returned to him and Moses talked with them. And afterward all the people of Israel came near, and he gave them in commandments all that the Lord had spoken with him in Mount Sinai. And when Moses had finished speaking with them, he put a veil on his face; but whenever Moses went in before the Lord to speak with him, he took the veil off, until he came out; and when he came out, and told the people of Israel what he was commanded, the people of Israel saw the face of Moses, that the skin of Moses' face shone; and Moses would put the veil upon his face again, until he went in to speak with him" (Exodus 34:29-35).*

So it is obvious that Moses was "a man of the glory." He bore God's glory physically and spiritually. He knew God deeply and most intimately. Out of this knowledge, he could speak to God in a language that could be misunderstood for rudeness; a language that people who do not know God with the same intensity should not use. Moses said to God,

> *"O Lord, why does thy wrath burn hot against thy people, whom thou hast brought forth out of the land of Egypt with great power and with a mighty hand? Why should the Egyptians say, With evil intent did he bring them forth, to slay them in the mountains, and to consume them*

from the face of the earth? Turn from thy fierce wrath, and repent of this evil against thy people. Remember Abraham, Isaac, and Israel, thy servants to whom thou didst swear by thine own self, and did say to them, I will multiply your descendants as the stars of heaven, and all this land that I have promised I will give to your descendants, and they shall inherit it for ever" (Exodus 32:11-13).

Moses was in a sense asking God questions as if to demand an answer: "Why does thy wrath burn hot against thy people?" "Why should the Egyptians say, With evil intent did he bring them forth?"

Very advanced intercessors can ask God such questions for they ask them from positions they occupy in God's heart, positions that have been well established and are recognized by the Lord. Others dare not ask God such questions. In fact they can only ask Him such questions to their undoing.

Moses did not only ask God questions that put Him in a position from which He more or less had to defend Himself. He commanded God. He said to Him, "Turn from thy fierce wrath." Then he gave God a second command, "Repent of this evil against thy people." To be in a position to command God to repent of an evil against His people is a most solemn thing. Who could tread such grounds easily? How many are there in the Church today who are qualified to speak to God that way? How many know God enough to flow to Him in this kind of way?

Moses finally preached a good sermon to God. He said to Him. "Remember Abraham, and Isaac and Israel, thy servants to whom thou didst swear by thine own self, and did say to them, I will multiply your descendants as the stars of heaven, and all this land that I have promised I will give to your descendants, and they shall inherit it for ever." Moses was saying, "God, do not forget what You promised with an oath. Do not forget that the land was to be given to them for ever. If You act in the way you in planning to act, You would have a forever that is not a forever

There are people whose speeches offend God. There are very few people who could have spoken this way and not have offended God. Moses was one such person and the proof of the fact that God was not offended is the fact that He hearkened to Moses. The Bible says, "And the Lord repented of the evil which he thought to do to his people" (Exodus 32:14).

An advanced intercessor labours to put God on the defensive. He labours to make God appear as planning action that is inconsistence with His nature, His promises, or His plans. He then commands God to become consistent by doing what the intercessor is burdened about.

THE ADVANCED INTERCESSOR AND SELF

No one can really become an advanced intercessor without knowing a radical dealing by the cross, of his self-life. In the type of intercourse that transpired between Moses the intercessor and the Lord God Almighty, it is obvious that Moses had died totally to self. He did not intercede so that some honour or some glory might come out of it for himself. He sought only the interests of the Lord and sought only the interests of the people of God. He was so oblivious of his own interest that he was prepared to give his place in the kingdom of God away eternally so that God's interest and the interest of the people of God were safeguarded. He pleaded,

> *"Alas, this people have sinned a great sin. They have made for themselves gods of gold. But now, if thou wilt forgive their sin - and if not, blot me, I pray thee, out of thy book which thou hast written" (Exodus 32:31-32).*

He was willing to suffer the loss of everything and even himself, not only in time but in eternity, so that the people might be forgiven! He really reached great heights in being delivered from self. May God raise many such in the Church today!

So the advanced intercessor knows that a commitment to God, God's interests and people means that he is prepared to pay the supreme price so that the Lord's interests and the people are spared.

I do not think that Moses attained this position in a short period of time. It was the fruit of many years of walking with God. It was the fruit of many years of God working to bring the "self" life in him to an end. It was the fruit of God smashing his own plans and standing in his way very often and very consistently until his will was broken and surrendered and his own plans and desires abandoned so that those of the Lord may be established. It was the fruit of his worldly career being broken at the age of forty and of forty years being spent in the wilderness as the shepherd of his father-in-law. The intercessor who had made such progress with God was not the same man who, as a potential Pharaoh, could have boasted because he was

"instructed in all the wisdom of the Egyptians, and he was mighty in his words and deeds" (Acts 7:22).

He was separated from his mighty deeds and from his opinion of his mighty deeds. He was separated from his mighty words and his opinion about his mighty words so much that he could say,

"Oh, my Lord, I am not eloquent, either heretofore or since thou hast spoken to thy servant; but I am slow of speech and of tongue" (Exodus 4:10).

God's dealing with him was deep and thorough. He was made humble. He became meek. He was very meek. He could minister in intercession at the plane that others could not.

All who aspire to become advanced intercessors must be aware that they will become advanced intercessors not only through spending much time in intercession but know also that they will be called upon to know the cross experimentally in its power to wound, cut deep, and then liberated from the self-life. Only those who are prepared both to intercede for endless hours and to be delivered them from the self-life can become advanced intercessors.

Are you prepared for this? Are you willing to pray to God along the lines below?

> *"Lord, I want to become an advanced intercessor. I am putting in the many hours that are needed everyday. I pray that You will accelerate my progress by delivering me from self quickly and completely. I give You full liberty to humble me by doing any of the following things that You find necessary:*
>
> ***1) Take away anything or any person from my life whose presence in my life stands in Your way, even in a slight way;***
>
> ***2) Expose my secret sins that I have hidden and that I do not want anyone to know about so that the desire of my heart to exalt myself will receive a fatal blow."***

Advanced intercessors are preoccupied with the glory of God and not with their own glory. Moses interceded many times for Israel, but when he pleaded for himself, he was told,

> *"Let it suffice you, speak no more to me of this matter. Go up to the top of Pisgah, and lift up your eyes westward and northward and southward and eastward, and behold it with your eyes, for you shall not go over this*

Jordan. But charge Joshua, and encourage and strengthen him, for he shall go over at the head with this people, and he shall put them in possession of the land which you shall see" (Deuteronomy 3:26-28).

Moses was rejected. He asked to be allowed to go over into the Promised Land. It was refused and he was told not to bring up the matter again in prayer. He was told to charge, encourage, and strengthen another to succeed where he had failed and he did it. Is there any question about the fact that his preoccupation was the glory of God?

Another advanced intercessor was Daniel. He knew God very deeply and there was much communion between God and him. The Bible says of him,

"Again one having the appearance of a man touched me and strengthened me. And he said, O man greatly beloved, fear not, peace be with you; be strong and of good courage. And when he spoke to me, I was strengthened and said. Let my Lord speak, for you have strengthened me. Then he said, Do you know why I have come to you? But now I will return to fight against the prince of Persia, and when I am through with him, lo, the prince of Greece will come. But I tell you what is inscribed in the book of truth: there is none who contends by my side against these except Michael your prince" (Daniel 10:18-21).

Daniel interceded and Daniel received abundant revelation. The Lord showed Moses and Daniel what He did not show the others. An advanced intercessor will know God and know the ways, methods, and plans of God. He will also know the Enemy and know the Enemy's ways, methods, and plans. He will intercede for the plans of God out of what the Lord has revealed to him and he will intercede against the plans of the Enemy out of what the Lord has also revealed to him. This will enable him to pray accurately and with deep insistence, for how can a person insist that

God does what he does not know God has planned to do? How can a person labour to destroy the plans of the Enemy that he does not know exist?

So the advanced intercessor lives in God's presence, hears God, knows what God has planned and prays them through. Knowing what God has planned, he may also be shown the counter plans of the Enemy that he labours to undo.

PART 4

28

THE INTERCESSOR AND THE OVERTHROW OF PRINCIPALITIES AND POWERS

The Kingdom of God is ruled and kept together by the supreme authority of God the Father, God the Son, and God the Holy Spirit. At their disposal, aiding them are archangels, angels, and spirit beings. These go on God's errands or serve in His immediate presence. They also carry out God's battles and protect God's people. A few verses from the Bible will make this plain.

> *"Now while he was serving as priest before God when his division was on duty, according to the custom of the priesthood, it fell to him by lot to enter the temple of the Lord and burn incense. And the whole multitude of the people were praying outside at the hour of incense. And there appeared to him an angel of the Lord standing on the right side of the altar of incense. And Zechariah was troubled when he saw him. But the angel said to him. Do not be afraid, Zechariah, for your prayer is heard, and your wife Elizabeth will bear a son and you shall call his name John" (Luke 1:8-13).*

> *"When Joshua was by Jericho he lifted up his eyes and looked, and behold, a man stood before him with his drawn sword in his hand, and Joshua went to him and said to him, Are you for us, or for our adversaries? And he said, No, but as commander of the army of the Lord I have now come.*

And Joshua fell on his face to the earth, and worshipped, and said to him, What does my Lord bid his servant? And the commander of the Lord's army said to Joshua, Put off your shoes from your feet for the place where you stand is holy. And Joshua did so" (Joshua 5:13-15).

"The same night he arose and took his two wives, his two maids, and his eleven children, and crossed the ford of the Jabbok. He took them and sent them across the stream, and likewise everything that he had. And Jacob was left alone; and a man wrestled with him until the breaking of the day. When the man saw that he did not prevail against Jacob, he touched the hollow of his thigh and Jacob's thigh was put out of joint as he wrestled; with him. Then he said, Let me go, for the day is breaking. But Jacob said, I will not let you go, unless you bless me. And he said to him, What is your name? And he said, Jacob. Then he said, Your name shall no more be called Jacob, but Israel, for you have striven with God and with men and prevailed. Then Jacob asked him, Tell me, I pray, your name. But he said, Why is it that you ask my name? And there he blessed him" (Genesis 32:22-29).

"In those days I, Daniel, was mourning for three weeks. I ate no delicacies, no meat or wine entered my mouth, nor did I anoint myself at all, for the full three weeks. On the twenty-fourth day of the first month, as I was standing on the bank of the great river, that is, the Tigris, I lifted up my eyes and looked, and behold, a man clothed in linen, whose loins were girded with gold of Uphaz. His body was like beryl, his face like the appearance of lightning, his eyes like flaming torches, his arms and legs like the gleam of burnished bronze, and the sound of his words like the noise of a multitude. And I, Daniel, alone saw the vision, for the men who were with me did not see the vision, but a great trembling fell upon them, and they fled to hide themselves.

"So I was left alone and saw this great vision, and no strength was left in me; my radiant appearance was fearfully changed, and I retained no strength. Then I heard the sound of his words; and when I heard the

> *sound of his words, I fell on my face in a deep sleep with my face to the ground.*
>
> *"And behold, a hand touched me and set me trembling on my hands and knees. And he said to me, O Daniel, man greatly beloved, give heed to the words that I speak to you, and stand upright, for now I have been sent to you. While he was speaking this word to me, I stood up trembling. Then he said to me, Fear not, Daniel, for the first day that you set your mind to understand and humbled yourself before your God, your words have been heard, and I have come because of your words. The prince of the kingdom of Persia withstood me twenty-one days; but Michael, one of the chief princes, came to help me, so I left him there with the prince of the kingdom of Persia and came to make you understand what is to befall your people in the latter days. For the vision is for days yet to come" (Daniel 10:2-14).*

The Enemy also has his co-workers. They are spirit beings who go on his errands and serve in his immediate presence. They carry out his battles and labour to destroy God's people. Sometimes, the devil himself carries out the operations personally. A few verses of Scripture will make this plain.

> *"Now there was a day when the sons of God came to present themselves before the Lord, and Satan also came among them. The Lord said to Satan, Whence have you come? Satan answered the Lord, From going to and fro on the earth, and from walking up and down on it. And the Lord said to Satan, Have you considered my servant Job, that there is none like him on the earth, a blameless and upright man, who fears God and turns away from evil? Then Satan answered the Lord, Does Job fear God for nought? Hast thou not put a hedge about him and his house and all that he has, on every side? Thou hast blessed the work of his hands and his possessions have increased in the land. But put forth thy hand now, and touch all that he has and he will curse thee to thy face. And the Lord said to Satan, Behold all that he has is in your power; only upon himself do not put forth your hand. So Satan went forth from the presence of the Lord.*

"Now there was a day when his sons and daughters were eating and drinking wine in their eldest brother's house; and there came a messenger to Job, and said, The oxen were plowing and the asses feeding beside them; and the Sabeans fell upon them and took them, and slew the servants with the edge of the sword, and I alone escaped to tell you. While he was yet speaking, there came another, and said, The fire of God fell from heaven and burned up the sheep and the servants and consumed them and I alone have escaped to tell you. While he was yet speaking, there came another, and said, The Chaldeans formed three companies, and made a raid upon the camels and took them, and slew the servants with the edge of the sword and I alone escaped to tell you. While he was yet speaking, there came another, and said, Your sons and daughters were eating and drinking wine in their eldest brother's house; and behold, a great wind came across the wilderness, and struck the four corners of the house, and it fell upon the young people, and they are dead; and I alone have escaped to tell you" (Job 1:13-19).

The Enemy has mighty spirits, demons, fallen angels and the like at his service. Some of them control winds, some of them control lightning, and others move men to steal and to do horrible deeds. The apostle Paul wrote,

"Put on the whole armour of God, that you may be able to stand against the wiles of the devil. For we are not contending against flesh and blood, but against the principalities, against the powers, against the world rulers of this present darkness, against the spiritual hosts of wickedness in the heavenly places" (Ephesians 6:11—12).

Satan has the following lineup working for him and going on his errands:

1. Principalities
2. Powers
3. Rulers

4. Spiritual hosts

These labour faithfully to ensure that the will of Satan is accomplished.

So there is conflict between the forces of God and the forces of Satan. It is quite obvious that God can destroy all of the powers of Satan in one second and win a neat victory. The question is, "Why does He not do it?" The answer is simple. God has decided that He will work with redeemed man as His co-worker. He has decided that although He can accomplish all His purpose unaided by man, He will not do it. He has decided to limit Himself in such a way that unless man cooperates, His purpose will be allowed to suffer loss for some time until He finds the person or persons who will cooperate with Him.

This is where the intercessor comes in. He is to be involved with God in the overthrow of the plans of Satan. He is to come against the principalities, powers, rulers, and spiritual hosts that constitute the Enemy's army and overthrow them. He is to wage war against them and uproot them. He is to put them out of the sphere of their activities. He is to do this through the principal instrumentality of intercession.

In writing about spiritual warfare, the apostle Paul names prayer as the final and most potent weapon. He wrote,

> *"Pray at all times in the Spirit, with all prayer and supplication. To that end keep alert with all perseverance, making supplication for all the saints, and also for me, that utterance may be given me in opening my mouth boldly to proclaim the mystery of the gospel, for which I am an ambassador in chains; that I may declare it boldly, as I ought to speak"* (Ephesians 6:18-20).

As the hosts of heaven fight against the hosts of hell, there is a sense in which the intercessor has a decisive role. He is to take sides with the hosts of heaven and by vigorous praying and supplication, with all alertness, bring the forces of hell to nought.

We know that there are principalities, powers, rulers, and spiritual hosts that have specific functions in the army of the evil one. There are principalities that are responsible for:

1. Continents
2. Regions of a continent
3. Nations
4. Regions of nations
5. Tribes
6. Provinces
7. Divisions
8. Subdivisions
9. Villages
10. Towns
11. Parts of towns, and so on

There are also powers and rulers that have specific functions. Some are in charge of various religions. There are spirits set up by Satan to control his affairs in Islam, Buddhism, Catholicism, Protestantism, Pentecostalism, and in everything imaginable. The devil always ensures that he sends a controlling spirit to command and control the other spirits that are sent by him to create a false religion or to turn true believers away from the Lord Jesus and His Word, to something else. When the Lord brings revival, Satan also sends a spirit and spirits to thwart it and turn it into something else or to weaken, confuse, and stop it. There is the host of wickedness everywhere. There is the presence of the hosts of wickedness even when consecrated believers meet to pray and to seek their God. This ought to be obvious from the passage in the Bible that says,

> "Now there was a day when the sons of God came to present themselves before the Lord, and Satan also came among them" (Job 1:6).

Again the Bible says,

> "Jesus answered, It is he to whom I shall give this morsel when I have dipped it. So when he dipped the morsel, he gave it to Judas the son of Simon Iscariot. Then after the morsel, Satan entered into him. Jesus said to him, what you are going to do, do quickly" (John 13:26-27).

It is obvious then that when the Lord Jesus was gathered with the twelve for the last supper, Satan came there personally. The job that was to be done that night was such that he could not trust it to someone else. He came himself.

If the Enemy was not afraid to appear before God and was not afraid to appear when the Lord Jesus was gathered with His own, we can be sure that in our day he will be present or be represented at every evangelistic meeting, at every prayer meeting, at every teaching meeting; at every meeting where the people want to receive the baptism into the Holy Spirit from the Baptizer, at every meeting of the elders, at every convention. ... This means that unless believers take control of things and oust him or his representative from their meetings they will surely come under his influence.

Because there are principalities and powers in charge of the devil's kingdom the world over, the success of God's programme today depends upon the presence of people in the Church who can overthrow these forces and release the captives under their control. The Lord Jesus taught saying,

> *"But no one can enter a strong man's house and plunder his goods unless he first binds the strong man, then indeed he may plunder his house"* (Mark 3:27).

In the overthrow of principalities and powers, an intercessor binds the principalities and powers that oppose God's move and gets them out of the way so that God's purpose can be accomplished. He is able to do this because of the triumph of the Lord Jesus over Satan. The Bible says,

> *"He disarmed the principalities and powers and made a public example of them, triumphing over them in it"* (Colossians 2:15).

Because the Lord Jesus has already disarmed the principalities and powers, intercessors can now overthrow them. It is the work of intercessors today to overthrow the principalities and powers which the Lord has disarmed. The Lord has disarmed them and triumphed over them. Having done that, He now waits for His co-workers to do by intercession that which is their part in the warfare - overthrow them. The Lord Jesus will not overthrow them. The intercessor must do so. Unless the intercessor overthrows the disarmed principalities and powers, they will remain disarmed but not overthrown.

Intercessors should identify various principalities and powers and through intercession overthrow them. As we have seen, not all principalities and powers have the same power and authority. The principality that is in charge of a continent is unquestionably more difficult to overthrow than the one in charge of a country or a town. Any intercessor can generally pray for the overthrow of any principality. In that way he is making his own contribution to a battle that involves many warriors. However, for a believer to single out a particular principality and focus on his overthrow, he has to weigh things carefully. He must ask himself some questions including, perhaps, the following:

1. Do I have the standing before God that will make such a principality heed my command for his overthrow?
2. Do I have experience in the overthrow of a smaller principality?
3. Am I not being moved by pride to come against spiritual forces that are stronger than my depth in the Lord and spiritual authority?
4. Have I the experience in prayer that it takes to wrestle until victory is won?
5. Do I have able co-workers in sufficiently large numbers to come against so mighty a host and maintain the grounds of victory for days, weeks, months, and perhaps years?
6. Do I have what it takes to plunder the strong man's house after he has been bound?
7. Has the Lord called me to it specifically or have I invited myself to it?
8. Am I prepared, if need be, to leave aside all other aspects of my ministry and concentrate on the battle against this principality until he is overthrown even if it demands that I labour at it for ten, fifteen, or twenty hours each day for the next ten or more years?

An honest facing of these questions and prayer to God will guide the intercessor to remain in the centre of God's will with regard to the overthrow of principalities and powers.

A beginner will start on a small scale, probably labouring to overthrow the principality or power that controls his life, then the life of another person, then perhaps his town, then tribe, and so on. As he pays the price and matures in spiritual warfare, God may call him to greater battles. Beginners may become partners with more advanced intercessors in the overthrow of some mighty principality and in that way grow.

God calls people to overthrow particular principalities. He gives them clear instructions and then commissions them. They then go out and stay within the call of God on their lives, overthrowing a specific principality or specific principalities. They keep at it until victory is won. Such warriors may be led by the Lord to invite others to join in the battle or they may be led by the Lord to battle alone. They may be led by the Lord to tell the story of their call and their conflicts or they may be called by Him to keep perfect silence, allowing the matter to remain between the Lord and themselves. The calls will vary and the demands will vary, but each one who is called will receive clear instructions from the Commander-in-Chief and obey them.

Amen.

29

INTERCESSION AGAINST A PRINCIPALITY OR PRINCE - 1

The first prince that the Lord called us to overthrow is the **Prince of Communism**. During my first forty-day fast I was carried in the Spirit for a tour of the world during which the Lord showed me the present power of the **Prince of Communism** and his plans for world conquest. He then gave me the key to the overthrow of this prince. He said to me,

> *"The secret behind the growth and expansion of communism is absolute commitment and utter sacrifice. If there are people who are prepared to commit themselves to Me in an absolute way and sacrifice everything for Me to an extent that measures up at least to that of the communist, I will work with them and ensure that the Prince of Communism is overthrown."*

Later on, after much prayer and waiting on the Lord, we sent the following letter to our co-workers in the Lord.

> *"We have decided, at the invitation of the Lord to fast for twenty-one days [drinking water only] from 10 to 30 December 1987. We shall be asking God to make us into the type of people who can co-operate with*

Him for the overthrow of the Prince of Communism. We shall also be asking that He should raise many others who, through absolute commitment to Him and utter sacrifice for Him, will be used to overthrow the Prince of Communism. I invite you personally to join with us in this fast. Some of us will fast for twenty-one days but any one who is prepared to fast for seventy-two hours (three days) or more can join us. We will pray for each warrior by name. If you intend to participate and would like us to pray for you, please fill the form below and send it to me. Thank you indeed.

— *ZACHARIAS FOMUM, B.P. 6090, YAOUNDE, CAMEROON.*

Dear brother Zach,

I will stand with you in the fast for the raising up of people who will co-operate with God for the overthrow of the Prince of Communism worldwide. I will fast, drinking water only, for ---------- days (from --- — to -------- December 1987).

The Lord can count on me. You too, count on me. My name and my address are ---------------------

One of my co-workers (Donald Ngonge) wrote the following prayer letter which we used as a guide:

THE TWENTY-ONE-DAY FAST (10 TO 30 DECEMBER 1987): THE OVERTHROW OF THE PRINCE OF COMMUNISM WORLDWIDE

Beloved brethren, we thank God who has led us to set aside a time of fasting for the overthrow of the Prince of Communism worldwide. We thank Him for enabling us to discern the secret of this Prince: total commitment and sacrifice.

When the communist says there is no God, this is falsehood because it opposes the existence of God. The average communist is loyal to its goal for world communism as what is better for mankind. If the communist is committed to falsehood then the believer's heart has to be committed to God, to total truth and honesty. This is the challenge before us. Our commitment and sacrifice has to be total in order to overthrow this Prince.

In the light of this, let us pray that each believer:

1. Will see that communism is a system against God.
2. Will understand that the secret of this system is total commitment and sacrifice.
3. Will see the price he has to pay in order to overthrow this Prince.
4. Will face the fact that an honest and pure heart before God is a prerequisite for warfare.
5. Will see the horror of loving a judged world.
6. Will have a spirit of repentance, separation, and judgment of the world and its offers in all forms.
7. Will repent of the terrible sin of coveteousness.
8. Will see that coveteousness is rooted in: a) lack of rest and satisfaction in the Lord, b) deep ingratitude, c) the pride of life.
9. Will examine his heart as to how far the fasting is for God's glory and God's glory alone.
10. Will examine every motive, every work, and every thought before the Lord in truth and honesty.
11. Will repent of every wrong attitude and every deed whose outward expression is different from the impression on the heart.
12. Will examine before the Lord if the impressions he gives of himself to others are true of his life before Him.

13. Will examine how far every confession of love and commitment is true and honest.
14. Will react immediately by putting things right where things have to be put right.
15. Will be totally committed to God's will and service.
16. Will cry out for deliverance from pride and self-love in all their forms.
17. Will judge any manifestation of the spirit of independence in his life.
18. Will examine his loyalty to whom loyalty is due. May every mark of disloyalty be exposed in every heart.
19. Will repent and restitute for every act of disloyalty in his heart.
20. Will forsake all purposelessness in his life.
21. Will repent of all prayerlessness for himself, servants of God and for others.
22. Will be disciplined in the redemption of time and will invest his time to the maximum, for God's work.
23. In a new way will invest his Finances for the urgent task of world conquest for Christ.
24. Will see the need to make long term goals, yearly goals, monthly goals, weekly goals and daily goals and labour to accomplish them.
25. Will have the spirit of the rapture, working hard and being ever prepared for the Lord's soon coming.
26. Will see that part of the sacrifice is a life of fasting.

On the seventeenth day of that fast, 20 December 1987, the Lord told us that the fast had accomplished its purpose, the Prince of Communism had been overthrown and we should stop the fast then. We rejoiced and praised the Lord, having stayed away from fifty-one meals. There were brethren from many countries involved in the battle, although 90 percent were from Cameroon.

On 23 October 1988, we sent out a letter to the brethren, part of which reads:

> "Beloved, you will remember that we fasted in December 1987 for the overthrow of the Prince of Communism. God has continued to do great things in opening up the Communist world to the glorious gospel of His love. However, we are not through with Communism. It is a religion that holds two billion people in captivity. We made inroads into Communism last year during the fast. This year, we must press on for total victory. We must open up all Communist lands to the glorious gospel. We must open the hearts of individuals to the Lord and we must pray that the Church in the Communist lands should never grow cold or lukewarm. We must pray hundreds of millions of Bibles into Communist countries. We must also pray in hundred of millions of top quality books. We must pray that many excellent Christian books will be translated into Chinese and Russian languages and into the other languages spoken where Communism has had a grip on the people. We must pray that the books are translated, produced and circulated. We must pray Communist leaders, intellectuals, and youth to our Lord and Saviour. We must pray multitudes of consecrated and sanctified apostles, prophets, evangelists, pastors and teachers into Communist lands. We must by prayer raise up apostles, prophets, evangelists, pastors and teachers from among believers in Communist lands for Communist lands. Finally, we must pray that the Church in the non-Communist lands will catch the flame and zeal of the Church in Communist lands. For these things we are going to fast for twenty-one days. It is a complete fast [water only]. You can fast for any number of days as you team up with us, but we suggest a minimum of three. Please fill the form below and send to us. Give the extra copies to others who are interested. The fast, **The Lord's Victory in the Communist Lands**, will begin on 5 and end on 25 December 1988. There is a team here that fasts and prays for those in the fast. Stand with us and do not hesitate to fast and to send in your form even if it gets to us long after the fast."

We wrote out the names of the following Communist countries that we know about and laboured in prayer throughout the fast that the Lord may have His way unhindered in each:

1. Guinea Bissau
2. Mozambique
3. South Yemen
4. Benin
5. Congo
6. U.S.S.R.
7. Afghanistan
8. Bhutan
9. Mongolia
10. Laos
11. Macao
12. Cuba
13. Vietnam
14. North Korea
15. Cambodia
16. Ethiopia
17. Nicaragua
18. East Germany
19. Yugoslavia
20. Poland
21. Bulgaria
22. Angola
23. Hungary
24. Surinam
25. Rumania
26. Albania
27. Finland
28. Czechoslovakia
29. Madagascar
30. China

The fast was the most difficult we had ever faced. Personally, I suffered the agony that I normally suffer between the thirty-fifth and fortieth day of a forty-day fast, between the seventeenth and the twenty-first day of the fast. Many people stopped short of their expected number of days, but a number of valiant men and women pressed through to victory. On the morning of the twenty-first day of the fast, 25 December 1988, the Lord spoke to me. The last thing He said concerned the fast. He said,

"Tell My children who have fasted that I have accepted their fast and accepted their contribution to ensure that My Exalted Son has total victory in the Communist world. I have accepted their fast. I exchange it for reward in My kingdom on that Day, each one according to what it has cost him. You will continue to lay hold on what you have conquered but it will be by prayer and literature [to Communist lands] but never again through long fasts."

Participation

We decided to look at our records in order to see what was the involvement of God's children in this second fast for the Lord's victory in communist lands. We had asked the Lord for fifteen hundred participants from twenty-five countries. The participants after giving reasonable time for the forms from other countries to get to us were:

Concluding Statistics: The Lord's victory in Communist Lands

	Participants
Total number of participating female	634
Total number of participating male	888
Total number of participants	1522
Total number of participating countries	23
Total number of participating continents	3

The Fasting Duration Details

Duration	Participants		Totals
Days	Males	Female	
03 - 05	475	359	834
06 - 09	200	151	351
10 - 13	97	60	157
14 - 18	52	30	82
19 - 21	59	27	86
14	0	1	1
20	1	1	2
21	4	5	2
Total	**888**	**634**	**1522**

Participants per Country

	Country	Number
1	Angola	2
2	Benin	2
3	Cameroon	1230
4	Congo	6
5	France	3
6	Gabon	5
7	Ghana	4
8	Ivory Coast	17
9	Kenya	1
10	Niger	5
11	Nigeria	86
12	Norway	1
13	RCA	29
14	Scotland	2
15	Sierra Leone	5
16	Tanzania	3
17	Chad	5
18	Togo	6
19	Uganda	1
20	USA	1
21	W. Germany	1
22	Zaire	35
23	Zambia	62
Total		**1522**

Cameroonian Participation per Province

	Province	Number
1	Adamawa	39
2	Central	583
3	East	105
4	Extreme North	46

5	Littoral	307
6	North	13
7	North West	58
8	South	1
9	South West	55
10	West	23
Total		**1230**

Central province Details

	Town	Number
1	Akono	4
2	Bot Makak	20
3	Endom	7
4	Eseka	6
5	Makak	7
6	Mbalmayo	24
7	Mfou	16
8	Ngoumou	5
9	Obala	31
10	Onguesse	19
11	Yaounde	444
Total		**583**

Littoral Province Details

	Town	Number
1	Douala	271
2	Edea	2
3	Loum	6
4	Mbarga	15
5	Melong	2
6	Njombe	11
Total		**307**

Was the Prince of Communism Overthrown?

The question must linger in many hearts as to whether the Prince of Communism was overthrown. All we can say is that the God who called us to fast and pray for his overthrow told us that he had been overthrown. This was on 20 December 1987. We believe we heard God correctly both about the fast and about the result of the fast. We, however, do not need to defend ourselves.

If God did speak to us and we heard Him correctly, then from 20 December 1987 and on, there should be changes – far-reaching changes in Communist lands in their attitude towards:

1. Communism.
2. The imprisonment of believers.
3. The barrier to the entry of Bibles and other Christian literature.
4. The refusal of the freedom of individuals.

5. And so many other changes.

If the Prince of Communism was indeed overthrown and if believers continue to stand in the gap, then millions of people in Communist lands should turn to the Lord Jesus Christ in a few years at a rate that is phenomenal. Many Communist leaders should move away, at least in practice, from the Communist approach to life and seek an approach that is more godly.

We look to the Lord to fulfil His word to us.

Amen

INTERCESSION AGAINST A PRINCIPALITY OR PRINCE - 2

As we have said earlier, the Lord called us to wage war against principalities and powers. We were told that the special weapons in this warfare were fasting and prayer. During the same period that the Lord told us to intercede against the Prince of Communism by two three-week fasts, we were told that we had to battle against the Prince of Islam. The Lord said to us,

"I want you to battle against the Prince of Islam. The Battle will not be an easy one but you will press on until I give you victory."

We decided to have a three-week fast each March as a part of this warfare. One month later as I was bathing, the Lord said to me,

"You cannot come against the Prince of Islam with a twenty-one day fast. He would not yield on those grounds. In fact, he would say that his worshippers fast for twenty-eight days and you were not able to fast that long and as such he would not yield. You should fast for twenty-eight days and all your fasts against him shall be twenty-eight days. You shall not accept any who carry out partial fasts to be involved. The Prince of Islam has received adoration from hundreds of millions of worshippers through

partial fasts for centuries. Fasting is his arena. The way to win is to ensure that all of you carry out a complete fast. This will give you an edge, the victory edge, over him. I will, however, accept a partial fast of twenty-eight days from those who, for medical reasons cannot carry out complete fasts. The battle will be rough and will need at least four fasts of twenty-eight days. You should recruit the largest army possible. You will receive special information that will be necessary for victory after you and your co-warriors have finished two fasts of twenty-eight days. Set your mind on victory and never look back."

When the Lord spoke to us in this way, I sent the following letter to brethren who stand with us in battle.

"I am inviting you to join me in the battle to overthrow the Prince of Islam. Together, we are going to fast for the Moslems out of love for them. We love the Moslems. We wish them God's best and God's best for them is that they may come to a saving knowledge of the Saviour - the Lord Jesus. Many Moslems would believe in the Lord Jesus were they not hindered by a power, a spiritual power, an unseen personality in the spirit world who controls all the affairs of Islam and causes Moslems to believe what they believe. This spiritual personality is the one we call the Prince of Islam. He is a mighty Prince and has been operative and fully functional for nearly fourteen hundred years. He holds nearly one billion Moslems under sway, all over the world, at the moment. This Prince is totalitarian. He holds all who are his with a most firm grip. The Prince of Communism is no match for him. First of all, the Prince of Communism only became operative in this century. Second, there are millions of true believers in the Lord Jesus in Communist lands. If you were well informed then you know too well that there are very, very, few Moslems who have ever believed in the Lord Jesus anywhere in the world, be it in the past or in the present! In coming against the Prince of Islam, we know that we are coming against a very mighty force. It will be a fierce battle. Another element of importance is that the Prince of Islam has led her subjects to 'fast' regularly and to 'pray' regularly and seriously for fourteen hundred years.

The truth is that millions of Moslems have fasted and prayed for hundreds of years. These are hard facts.

"Were it not that we know the One who went to the Cross and there 'Disarmed the principalities and powers and made a public example of them, triumphing over them in it [that is, the cross]' (Colossians 2:15), we would not dare to go into such warfare. Were it not for the fact that I received very clear instructions from the Lord God of heaven to wage war against this Prince and overthrow him, I would not get involved in such conflicts. Were it not for the fact that on 20 January 1988 when I was in the Spirit, I battled furiously with this Prince with my hands on a world map over North Africa and the Middle East and after utter conflict that nearly cost my life, saw him overthrown by the power of the Cross, I would continue to tremble. The battle will be fierce but the Lord will grant us victory. I do not know at the moment if we shall overthrow him in one or in many fasts but we shall keep fighting until the victory is won. I had initially intended that the fast would be twenty-one days. The Lord has however asked me that it be twenty-eight days. He has also told me that the Prince of Islam will react and try, if possible to take the lives of some of those who will come against him in this way. There is need for much protection, much hiding under the blood of the Lion-Lamb. Pray very much for yourself and for all who will be in the battle. During the fast, we shall ask the Lord to bless Moslems and to give them His best Gift - the Lord Jesus. We shall ask the one who holds them captives [the Prince of Islam] to make way for the Lord Jesus. We shall labour at this, knowing that we are fighting from the victory of the Cross. We shall fight knowing that 'The weapons of our warfare are not carnal [worldly] but have divine power to destroy strongholds' (2 Corinthians 10:4). We shall look to the Lord and we shall 'wax strong.'*

"I invite you to stand with me in this battle for the glory of God. The fast is from 29 February to 27 March. Some of us will fast completely [water only] and others may fast partially [one meal each evening about 6 P.M.] Those on the complete fast [only water] may enroll for three or more days. Those on the partial fast [one meal after 6 P.M each day] will fast for all *the twenty-eight days. There is need, great need for many to go on for twenty-eight days of the complete fast [water only]. The spiritual repercussions are obvious, Please, I plead with you not only to come into this battle but to seek other believers to join with you. Fill the form below and send it to me as soon as possible. There are prayer warriors who will lift you up to the Lord daily as you fast. I enclose a second form that you should give another believer whom you have encouraged to join you in the fast. You can copy out the form by hand if you have more people who are willing to join you in the battle than the number of forms available. The Lord alone will reward each one of us on that day. May you so labour that when the books shall be opened on that day and the book on fasting is opened, you shall receive a full reward."*

— YAOUNDE, 28 JANUARY 1988.

The form that was to be filled was as follows:

Zach Fomum

B.P. 6090

Yaounde, Cameroon.

Dear brother Zach,

I am standing with you in the fast so that the Lord will bless and visit the Moslems. I will fast for ___ days drinking only water or for all twenty-eight days (29th February-27th March) eating one meal a day after 6 p.m.

Name -----------

Adress-----------

Date -----------

One of my co-workers, Roger Forteh, wrote the following prayer topics as a guide for those of us who were preparing to get into the battle.

PREBATTLE PRAYER FOR THE TWENTY-EIGHT-DAY FAST AGAINST THE PRINCE OF ISLAM

Praise and Thanksgiving.

1. We bless, praise and thank You Lord for revealing to us a need of Your heart: the overthrow of the Prince of Islam.
2. We thank You for opening Your heart to us and revealing to us Your eternal purpose.
3. Father, thank You for this confidence You have in us men.
4. Thank You for the zeal, courage, and jealousy You have aroused in our hearts to respond to Your need, Your purposes promptly.
5. Blessed be Your name for none will thwart any purpose of Yours that You have purposed (praise as per Isaiah 14:27).
6. Thank You for raising an army of God to fight this battle even against unnumbered foes.
7. Lord, continue to speak to us about the battle. Give us more details, specific instructions.

Preparation

1. Lord, continue to speak to us about the battle. Give us more details, specific instructions about our personal preparation for and conduct of the battle.
2. Lead us into preparation for it. Constrain us to prepare physically in the choice, quality, and quantity of food we eat, physical exercise, vitamins, minerals intake . . . Deliver us from all gluttony.

3. Constrain us to prepare spiritually. Separate us from all sin, from all that is common
4. Cause Your Spirit to work out blamelessness in each of Your warriors.
5. Lord, carefully select Your warriors from the ranks of Your army and equip them for battle.
6. Lord, cause Your elite army to embrace the harsh preparations and training prior to the battle (your discipline, loneliness and faithfulness in prayer, mock attacks by the Enemy, faithful dynamic encounters with You daily).
7. Lord, train our hands for war, train us in the tactics of spiritual offensive and defensive warfare.
8. Lord, reveal to us the war strategy of the enemy now.
9. Reveal to each warrior, Lord, that our war against the Prince of Islam is not a worldly war.
10. Reassure Your warriors that the weapons You have given us are mighty and dreadfully destructive for they have divine power.
11. Lord, we beseech You for special, continuous and triumphant protection against the fury of the Enemy. Protect Your heritage, Lord.
12. Teach and lead us to bring all our beings and all that we have for protection under the blood of Jesus on a daily basis as from now.
13. We bring our spirits, souls and bodies for Your mighty protection under the blood of Jesus Christ.
14. Lord, please, as a token of Your overflowing grace and goodness and love for us, and as part of our own preparedness for mighty conflict, heal all the diseases, sicknesses, and pain and infirmities that afflict us. Reveal Yourself to us now as the Almighty, our healer. Then clothe each of us permanently with the health of Christ.

15. Lord, grant to us gifts of tough, resistant bodies for warfare.
16. Forbid, Lord, that any of Your warriors would faint or suffer any unwanted crippling effects as a result of the fast.
17. Grand to each warrior spiritual buoyancy, alertness, strength, and might and integrity from now onwards.
18. Lord, in the name of Jesus Christ, do not permit the premature death of any of Your children. Protect Thy heritage, Lord.
19. Lord, arise now as never before against our enemies that they may melt like wax before Thee. Deliver us from wicked men, Satan-generated circumstances, and other agents of the devil.

The Active Battle

1. Fill us with divine jealousy for You and Your glory and divine hatred for the devil and the Prince of Islam.
2. Move us to pray fervently and to believe You as we pray throughout the fast.
3. Strenghten our weak knees, our drooping hands, uphold, strengthen and sustain us during the fast.
4. Lord, show us Your glory. Grant that we would trust You and You alone throughout the battle.

Offensive Warfare

1. Grant us constant revelation of Your fighting tactics through out the fast.
2. Reveal to us all the prayer topics and may Your Spirit help us to pray each of them through.
3. Lord, grant that the twenty-four hours of each day, from

day one to day twenty-eight, would each be covered in prayer.
4. Blessed Holy Spirit grant to us the right burdens and the right direction in prayer.
5. Lord, protect us even in our errors during the battle.
6. Lord, raise a mighty back-up army of praying men and women interceding for those at the battle front and providing them the necessary supplies of encouragement, blessing, visits ... in the heat of battle. Forbid that there would be spectators when an all-out war has been declared.
7. Grant that in Your army there would be: a) experienced warriors, expert in using all the spiritual weapons You have equipped us with; b) Warriors with faces like lions; c) Daring warriors who would cross over all obstacles and put the hosts of the enemy to flight; d) Warriors who though faint, yet pursue the enemy until he is cut-off and despoiled.
8. Lord, make Your warriors resolute in their overthrow of enemy strongholds and high places.
9. Reveal to us in astonishing detail every stronghold of the Prince of Islam and any evasive, misleading suggestion he makes to us, however good.
10. Lord, grant that even the youngest and weakest of us would be a man of valour capable of each putting to flight millions of demons.
11. Grant that we would use the weapons You have given us to destroy the arguments and age-old doctrines perpetuated and handed down over the centuries by the Prince of Islam.
12. Grant that we would punish every disobedience to Christ and smash the doctrine that says Mohammed is the way to God.
13. Grant that we would take every Islamic doctrine,

thought, argument, custom, and philosophy captive to obey Christ.

14. Lord grant that we would utterly despoil the Prince of Islam and smash the bars, iron gates, and bronze doors that keep hundreds of millions of people imprisoned in: a) all koranic, cultural and religious centres; b) every single mosque or place of prayer existing, planned or being built; c) the Kaaba, the chief Moslem Shrine in Mecca; d) Islamic political and legal systems; e) each fence, country (e.g., Iran), custom, that denies women the opportunity to come into contact with the gospel of Jesus; f) abject ignorance, lies, and fear of the consequences of confessing Christ.

15. Lord, grant that in the Name of Jesus Christ, we would release hundreds of millions of Moslems from the prison cells and dungeons of Islam and bring them all and their possessions to You as the great spoils of war.

16. Lord, we deny them the use of any propagating mechanism for spreading Islam. We deny them the use of leaflets, brochures, paper, machines, the TV and the radio. We come against the use of CRTV for the advertisement of Islam, in the name of Jesus.

17. Lord, grant that Your victory and our victory over the Prince of Islam and his government here and in the world would be resounding, definitive, and irreversible and that all the spoils of war will be Yours until You return.

18. Unto Him who is seated on the great white throne, Our Father, from whose presence earth and sky will flee away, unto Him who is God Almighty, Our dread warrior, and Jesus, be praise, honour, blessing, majesty, dominion and authority, before all time and now and for ever. Amen.

Another co-worker (Donald Ngonge) led us to pray as outlined below:

THE TWENTY-EIGHT-DAY: FAST THE OVERTHROW OF THE PRINCE OF ISLAM WORLDWIDE

Beloved brethren in the battle, it is sad to learn that there are slightly over 890 million Moslems in the world of 5 billion people. It is presently the most populated religious system occupying West and North Africa, the Middle East and around the Mediterranean Sea, and Central and South Asia mostly.

Islam and the prince of Islam stand as the violent opposers of the gospel of Christ. It is a rapidly growing religion. It is time for us to wage war furiously against this prince with the jealousy of the Lord.

God has to move! The outpouring of His Spirit has to be mighty to sweep millions of Moslems into His kingdom.

The opposing strength of this prince shows it is under the special charge of Satan himself.

1. May we remind Satan of the Lord's victory over him on the cross.
2. May we praise God for a standard against Satan; the cross of Christ, which is His answer of the Lord's victory over him.
3. May we overthrow him and bring his powers and influence to nought, liberating the 890 million Moslems in the world, held captive by him.
4. The Overthrow of the Prince of Islam in the Middle East: There are about 163 million Moslems in this part of the world.
5. Let us remind the Lord that this part of the world was once the home of the early churches during the apostolic age.
6. May we bind and overthrow the Prince of Islam and his

actions in the Middle East, the land of its birth and propagation.

7. May we judge the spirit behind the Arabic language as the main Islamic tongue. May we also judge its influence and grip over millions of people.
8. May we neutralize the power behind the Arabic language and its influence in the advance of Islam in the world since ages past.
9. May we judge the Moslem militancy's and tendencies to islamize the world from the Middle East.
10. May we judge the power of petrol as a means to finance world Islamic evangelization and advances in the construction of mosques.

In a period of ten years two hundred new mosques and a theological college for Islam were financed and built in Yugoslavia .

There are fifty mosques at least in New York City in the U.S.A.

The mosque in Paris now registers six hundred to seven hundred converts annually.

During an inauguration ceremony of a mosque in Sweden, a Moslem leader told a journalist that Europe will be conquered for Islam in fifty years. He said again, "We have the means, the men to do the work, and we have begun!"

1. May we judge the power of the rulers of each Moslem state to propagate Islam.
2. May we bring their counsels to nought. May we disunite and put to flight the forces that unite them. May we sow confusion in their camps.
3. May we judge the lie that Islam is the only true religion for mankind today.

4. May we judge the violence and warlike spirit behind the spread of Islam.
5. May we judge the yearly Moslem pilgrimage to Mecca: to the Kaaba. May we release the millions of captives all over the world who yearly flock to Mecca.
6. May we judge the Prince of Islam behind the Kaaba in Mecca holding captive the 890 million Moslems all over the world.
7. May we judge the power released through the yearly one month Moslem fast. May we frustrate the fast henceforth and nullify its effect in the propagation of Islam.
8. May we judge the lying spirit that make Moslems believe that their sins are forgiven whenever they fast.
9. May we cry out to God to pour out His power anew. May we pray that He will revive His work in this part of the world.

Pray that:

1. He will grant a rebirth of living churches in this land. God will open their eyes to see that Jesus is the only solution to the world today.
2. A mighty Spirit of conviction of sin, judgment, and righteousness will grip the people.
3. He will move mightily and greatly sweep millions of Moslems into His kingdom.
4. God will grant the many Arabs outside the Middle East to come in touch with the gospel and believe. Churches will be established in many towns of the Middle East.
5. Doors will be open for the gospel through men, literature, Bibles, radio, correspondence courses, cassettes, and tracts. The women will be released from seclusion imposed by the men.

6. The Lord will strengthen the faith of all who belong to Him in spite of the heavy persecutions.
7. Doors will be open for churches to be established in countries with no churches such as Saudi Arabia, Qatar, Kuwait, the United Arab Emirates, North Yemen.
8. God will strengthen the few who confess Christ by visiting them mightily with His Spirit of revival and to give them boldness to preach Christ in Afghanistan, Bahrain, Oman, Turkey, South Yemen.
9. The Lord of the harvest will raise apostles, evangelists, pastors and teachers and many labourers for the conquest of the Middle East for Christ.

One thousand people were involved in this fast. Nine hundred of them from Cameroon and the other one hundred from other countries. Ten of us in Cameroon did the complete fast, drinking water only.

As this was just the beginning of our warfare with the Prince of Islam we cannot say much about the battle and the repercusions in enemy territory. We can only say that we shall keep at it. I am writing this chapter on 29 January 1989. The second fast for the salvation of the Moslems through the overthrow of the Prince of Islam will, God willing, be carried out from 22 February 1989 to 21 March 1989. We are asking the Lord to give us two thousand warriors from thirty countries. We are also praying that at least one hundred believers will complete the twenty-eight days fast, drinking water only. The prayer letter for the second fast follows. We are looking to the Lord for His enabling. God enabling, we shall tell the the whole story in the book *The Overthrow of Principalities and Powers*. Praise the Lord!

PRAYER LETTER NO. 19

My Beloved Co-labourer,

Praise the Lord!

A very Happy New Year to you. May this be the year that you draw closer to the Lord Jesus more than ever before. May this be the year in which you know complete deliverance from sin. May this be the year when the Spirit of the Lord roots out the last traces of the love of the world from your heart. May this be the year during which you consecrate all that you are; all that you will ever be, all that you have, and all that you will ever have, to the Lord Jesus in an irrevocable way. May this be the year when you do all that you can to love Him and serve Him. May this be the year when you do all that you can, be it praying, giving, and perhaps going, to tell the story of God's love revealed in the Son, the Lord Jesus, to all on Planet Earth; to everyone as far as the curse, brought in by the fall, is found. And, oh, how I wish it really was that. May this be the year when the Lord Jesus returns to take His Bride to Himself! How wonderful it would be to change earth for heaven; to change seeing Him as through a veil to seeing Him face to face, to change being in His service to being at His table—always in His immediate presence. I confess that the Lord has began to create deep desires for the return of the Lord Jesus in my heart that I never had before. Something deep down in me yearns and burns for His immediate presence. The power of the things of the world to satisfy seems to have disappeared from my spirit, soul, and body. I want the Lord, our Lord back. Maybe you, too, are experiencing what I am going through. Maybe you, too, want Him back. Maybe you are no longer satisfied with all that you have while He, your Beloved, is absent. If that is the case, should we not together cry out: "Come, Lord Jesus?" I believe we should do that every clay of this year, and many times each day until the passion for Him and His return, becomes a flame that will ignite others to desire Him.

Even though there is the new flame for the Lord Jesus and this increasing yearning for His return, I am an unhappy man. We have gathered the following facts from the book Operation World about the dominance of Islam. I will give you the figures of the percentage of Moslems in only twenty-eight countries. I will give them to you, with prayer that God will speak to your heart about them and cause you to respond.

1 -> North Yemen -> 100%

2 -> Somalia -> 99.8%

3 -> Comoros Islands -> 99.7%

4 -> Mauritania -> 99.6%

5 -> Morocco -> 96.6%

6 -> Algeria -> 99.5%

7 -> Tunisia -> 99.5%

8 -> Turkey -> 99.5%

9 -> Afghanistan -> 99.0%

10 -> Iran -> 98.0%

11 -> Oman -> 97.4%

12 -> Pakistan -> 96.6%

13 -> Djibouti -> 96.0%

14 -> Iraq -> 95.8%

15 -> Saudi Arabia -> 94.0%

16 -> Jordan -> 93.0%

17 -> Libya -> 93.0%

18 -> Qatar -> 92.0%

19 -> Senegal -> 92.0%

20 -> South Yemen -> 92.0%

21 -> Bahrain -> 90.8%

22 -> Kuwait -> 90.0%

23 -> Syria -> 90.0%

24 -> Bangladesh -> 87.0%

25 -> Gambia -> 87.0%

26 -> Niger -> 86.0%

27 -> United Arab Emirates -> 85.0%

28 -> Egypt -> 82.4%

The grip of Islam on these nations is more or less total. In the Comoros Islands, there are over 780 Mosques. Cairo is the intellectual capital of Islam. There is an Islamic revival going on in many places in the world at the moment. There are.nearly one billion Moslems in the world today. That means that 20 percent of all the people in the world are Moslems. Moslems are far more committed to their faith than many believers who have received the Lord Jesus as their Saviour. They are not ashamed, of what they believe. Spiritual values are more important to a Moslem father than the materialistic values that rule the hearts of many who claim to know the Christ who saves. The reality is that, without divine intervention Islam could conquer the whole world. There are plans, carefully made plans, for the universal conquest of the world for Islam. Everything is being put in: money, personnel, time, energy, indoctrinating systems ... to ensure that the plan succeeds. The normal Christian has nothing to offer to a Moslem at the spiritual level.

The question then is, "Why bother?" There is a sense in which it would be easier not to get involved. However, when I turned to the Bible and read the declaration of Jesus,

> *"I am the Way, and the Truth and the Life; no one comes to the Father, but by me" (John 14:6)*

and the proclamation of the apostles,

> *"And there is salvation in no one else, for there is no other name under heaven given among men by which we must be saved" (Acts 4:12)*

and

> *"For there is one God, and there is one mediator between God and men, the man Christ Jesus, who gave himself as a ransom for all, the testimony to which was borne at the proper time" (Timothy 2:5),*

I know that the Moslem needs Jesus Christ. He is the Saviour of the whole world. He is the Saviour of the Moslem. He is the Saviour of everyone born of woman. It is imperative that every Moslem in the world clearly hears the gospel of God's redeeming love manifested in the Lord Jesus and that, upon hearing the gospel, he turns to the Lord Jesus for salvation.

Why has this not happened to any significant extent over the last thirteen hundred years? There are many reasons for it, but the central reason is that Islam was conceived by a spirit being and it is being controlled by that being. I received this information in a personal revelation from the Father, the details of which must not be given here. Because Islam was so conceived and is being propagated by a spirit being who has other spirit beings under control, the battle is purely spiritual. This spirit being holds everything that concerns the propagation of Islam, under sway. The deep commitment of the Moslems to Islam is the work of this spirit being whom we call "The Prince of Islam." He has blinded the Church from seeing her debt to the Moslems. He ensures that many of those who go to work among the Moslems are ill-equipped spiritually for the task and easily get discouraged. He ensures that those who do not withdraw, spend five, ten, fifteen, and even twenty years in an Islamic country without seeing some real Moslems receive the Lord Jesus. He ensures that the Church is preoccupied with worldly things and worldly values. He is the mind and the power behind the Islamic revivals that are on throughout the world.

The truth is that there will be no significant progress for the cause of Christ among the Moslems until the Prince of Islam is overthrown. (He has power to strengthen the Moslems and power to weaken, confuse, divert, and ground any real attempt to get the gospel to the Moslems and see many Moslems receive Christ). The Bible says, "How can one enter a strong man's house and plunder his goods, unless he first binds the strong man? Then indeed he may plunder his house" (Matthew 12:29). The strong man of Islam is the Prince of Islam. He must be bound. Binding him is what we call his overthrow from authority. When he will be bound (overthrown), in a short period of time, Moslems will turn readily to the Lord Jesus in their millions and perhaps hundreds of millions. When he is overthrown (removed from authority in the spiritual realm) the Church's attitude to the Moslems will change overnight.

The most urgent task then is the overthrow of the Prince of Islam. The weapons that the Lord has given as effective against this Prince are the following:

1. Fasting (the ground on which the Prince of Islam is very strong).
2. Praying (the ground on which the Prince of Islam is very strong also).
3. Faith in the triumph of the Lord Jesus over Satan and Satan's hosts on the cross (Colossians 2:15) and in the

ultimate victory of the Lord Jesus over all that has not yet bowed to Him now (1 Corinthians 15:24-25).
4. Utter love for the Lord Jesus and His glorious cause without which the battle will lose the power to captivate.
5. Utter love for the Moslems without which it will be difficult to go hungry so that they may come into a saving experience of the Lord Jesus.
6. Utter faith that the Prince of Islam can be overthrown and will be overthrown and multitudes of his captives brought to the Lord Jesus.
7. Utter separation from the love of the world and the things of the world (1 John 2:15-17).
8. Utter holiness unto the Lord (the indispensable consecration of spirit, soul, body and all to the Lord Jesus).
9. Utter purity before the Lord (the indispensable separation from all known sin). With these weapons, victory will come through even if it takes long; victory will come even though the fight will be fierce and the foe strong and resistant.

As can be seen from the weapons above, all who want to acquire them can do so. They are within the reach of all believers. All who want can become a part of God's army for the binding of the strong man and the release of his captives. Of course, there is a price to pay, but which believers cannot pay the price outlined above?

I invite you to team up with me for the overthrow of the Prince of Islam. In order to team up with me, separate yourself from every known sin in your life and consecrate yourself without reserve to the Lord. Pray that the Lord will work out the other weapons in you and believe Him to do it. Then join me in the fast titled "WITH THE LOVE OF JESUS CHRIST TO THE

MOSLEMS." THE FAST IS A COMPLETE FAST (WATER ONLY), IT WILL BEGIN ON 22 FEBRUARY 1989 AND END ON 21ST MARCH 1989. YOU MAY NOT BE ABLE TO FAST FOR ALL THE TWENTY EIGHT DAYS. HOWEVER, I ENCOURAGE YOU TO JOIN IN THE FAST AND PUT IN ANY NUMBER OF DAYS THAT YOU CAN.

I beseech you to get involved. I humbly beg you not to stand aloof. The salvation of one billion people is involved. How can you be indifferent? I beg you not only to join in the fast but also to influence all you can to join in your family, your friends, your church members, the churches under your leadership ... so that there will be a mighty army of able soldiers to do this needed work for our Lord and for our fellow human beings, the Moslems. Fill the form below and send it to me at once. Give the others to others whom you have convinced to join in. Copy it by hand, photocopy it or type more examples as your need may be. The Lord sees your contribution and will reward you on that day. There is another issue attached to it: hundreds of souls of Moslems won to Christ will make the return of Jesus and the Marriage Supper such a joy. So, brother and sister, the Lord is counting on you . I, too, am counting on you. God bless you abundantly.

With deepest gratitude.
Your servant in the service of the Lord Jesus
Zacharias Tanee Fomum

Zacharias Fomum

B.P. 6090

Yaounde, Cameroon

Dear Brother Zach,

I love the Moslems. I desire that Jesus might be revealed to them. I want the obstacle which is the Prince of Islam overthrown. I am teaming up with you in the fast titled, "WITH THE LOVE OF JESUS CHRIST TO THE MOSLEMS" from the 22nd February to the 21st March 1989.

I will fast for ----- days beginning from ---- and ending on ----

I am separating myself from all sin and consecrating myself unconditionally to the Lord for ever. Count on me.

My name is -----

My address is -----

Zacharias Fomum

B.P. 6090

Yaounde, Cameroon

God enabling, we shall complete the story of God's attack and His overthrow of the Prince of Islam, after we have seen this happen, in a subsequent book titled *The Overthrow of Principalities and Powers*.

Praise the Lord!

PART 5

AN INTERCESSIONAL PRAYER CHAIN

THE BIBLICAL BASIS OF A PRAYER CHAIN

The Bible commands,

> *"Pray without ceasing"* (1 Thessalonians 5:17).

The prayer chain is one method of praying without ceasing. It is a corporate method of praying without ceasing. The Enemy is constantly looking for opportunities to attack. The vital force that opposes him has to be on duty night and day. This is the force of intercessors. They stand in the gap without ceasing. They plead with God without ceasing as in the battle with Amalek, the prayer chain ensures that the hands of Moses are permanently raised up and so guarantees the victory of Israel.

A PRAYER CHAIN MUST BE GOD-ORIGINATED AND GOAL-DIRECTED

The Lord said,

> *"Upon your walls, O Jerusalem, I have set watchmen, all the day and all the night they shall never be silent. You who put the Lord in remembrance, take no rest, and give him no rest until he establishes Jerusalem and makes it a praise in the earth"* (Isaiah 62:6-7).

Part of the function of people praying on a prayer chain is to monitor the activities of the wicked one and all of his allies. They are to serve as watchmen. God is the One who sets up watchmen. God must be the One who initiates each prayer chain. It is not just a matter of someone waking up one day and saying, "I have heard of the prayer chain that is in that church and of its impact. We are going to have our own." Such a thing would be an activity of the flesh for it would lack mandate from above. It may even be the fruit of jealousy or of competition and strife. God must give the vision of what He wants to do. That vision will be given to a person who seeks God's face and waits before Him. The vision from the Lord will result in burden. The burden itself must be from the Lord. If not, it will be short-lived. What God does lasts. It cannot be overthrown. It cannot vanish like a mist.

The burden will grow until it becomes such that were it not executed, the person bearing it would feel like collapsing. When God puts the burden to have a prayer chain on a heart and it grows until the man becomes restless with it, the burden will give way to action and that action is the establishment of the prayer chain: So there must be vision that gives birth to burden that results in action.

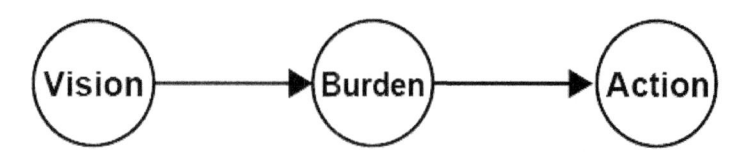

Vision ⟶ Burden ⟶ Action

As we have seen, it is God who sets up watchmen. It is God who places the burden to pray on the hearts of people. An individual may, out of personal reasons, establish his chain but he will not be able to draw to it men and women who are burdened to see God's glory established. Human authority and planning can get people to register on a prayer chain and the shame and fear of failure can keep them coming week by week but only the Lord can lodge the burden to see God's glory in a heart and only He can translate that burden into prayer that may become tears, cries, and groans unto God. Only the Lord's doing ensures that the burden is maintained and that it grows until the goal is accomplished.

The vision may be a revival in a local assembly or it may be revival in the churches in a region. It could also be the revival of the churches in a continent or on all of Planet Earth. The vision may be the penetration of some unevangelized tribes or it may be the overthrow of some principality that prevents its subjects from coming to a saving knowledge of the Lord Jesus. Whatever is the vision, it must begin in the heart of God and be revealed to someone by the Lord. The person who receives the vision must be one who has proven spiritual authority to call people to a spiritual work. He will then share the vision and those who hear him will receive the witness in their hearts that what they are hearing is of the Lord! Could there be a greater vision in our time than to pray that the heavens would be closed no more but that they would release the Exalted Son of God, the Lord Jesus, to come for His Bride? Are there any people who hunger enough for Him and are desperate enough for His return to pray the Spirit-breathed prayer, "Come, Lord Jesus!" without ceasing and at the call of God establish a prayer chain of Jesus' lovers who would cry out in hot pleading until He comes? Are there some who would give God no rest and take no rest, night and day until the Father has released the Son to make His second journey to earth a historical fact?

GIVING GOD NO REST AND TAKING NO REST

The goal to be accomplished by the prayer chain must be such that the people praying are compelled to pray, giving God no rest and taking no rest themselves. This means that those who are to be involved in praying on a prayer chain must be men and women of war - spiritual war. They must be people who must win or perish. They must have decided that they must receive an answer from the Lord and having so decided they put their all into it night and day.

It is not possible for one person to intercede without ceasing every minute of every day for years. That is why other warriors are indispensable so that each may stand in the gap for some length of time and then give way to another when his turn is over. There are times when the burden is so heavy that after a short period of praying, the intercessor is at the brink of collapsing. This again is the reason why there must be other intercessors involved. They will each take turns to give God no rest until He has moved.

A prayer chain is not only established to deal with God. It is also established to deal with Satan. This makes it imperative for those involved in praying on a prayer chain to have experience in spiritual warfare. They will have to intercede with the Father for the work to be done or the work being done and intercede with the Father against the devil. They will pray to God and they will pray against Satan. They will carry the weapon for building the kingdom of God on the one hand and on the other hand carry the weapon for the destruction of the work of Satan, and at times they will use both weapons simultaneously. Nehemiah did this. The Bible says,

> *"From that day on, half of my servants worked on the construction, and half held the spears, shields, bows, and coats of mail; and the leaders stood*

behind all the house of Judah, who were building the wall. Those who carried burdens were laden in such a way that each with one hand laboured on the work and with the other hand held his weapon. And each of the builders had his sword girded at his side while he built" (Nehemiah 4:16-18).

THE GOAL MUST BE MAINTAINED

When a prayer chain is established to accomplish a certain desire that is in the heart of God, that goal must be jealously guarded. If not, it will be stolen by the Enemy. One of the chief tactics of the Enemy is to confuse the vision. He may take it away completely or he may add so many other issues to it that a thousand and one things are being pursued at once. When that happens, he has gained ground significantly. To avoid the Enemy from wreaking havoc in this way, the goal of the prayer chain should be written on the wall of the room being used for the chain and only prayer topics that when answered will contribute to that goal should be prayed on the chain.

Then there must be some way of monitoring the progress of the prayer chain. The Lord said that those who put Him in remembrance would take no rest and give Him no rest until He established Jerusalem and made it a praise in the earth. This signifies that there was a way to know when the work was accomplished. Each prayer chain must be so goal oriented that it would be possible to know when it should start.

It will be possible to have the initial goal enlarged but the goal will have to be maintained and it will have to continue to be precise.

Because the prayer chain can really continue only as long as the burden lasts, the vision and the burden must be protected by violent praying. The heart must be helped to be steady and not just be open to every idea floating around, in the name of a work for God. In fact every watchman must not be broad hearted but should be narrow-minded. He must stick to one thing and keep to it even if it takes years for it to be realized. When Anna set out to intercede, possibly for the first advent of our Lord and Saviour Jesus Christ, she remained with one goal for sixty years of intercession. She did not move to other pressing issues. She was not moved to start praying for something else by the spiritual condition of the day. She carried one burden and allowed only that one burden to envelop her, possess her, and cause her to burn as a flame that could not be extinguished for the next sixty years! Then her goal was accomplished! The Saviour came and she spoke of Him before returning to spend the rest of her life in unceasing thanksgiving:

THE PRACTICE OF A PRAYER CHAIN

The prayer chain is a method of accomplishing a particular work that is in God's heart and that has been revealed to a people. How is it to be practised?

The Bible says that the watchmen were to give God no rest and take no rest all day and all night. All day means from 06.00 to 18.00 and all night means from 18.00 to 06.00. This means that a prayer chain that is all day and all night must go from 00.00 hours on Monday morning to 24.00 hours on Sunday night. It means 168 hours of praying without ceasing each week.

We recommend that although it is possible to have a partial chain, i.e., for six or twelve or eighteen hours of prayer each day, the best thing is to have a complete chain. The reality is that the Enemy is likely to step in during the hours during which no one is watching and do great harm. Partial prayer chains are acceptable as good starts but the start should not be made an end.

The practical outworking of a prayer chain needs to be carefully sorted out with the Lord of the harvest who alone sends out labourers into His harvest. The spiritual leadership of each prayer chain or each group of prayer chains needs to have taken some elementary and some advanced courses in the school of waiting on God. He has to be able to receive revelation, ask God questions, receive answers from Him and hence be in a position to say with full assurance "This is what God wants done and it must be done."

We present the following possibilities as being convenient for possible use on a prayer chain.

A. Two periods of twelve hours each or two periods of six hours each per person per day.

1. 00:00-18:00 hours
2. 18:01- 06:00 hours

This means that two people can keep a prayer chain going. This will be possible for mature intercessors who have a full-time ministry of intercession. They will have to be mature, in fact, they will have to be very mature to stand in God's presence every day for twelve hours. This is certainly not work for spiritual babies even if they be babies who believed in the Lord fifty years ago. It is possible for the same two people to maintain a chain by having each occupy two periods of six hours for each twenty-four hours. This should be more refreshing and more effective.

B. Three periods of eight hours each:

1. 00:00 to 08:00 hours
2. 08:01 to 16:00 hours
3. 16:01 to 24:00 hours

Again this means that three people can keep a prayer chain going. They will need to be fully given to the ministry of intercesion so that no other affair is allowed to interfere. The three-period chain of full-time intercessors has the advantage that in cases of emergency, when one of the intercessors is indisposed, the other two can step up their praying time and cover up the gap, a thing which is more difficult, although not impossible in the two period chain.

C. Four periods of six hours each:

1. 00:00 to 06:00 hours
2. 06:01 to 12:00 hours
3. 12:01 to 18:00 hours
4. 18:01 to 24:00 hours

This is again a chain for mature intercessors. The only difference is that it is possible for people to be involved in it who earn their living by working somewhere else. For example, a group of people, some who work in the mornings and others in the afternoons and evenings, while others who work at night, can easily keep such a chain going, provided they are sold out to God and are prepared to invest sacrificially in this way.

D. Six periods of four hours each:

1. 00:00 to 04:00 hours
2. 04:01 to 08:00 hours
3. 08:01 to 12:00 hours
4. 12:01 to 16:00 hours
5. 16:01 to 20:00 hours
6. 20:01 to 24:00 hours

Again this requires people who can usefully and aggressively spend four hours in God's presence and are not carried away by sleep, hunger and all the like.

E. Eight periods of three hours each:

1. 00:00 to 03:00 hours
2. 03:01 to 06:00 hours
3. 06:01 to 09:00 hours
4. 09:01 to 12:00 hours
5. 12:01 to 15:00 hours
6. 15:01 to 18:00 hours
7. 18:01 to 21:00 hours
8. 21:01 to 24:00 hours

F. Twelve periods of two hours each:

1. 00:00 to 02:00 hours
2. 02:01 to 04:00 hours
3. 04:01 to 06:00 hours
4. 06:01 to 08:00 hours
5. 08:01 to 10:00 hours
6. 10:01 to 12:00 hours
7. 12:01 to 14:00 hours
8. 14:01 to 16:00 hours
9. 16:01 to 18:00 hours
10. 18:01 to 20:00 hours
11. 20:01 to 22:00 hours
12. 22:01 to 24:00 hours

This is the easiest of the time allocations, for it permits even young believers to participate in the praying on the prayer chain. We do not recommend the one-hour period prayer chains unless it is for children. When a person comes into God's presence, it does take some time to really "plug in" and begin to commune with God in prayer. The one hour-period means that the intercessor will often leave just at the point when he is entering into sweet intercourse with his

Maker. There are two prayer chains in our city which run as follows:

1. 00:00 to 06:00 hours
2. 06:01 to 08:00 hours
3. 08:01 to 10:00 hours
4. 10:01 to 12:00 hours
5. 12:01 to 14:00 hours
6. 14:01 to 16:00 hours
7. 16:01 to 18:00 hours
8. 18:01 to 20:00 hours
9. 20:01 to 24:00 hours

The third one runs on one-hour periods. The only difference is that no one ever comes for one hour. The intercessors take praying periods of two, three, four, five, six hours in succession. The fourth chain is like the third. The difference is that it is not yet full (as of 28 January 1989). We are asking God to fill the hours by stirring and raising up intercessors in the assembly. The fifth chain will begin on 1 February 1989. It will be a chain of six-hour praying periods for advancing intercessors. We are wrestling with God to raise up the sixth chain and then the seventh and eighth and . . . until the fiftieth.

In most of the prayer chains intercessors pray in twos. This means that when one is unable to turn up, the watching is maintained by the partner.

THE VISION OF THE YAOUNDE PRAYER CHAINS

God began to lay a burden on our hearts for the prayer chain in 1982. We prayed about it but He still had so many things to deal with us about our walk with Him that He did not allow us to start. Had we started then, we would have built a big building and called it a centre for prayer and so much money would have gone into it with people coming to admire our "Tower of Babel."

After much dealing with us and the enlargement of our hearts to be concerned with the global purposes of God, the Lord enabled us to start the first prayer chain at 0000 hours on 1 January 1988. We have had a year at it and last year closed with four prayer chains being established. We are looking to God to increase our vision of Him, His Bride and His world and consequently pray more. The goal of the prayer chains is "to labour by prayer to ensure that all over the world one billion people come to the Lord Jesus and render to Him a total obedience in all things." The chains are rooms in the homes of believers and as such no additional expenses are put into them. Many believers who are building houses in the city now think of including two rooms for a prayer chain.

We are planning to set up other prayer chains that will function only on the week-ends and holiday periods in order to provide additional opportunity for believers to pray.

Those who have prayed on the prayer chain, testify to the fact that because they could not do anything else but come and pray on the chain, their unfaithfulness in praying has been taken away not only for the period spent on the chain but for other prayer periods during which they have prayed elsewhere.

The inner life of the assembly is changing and the burden to walk close to the Lord is increasing. Our prayer is that each one of us who prays will be fully revived and that the flames of revival will sweep through the entire body of Christ and then multitudes will be swept into the kingdom of God, and while in the kingdom of God (while the Bride is still on earth), those added will be as revived as the Body to which they have been added.

The Lord is raising up similar prayer chains in other cities and we thank Him for this and give Him all the honour and glory. Amen.

PART 6

INTERCESSION FOR AN INDIVIDUAL - 1

The intercessor who is growing normally will begin his ministry by interceding for individuals. He may spend a long time at this level and learn many valuable lessons. After some time two pathways will be open to him. The one will be to continue to intercede for a special individual whose ministry has consequence or to go on and pray for groups of people and so forth. The Lord will guide the faithful intercessor as to how his ministry will develop. Each must ask the Lord and receive what to do from Him. Each must seek God's will ardently about this matter and be sure that he has clearly come to a true knowledge of what God would have him do. The man who later on became the apostle Paul asked from the onset of his experience of the new birth,

> *"What shall I do, Lord?" (Acts 22:10).*

The Lord was not silent. He said to him,

> *"Rise, and go into Damascus, and there you will be told all that is appointed for you to do" (Acts 22:10).*

There was something appointed for him to do. There is something appointed for every believer to do. There is a particular area of intercession mapped out by the Lord for each intercessor. That particular area must be sought out and accomplished.

There are many areas in an individual's life that need to be prayed through. In this chapter, we shall outline areas of intercession that are specially a part of his spiritual life, and in the next chapter we shall consider those areas that are linked to the other aspects of his life. Both his spiritual, physical life, and soul are important.

Below are some areas, but we confess that the list is in no way exhaustive.

A. HIS CONVERSION:

1. That the gospel will get to him.
2. That the gospel messenger will be filled and led by the Spirit.
3. That the gospel messenger will contact him at the right moment
4. That there would be communication between the two.
5. That he would be receptive.
6. That he would understand the facts of the gospel.
7. That he would receive the revelation that Jesus is the Christ.
8. That he would respond to the Savior and thus receive power to become a child of God at once.
9. That he would receive assurance that he has passed from death unto life in Christ.
10. That he would see the sinfulness of sin.
11. That he would hate sin with all his heart'.
12. That he would terminate radically with the past, putting away everything that does not please God.

13. That he would be taught about baptism in water.
14. That he would receive baptism into water.
15. That he would be taught on baptism into the Holy Spirit.
16. That he would receive the baptism into the Holy Spirit.
17. That he would be led to and introduced to the local church.

B. HIS LIFE AS A YOUNG BELIEVER:

1. That he will desire the sincere milk of the Word of God.
2. That he will read his Bible every day.
3. That he will read many chapters at a time.
4. That he will be taught to meditate on the Word.
5. That he will begin to meditate on the Word every day.
6. That the Lord will speak to him through His Word.
7. That he will learn to pray.
8. That he will pray honestly.
9. That he will pray simply.
10. That he will record prayer topics and the answers received and therefore thank the Lord for each answer.
11. That he will learn to bring everything to God in prayer.
12. That he will witness to others.
13. That he will bring some to the Lord.
14. That he will find fellowship and acceptance in the local Asembly .
15. That he will be loyal and obedient to the elders and other leaders of the local assembly.
16. That he will learn to serve in all the ways that are open to him, especially in practical things.
17. That he will continue in the attendance of the teaching, fellowship, worship, breaking of bread, and prayer meetings of the local assembly.

18. That he will know how to repent and seek forgiveness from God when he has sinned.
19. That he will learn how to repent and receive forgiveness from man when he has sinned.
20. That he will be taught on restitution.
21. That he will carry out restitution on anything in his past life that needs restitution.
22. That he will hate sin increasingly.
23. That he will know the fear of the Lord.
24. That he will be zealous for the Lord.
25. That he will learn to give sacrificially to the Lord.
26. That he will learn to be faithful in little things.

C. HIS LIFE AS A MATURING BELIEVER:

1. That he will know an intense hatred for sin.
2. That he will be taught deliverance from sin.
3. That he will be delivered from sin.
4. That he will gain grounds as one delivered from sin.
5. That he will receive a gift from the Lord with which to minister to the body.
6. That he will grow in the use of the gift.
7. That he will begin to seek his special area of ministry.
8. That the Lord will show him the area in which he is called to serve.
9. That he will grow in waiting on the Lord.
10. That he will grow in discerning the voice of the Lord.
11. That he will grow in knowing the tactics of the devil.
12. That he will grow in hating the devil.
13. That he will grow in rebuking the devil.
14. That he will begin to cast out demons.
15. That he will begin to withdraw increasingly for some days, say, two or three, to seek the Lord.

16. That he will grow in knowing the Lord as his sanctification.
17. That he will begin to make others into disciples.
18. That he will begin to exercise his ministry.
19. That he will grow in resisting the devil.
20. That he will grow in the life of fasting.
21. That he will grow in the prayer life.
22. That he will grow in Christian character.
23. That he will spot the areas of weaknesses in his character and work out how to get rid of each.
24. That he will find out if women are a point of weakness in his life and build a wall of defense if need be.
25. That he will find out if money is a point of weakness in his life and build a wall of protection if need be.
26. That he will find out if the love of fame (worldly glory) has a hold in his life and do something to be delivered.
27. That he will grow in not loving the world.
28. That areas in which the flesh rules in his life will be revealed to him.
29. That he will do something to crucify the flesh.
30. That he will see if he is governed by the love of food.
31. That he will be delivered from gluttony.
32. That he will see if sleep rules in his life.
33. That he will grow in controlling how much sleep his body needs.
34. That he will grow in disciplining himself in all things.
35. That he will learn the basic lessons on persecution.
36. That he will be aimed with a mind to suffer.
37. That he will know basic deliverance from being ruled by his emotions.
38. That he will know basic deliverance from being ruled by his will.
39. That he will know basic deliverance from being ruled by his mind.

40. That his emotions will be set free to be ruled by his spirit.
41. That his mind will be set free to be ruled by his spirit.
42. That his will will be set free to be ruled by his spirit.
43. That he will learn the art of working hard.
44. That he will learn how to give thanks in all circumstances.
45. That he will begin to learn how to lead others.
46. That he will begin to learn how to delegate authority.
47. That he will begin to seek spiritual power.
48. That he will begin to grow in longing after the Lord.
49. That he will begin to grow in longing for a more intimate daily relationship with the Lord.
50. That he will grow in humility.
51. That he will grow in brokenness.
52. That he will grow in exposing his faults and hiding his virtues.

D. HIS LIFE AS A MATURE BELIEVER:

1. That he will be totally delivered from lust.
2. That he will be totally delivered from covetousness.
3. That he will be delivered from serving the Lord partly for the Lord's glory and partly for his own glory.
4. That he will be totally set free from the last traces of the love of the world and the things in the world.
5. That he will know total obedience to the Word.
6. That he will know total obedience to the slightest desire of the Lord regardless of how it might come to him.
7. That he will know how to suffer without complaining.
8. That he will know how to accept being put aside and others preferred.

9. That he might be delivered from the last traces of jealousy when others are preferred or used.
10. That he will grow in labouring for the glory of God regardless of who gets the glory from men.
11. That he will know total conquest of himself.
12. That he will have his spirit released.
13. That he will develop a sensitive but strong conscience.
14. That his intuition will develop so that he can discern the will of God more readily.
15. That he will know unceasing communion with God.
16. That his soul will cooperate with his spirit.
17. That he will maintain his first love for the Lord.
18. That he will mature in his willingness to deny himself, take up his cross, and follow the Lord.
19. That he will mature in counting all earthly things as refuse when compared with the excellence of knowing the Lord.
20. That he will mature in having the courage of his convictions.
21. That he will mature in delegating responsibilities.
22. That he will press on for perfection in Christian character.
23. That he will grow in maturity in discerning the difference between the acceptable will and the perfect will of God.
24. That he will labour increasingly to be in the perfect will of God
25. That he will grow in discerning the difference between spiritual issues that have an impact only in time and those issues whose impact is eternal.
26. That he will labour to serve the Lord in such a way that the impact will outlive time.
27. That he will know the difference between passing emotional issues and deep spiritual impact.
28. That he will increasingly prefer the Giver to the gifts.

29. That he will earnestly desire spiritual gifts, but regard the fruit as of greater importance.
30. That he will serve the Lord with all his might but prefer the knowledge of the Lord to the service of the Lord.
31. That he will know deliverance from dispositional sins like being difficult to please, irritable, and so on.
32. That increasingly he will yearn for the return of the Lord.

33

INTERCESSION FOR AN INDIVIDUAL - 2

Anyone interceding for someone will have to face the fact that man is tripartite: spirit, soul, and body and that intercession would have to be for the whole man, if he is to function properly as God meant him to do. We considered what may be called "the spiritual aspects" in the preceding chapter. In this chapter we want to make some suggestions for intercession on what may be called the more earthly issues. We have divided them into two chapters for ease of presentation and not because we want to dissect the spirit from the soul nor the soul from the body and keep each apart. Below are some areas of intercession for an individual. In setting forth these areas of intercession, we are bearing in mind the fact that the devil is a destroyer. The apostle writes,

> *"Be sober, be watchful. Your adversary the devil prowls around like a roaring lion, seeking someone to devour. Resist him, be firm in your faith"* (1 Peter 5:8-9).

We believe that the devil will strike where he can and that what he strikes, he aims at destroying completely. If he cannot destroy a man's walk with God, he will try to destroy his finances or his health. This means that part of the work of an intercessor for an individual will be to build a hedge around the person so that Satan may have no access to him. Satan complained to God about Job saying,

> *"Does Job fear God for nought? Hast thou not put a hedge about him and his house and all that he has, on every side? Thou hast blessed the work of his hands, and his possessions have increased in the land" (Job 1:9-10).*

The Lord has put a hedge around the believer and blessed the believer. The believer must reinforce the hedge and also bless. When the believer thus cooperates with God, the devil is put out of action.

A. BUILDING A HEDGE AROUND HIS PHYSICAL BODY

1. Pray that no disease will attack his head, nose, eyes, mouth, ears, neck, chest, hands, back, waist, feet, toes, fingers, nails, sexual organs, skin, hair, lungs, liver, heart, kidneys, arteries, veins, glands, vascular system, alimentary canal, reproductive system, brain, and the rest.
2. Pray that all attempts of the Enemy to make him overeat and therefore put on excess weight that is disastrous will be stopped. Intercede for him so that he may be delivered from overeating or under eating. Pray that he will have a balanced diet. Protect his health during the times of fasting. Pray that he will be protected from insect, scorpion, and snake bites.
3. If he is sick in any way, pray that the Lord will heal him. Pray that he will know the Lord Jesus as his Healer and the source of his health.
4. Pray that he will live until his ministry is completed.

B. BUILDING A HEDGE AROUND HIS FINANCES

Pray that his finances will be protected from destruction through any of the following:

1. Laziness on his part.
2. Wrong investments.
3. Theft.
4. Loss of job.
5. Fire destroying his home, his farm, his car.
6. His car being involved in an accident.
7. His falling sick.
8. Some member of his family falling sick.
9. His company becoming bankrupt.
10. His cattle, poultry, farm, failing to produce as they ought.
11. His promotion failing to come through.
12. And so on.

Pray that the Lord will bless him financially by:

1. Causing him to work very hard.
2. Granting him promotion.
3. Causing his crops to grow and produce abundantly.
4. Providing him with a market for his goods.
5. Blessing the company in which he works.
6. Saving him from hasty moves in investment.
7. Providing scholarships for his children's education.
8. And so on.

The Lord does indeed bless materially. The Bible says,

> *"And Isaac sowed in that land and reaped in the same year a hundred fold. The Lord blessed him, and the man became rich, and gained more and more until he became very wealthy" (Genesis 26:12-13).*

Of Abraham the Bible says,

> "Now Abram was very rich in cattle, in silver, and in gold" (Genesis 13:2). Of Job the Bible says, "And the Lord blessed the latter days of Job more than his beginning; and he had fourteen thousand sheep, six thousand camels, a thou sand yoke of oxen, and a thousand she-asses" (Job 42:12).

However, there is something greater than material blessing that the believer may receive from the Lord. It is a spirit of contentment. The Bible says,

> "There is great gain in godliness with contentment; for we brought nothing into the world and it is certain that we cannot take anything out of the world; but if we have food and clothing, with these we shall be content. But those who desire to be rich fall into temptation, into a snare, into many senseless and hurtful desires that plunge men into ruin and destruction. For the love of money is the root of all evils; it is through this craving that some have wandered away from the faith and pierced their hearts with many pangs" (1 Timothy 6:6-10).

Finally,

> "Keep your life free from love of money, and be content with what you have; for he has said, I will never fail you nor forsake you" (Hebrews 13:5).

So God does bless with money and property but the greatest blessing that a man can receive from Him is not money but God Himself as man's source and wealth. When a man has not money but God as his wealth, he is content and because it is impossible for God to fail, the man will always have his needs met.

C. BUILDING A HEDGE AROUND THE MAN'S RELATIONSHIPS WITH OTHERS

1. Pray for his relationship with his wife, son, daughter, father, mother, grandfather, grandmother, cousins, aunts, uncles, in laws, grandchildren, neighbours, employer, employee, friend, co workers, and so on.
2. Pray that each relationship will be edifying and free from unnecessary strains. Pray that he will be given the capacity to give himself away. Also pray that he will be given the capacity to accept himself and accept others.
3. Pray that he will be delivered from any complexes of inferiority or superiority; that he will be delivered from the dangerous sin of comparison and that he will accept his station in life with gratitude.
4. Pray that he will be given the capacity to live happily in disagreeable circumstances, being unmoved by the external environment.
5. Pray that he will know the peace of God that comes from the Holy Spirit and which is not dependent on outward circumstances. Pray that he will be healed of any hurts that he received along life's journey but which he buried instead of abandoning to the Lord. Pray that the Lord will provide someone to whom he will open up completely and who will be able to minister "inner healing" to him.
6. Pray that he will forgive all who have hurt him and bless his enemies.

Praise the Lord!

34
INTERCESSION FOR A FAMILY

Each family must learn how to intercede for itself. In addition to this, one member of the family may be called by the Lord to become the intercessor for the family. Besides this, the Lord may raise up someone who is not a member of the family to become an intercessor for the family. In the case where the Lord raises someone outside the family to make it his life's preoccupation to intercede for some family, it is often because that family has a special responsibility in God's programme. Take, for example, a family in which the husband has a ministry of national or international repercussions. The man's ministry makes him to become a marked man. The forces of the enemy will be arrayed against him with the goal of destroying his spirit, soul, or body or that of his wife or children. We know that the Enemy will do anything he can in order to bring the man and his ministry to nought or to reduce its potential for good. If the Enemy cannot accomplish this by attacking the man directly, he will labour to see if he can do so by attacking the wife, the children, or his co-workers. In such a case, investment in intercession for the family of the man becomes a real contribution to God's global interests. We shall consider intercession for such a man and his family in another chapter. Here we want to look at intercession for an ordinary family.

The question that arises is, *"What are the possible areas for intercession for a family?"* Below are some:

1. The husband's walk with God.
2. The husband's study and knowledge of the Scriptures.
3. The husband's prayer life.
4. The husband's separation from the love of the world and the things in the world.
5. The husband's ministry to the Lord.
6. The husband's ministry to the local assembly.
7. The husband's contribution to the conquest of the world for Christ.
8. The husband's relationship with his wife - communication.
9. The husband's relationship with his wife - sexual.
10. The husband's relationship with his wife - spiritual.
11. The husband's relationship with other men.
12. The husband's relationship with the opposite sex.
13. The husband's relationship with his son(s).
14. The husband's relationship with his daughter(s).
15. The husband's relationship with his relatives - father, mother and others.
16. The husband's relationship with his in-laws.
17. The husband's relationship with his friend(s).
18. The husband's relationship with the one above him spiritually.
19. The husband's relationship with the ones below him spiritually.
20. The husband's job.
21. The husband's relationship to his boss, his equals and his juniors, at his place of work.

22. The husband's productivity and promotion at his job.
23. The husband's witness at his job.
24. The husband's growth in Christian character.
25. The husband's peculiar strength(s).
26. The husband's peculiar weakness or weaknesses.
27. The husband's spiritual gift(s).
28. The husband's emotional health.
29. The husband's physical health - inheritable diseases.
30. The husband's physical health - other diseases.
31. The husband's physical health - the Lord Jesus as his Healer, healing, and health.
32. The husband's relationship with visitors.
33. The husband's attitude to food.
34. The husband's altitude to those in political and administrative Authority.
35. The husband's attitude to money.
36. The husband's altitude to time.

These areas of intercession most probably apply to the wife and so we will state them clearly.

1. The wife's walk with God.
2. The wife's study and knowledge of the Scriptures.
3. The wife's prayer life.
4. The wife's separation from the love of the world and the things that are in the world.
5. The wife's ministry to the Lord.
6. The wife as a helper to her husband - his spiritual needs in knowing the Lord.
7. The wife as a helper to her husband - his spiritual needs in serving the Lord.
8. The wife as a helper to her husband - his emotional needs.

9. The wife as a helper to her husband - his professional needs.
10. The wife as a helper to her husband - his social needs.
11. The wife as a helper to her husband - his sexual needs.
12. The wife as a helper to her husband - his financial needs.
13. The wife's ministry to her son(s).
14. The wife's ministry to her daughter(s).
15. The wife's ministry to the local assembly.
16. The wife's relationship with her spiritual authority.
17. The wife's relationship with those under her spiritual care.
18. The wife's special ministry to the Body of Christ.
19. The wife's special ministry to those who are yet to belong to the household of faith.
20. The wife's relationship with her boss.
21. The wife's relationship with her colleagues.
22. The wife's relationship with the neighbours.
23. The wife's relationship with her relatives.
24. The wife's relationship with the husband's relatives.
25. The wife as the cook of the family.
26. The wife as the housekeeper of the family.
27. The wife and the family budget under her control.
28. The wife and visitors.
29. The wife's relationship with her friend(s).
30. The wife's relationship with her husband's friend(s).
31. The wife's growth in loving and serving the Lord.
32. The wife's growth in Christian character.
33. The wife's spiritual gift(s).
34. The wife's motivational gift(s).
35. The wife's talent(s).
36. The wife's emotional health.
37. The wife's physical health.
38. The wife's physical appearance.
39. The wife's attitude to food.

40. The wife's attitude to time.
41. The wife's relationship with other men.
42. The wife's peculiar weakness or weaknesses.
43. The wife's special strength(s).
44. The wife's low moments.
45. The wife and old age.

Other areas of intercession for the family include:

1. The conversion of a son.
2. The conversion of a daughter.
3. The restoration of a backslidden husband.
4. The restoration of a backslidden wife.
5. The restoration of a backslidden child.
6. The conversion of the husband's relatives.
7. The conversion of the wife's relatives.
8. The conversion of neighbours.
9. The son's choice of a career.
10. The daughter's choice of a career.
11. God's call on the son.
12. God's call on the daughter.
13. The family altar.
14. The praying husband and wife together.
15. The home as the meeting place of the local church.
16. The home as the place for winning the lost.
17. The home as the place for restoring backsliders.
18. The home as the place for communicating spiritual vision.
19. The home as the place for entry into new experiences with the Lord.
20. The home as the place for rest for weary and worn out soldiers of Christ.
21. The home and visitors who are passing.
22. The home and visitors who are resident.

23. The home and nonfamily members who are resident.
24. Family goals.
25. Family finances.
26. Family properties.
27. Family councils.
28. Family retreats.
29. Family recreation.
30. Family's weekly programme.
31. Family's annual programme.
32. Spiritual health of the children.
33. Emotional health of the children.
34. Physical health of the children.
35. Marriages of the children.
36. Strengths of the family.
37. Weaknesses of the family.
38. Friends of the family.
39. Enemies of the family.
40. Future of the family.

Other areas of intercession that may apply to some families and not to others may include:

1. Handicapped wife.
2. Handicapped husband.
3. Handicapped child.
4. Husband on drugs.
5. Husband who has run away from home.
6. Wife on drugs.
7. Runaway child.
8. Bereaved family.
9. When a husband dies.
10. When a wife dies.
11. When a child dies.
12. A barren family.

The list is not exhaustive in any way. For example, we have not included topics for intercession such as:

1. the husband as the disciplinarian of the home;
2. the authority of the husband;
3. the love of the husband for his wife;
4. the submission of the wife to the husband;
5. the obedience of the children,
6. and so forth.

It is possible to write out ten, twenty, fifty or a hundred prayer topics on each of the headings outlined above. We shall not do so here. We shall attempt it in our next book *Practical Helps for Praying Believers*. The intercessor will take each topic and labour patiently at it with God. He will know the family very thoroughly and have the details that are needed to intercede in such a way that God is "compelled" to answer.

35
INTERCESSION FOR AN ASSEMBLY (CHURCH)

God is concerned about the Church. He is also concerned about the churches. The reality is that the Church causes more problems to the Lord than does the world. This is obvious when you consider the fact that the world was judged on the cross and can never have any future. However, the Church is the Bride-elect of the Lord Jesus. All of God's purposes arc tied to her. She is the purpose of creation and redemption. This being so, it is important that the Church becomes what God intended it to be. We shall write in more detail on how to pray for your assembly elsewhere. In this chapter, We shall present just some key areas in which an intercessor for an assembly will have to work.

A. INTERCESSION FOR THE GOAL OF THE ASSEMBLY

It is important for each assembly to receive a clear goal from the Lord and labour to accomplish it. One assembly that I know of has the goal of growing to two hundred thousand members in a period of fifty years. She is in a modern city that will grow to about 4 million people in fifty years. Her present membership is about one thousand in a city of six hundred thousand people. The goal includes the training and establishing of two thousand elders and twenty thousand deacons and deaconesses. Since it would be near impossible to have the two hundred thousand people meet together, the functional unit of the assembly will be the homes of the members (House Churches) where twenty people will gather to pray, receive the ministry of the Word, break bread, and carry out other functions that are conducive to spiritual growth.

It is obvious that if such a goal is accomplished, the kingdom of darkness will suffer great loss. It is therefore obvious that the kingdom of darkness will do everything to destroy this vision. It is even more obvious that unless God moves in great might and power, the goal will never be accomplished. It is then imperative that intercessors be raised in the assembly who will take no rest and give neither the Lord almighty nor the Enemy rest, until the goal is accomplished. Such intercessors will plead with God to pour out His Holy Spirit upon the saints so that they will walk in purity and power. They will also wrestle against the Satanic forces arrayed against the Assembly. They will be like the people who were rebuilding the wall of Jerusalem with Nehemiah, of whom it was said,

> *"When our enemies heard that it was known to us and that God had frustrated their plan, we all returned to the wall, each to his work. From that day on, half of my servants worked on the construction, and half held the spears, shields, bows, and coats of mail; and the leaders stood behind all the house of Judah, who were building on the wall. Those who carried burdens were laden in such a way that each with one hand laboured on the work and with the other held his weapon. And each of the builders had his sword girded at his side while he built. The man who sounded the trumpet was beside me. And I said to the nobles and to the officials and to the rest of the people, The work is great and widely spread, and we are separated on the wall, far from one another. In the place where you hear the sound of the trumpet, rally to us there. Our God will fight for us.*

> *So we laboured at the work, and half of them held the spears from the break of dawn till the stars came out. I also said to the people at that time, Let every man and his servant pass the night within Jerusalem, that they may be a guard for us by night and may labour by day. So neither I nor my brethren nor my servants nor the men of the guard who followed me, none of us took off our clothes; each kept his weapon in his hand"* (Nehemiah 4:15-23).

It seems to me that this passage is descriptive of what ought to be typical of intercessors. For a group of intercessors, half ought to be involved in building with God in prayer and the other half in protecting the work from the Enemy and tearing down the Enemy and his plans. For an individual intercessor, half of his time ought to be spent pleading with God and the other half spent pleading against the devil. It is only in this way that the purpose of God can fully be accomplished.

I also see that if the Assembly is prepared to put some people, say two, on some full-time aspect of the work like preaching, teaching, or any other such thing, the Assembly ought to put aside some people for a full-time ministry of intercession. Could a part of the failure of the Church in our day be the fact that in some assemblies there are full-time pastors and no full-time intercessors? How many of the pastors divide their twelve hours of daily ministry into six hours of teaching, preaching and the other aspects and six hours of intercession? I believe that that is how it was meant to be.

I believe that every apostle ought to give 50 percent of his ministering time to prayer and 50 percent to the ministry of the Word. I further believe that we will make faster progress in conquering the world for Christ if there are five full-time intercessors to back the ministry of each apostle, in addition to the many others who will intercede on a part-time basis. The same ought to be true of prophets, evangelists, pastors, and teachers.

B. AREAS OF INTERCESSION FOR AN ASSEMBLY

Below are some suggestions and it is obvious that the list is far from being exhaustive:

1. For each elder by name
2. For the presiding elder in particular
3. For each deacon by name
4. For each deaconess by name
5. For each leader of a house assembly. In praying for these leaders, the following areas ought to be covered: a) ministry; b) vision c) burden d) action, and e) knowledge of the Lord Jesus, His Word, the power of the Cross, power of the Holy Spirit, and methods and plans of the devil f) Discernment g) Separation from sin, self, and the world h) Separation from the common I) Separation unto God j) Deliverance from sin k) Humility l) The possession of a broken and contrite heart m) Authority with God n) Authority over Satan and his hosts, natural forces, and human systems o) Courage and boldness p) Love of God, the brethren, and his enemies q) Patience and self-control in the inner man with God, man, and circumstances r) Co-workers s) Health t) Marriage u) Children v) Finances w) Discipline x) Protection from the Enemy y) Growth in leadership.
6. For the training of leaders, including a) the choice of future leaders; b) the training of these by example, by the ministry of the Word and by prayer.
7. For the reception of spiritual gifts in the Assembly: a) **The gifts of men:** apostles, prophets, evangelists, pastors, and teachers; b) **Spiritual gifts:** a word of wisdom, a word of knowledge, discernment of spirits, tongues, interpretation of tongues, healings, prophecy, faith, and miracles; c) **Motivational gifts:** prophecy, government

(ruling, administration), teaching, exhortation, giving, mercy, and helps (services)
8. For the growth and maturation of the fruit of the Spirit among the members including the following: love, joy, peace, patience, goodness, faithfulness, longsuffering, kindness, and self control
9. For the evangelistic ministry of the Assembly
10. For the building up of young converts
11. For the establishing of maturing believers
12. For the teaching ministry
13. For the weekly prayer meetings
14. For the all-night prayer meetings
15. For the prayer chains
16. For the fellowship meetings
17. For the breaking of bread service
18. For the fasting life of the Assembly
19. For the restoration of backsliders
20. For the baptism into the Holy Spirit
21. For the ministry to the children
22. For the ministry of the sisters
23. For the unmarried men in the Assembly
24. For the unmarried women in the Assembly
25. For the students in the Assembly
26. For the married couples in the Assembly
27. For the husbands in the Assembly
28. For the wives in the Assembly
29. For the divorced in the Assembly
30. For the widows in the Assembly
31. For the widowers in the Assembly
32. For the orphans in the Assembly
33. For the pupils in the Assembly
34. For the unconverted in the Assembly
35. For the handicapped in the Assembly
36. For the jobless in the Assembly

37. For the sick in the Assembly
38. For the weak brethren in the Assembly
39. For the spiritually crippled in the Assembly
40. For the spiritually sick in the Assembly
41. For those who have gone astray in the Assembly or from the Assembly
42. For those who are lost from the Assembly
43. For inner healing in the Assembly
44. For the deliverance ministry of the Assembly
45. For the aged in the Assembly
46. For the barren in the Assembly
47. For the homes where the Assemblies are housed
48. For the relationship between the leaders and those they lead
49. For the ministry of any elder who may also be an apostle.
50. For the relationship of the Assembly and the apostle who was used by the Lord to plant the Assembly.
51. For the relationship between the Assembly and other Assemblies in the region
52. and so on.

It is quite obvious that an intercessor for an Assembly has an enormous task before him. It is also obvious that the success of the Assembly will depend on him or her even as it would depend on the elders, deacons, and deaconesses. My prayer is that each Assembly will have full-time intercessors whose livelihood is provided for by the Assembly. In addition to this. I pray that every minister will spend 50 percent of his time in prayer and 50 percent in other aspects of the ministry. I further pray that the Assemblies will provide places where those who want to intercede but cannot do so in their homes, will withdraw to pray.

Glory be to the Lord Jesus, the interceding Head of the Church.

36
INTERCESSION FOR A CITY

An intercessor for a city will be caught up with God's interest in that city. He will, therefore, intercede for the people of God in the city and pray against the works of the wicked one in the city.

There is a Satanic Principality or Prince who rules and controls, coordinates and executes the interest of Satan in every city. He is aided by a number of senior Satanic spirits and multitudes of demons. An intercessor for a city will have to intercede that the Satanic ruler of that city be overthrown and that the other spirits be put into confusion. He will bind the following wicked spirits that hold the citizens captive in:

- pride
- drunkenness
- sexual immorality
- alcoholism
- animism
- idolatory
- traditional religions
- laziness

- ease
- indulgence
- bribery
- corruption
- violence
- theft
- the love of money
- unbelief
- indiscipline
- worldliness
- vanity
- tribalism
- racism
- sorcery
- worldly music
- satanic worship
- drugs
- abortion
- divorce
- child abuse
- bitterness
- jealousy
- anger
- pride
- class consciousness
- greed
- wickedness
- murder
- gluttony
- covetousness
- lying
- falsehood
- adultery
- malice

- witchcraft

The intercessor will not only bind the wicked spirits. He will release the captives and upon releasing them he will bring them by prayer to the Lord Jesus and cause them to yield to Him. Then as they are in Christ, he will by prayer cause them to love the Lord Jesus completely and for all time.

He will intercede for the following:

- Head of State
- Ministers in the government
- Permanent Secretaries
- Directors
- Technical Advisers
- Deputy Directors
- Chief of Services
- Assistant Chiefs of Services
- Senior Administrative Officers
- Administrative Officers
- All the graduates in the civil service
- All the non-graduates in the civil service

He will plead with the Lord to open their eyes that they may see Christ their Saviour and come to Him for salvation.

He will intercede for Ambassadors and all in the diplomatic services, businessmen at all levels, bankers at all levels, and the rest and labour for their salvation.

He will pray for:

1. University teachers and university students
2. High School teachers and High School students.
3. Secondary School teachers and Secondary School

students.
4. Primary School teachers and primary school pupils.
5. Nursery School teachers and nursery school pupils.
6. He will plead with the Lord that Christ may be revealed to multitudes.
7. He will single out centres where Satan is worshipped and come against them in the name of the Lord. Such centres will include: a) pornographic shops and halls; b) gambling places; c) sex centres, hotels, beer parlours and breweries; d) cigarette factories; e) drug centres; f) meeting places for the occult; g) abortion clinics

He will intercede for people in religions where people are helped to labour to save themselves instead of turning to the Lord Jesus:

1. Islam
2. Buddhism
3. Transcendental meditation
4. Yoga
5. Communism
6. Hinduism
7. Hare Krishna
8. Jehovah's Witnesses
9. Ba'hai faith
10. African traditional religions especially those that abound in that city

He will not only pray. He will war against the wicked spirits that rule in those religions. He will identify, bind and overthrow the strong man of each of these religious systems that are opposed to the cross of Christ where the righteous Son of God poured Himself as a libation for the sins of all men. As the various principalities and powers are bound, their captives are then fettered by the love of God and brought to the Lord Jesus. This is all done by prayer. The psalmist describes what should be done as follows:

> *"Let the faithful exult in glory; let them sing for joy on their couches.*
>
> *Let the high praises of God be in their throats and two-edged swords in their hands, to wreak vengeance on the nations and chastisement on the people, to bind their kings with chains and their nobles with fetters of iron, to execute on them the judgment written" (Psalms 149:5-9)!*

The intercessor will then intercede for all who are Roman Catholics, Presbyterians, Methodists, Anglicans, Baptists, Pentecostals, the Brethren, and all others who do not know the Lord Jesus as their Lord and Saviour so that they may be saved.

He will pray for the various ministries that God has raised in the city for the work of the gospel: Bible-producing ministries, Bible translating ministries, Bible distributing ministries, Tracts producing and distributing ministries, Literature producing and distributing ministries, Bible Correspondence ministries, Special Prayer Ministries, and the like. As he prays for these, he will ask the Lord to show him the plans that Satan is making against these ministries and against the people who have been raised up by God to lead them. As he is shown Satan's plans, he will pray and bring them to nought.

He will watch out for any special meeting of Satanists that may be planned to take place in the city. For example the Free Masons, Yogis, Transcendental meditation followers. Rosicrucians, and other local Satanist movements may be planning to hold a meeting in the town. The intercessor will contend with the wicked spirits behind the meeting until they are defeated and the meeting cancelled. The reality is that the grip of Satan over a city is strengthened by such meetings.

In order to do this, the intercessor needs to be well informed. He cannot close his ears to information and only hear two weeks after that Satanists met for three days in one of the leading hotels and transacted business in the Enemy's name, and then rejoice in his ministry as an intercessor. Intercessors are to detect and frustrate all plans of Satan against the city. He is responsible to God to ensure that Satan does not have his way in anything.

He should study the map of the city and see the principal entrances into the city by sea, by land, and by air. He should set a watch over each of these places to ensure that Satanic forces are refused entrance. He should daily pray,

> *"In the name of the Lord, I build a wall at this airport, seaport, road entrance, and bring to nought all Satanic hosts that may attempt to enter."*

The intercessor may walk round the city, claiming it for the Lord Jesus and building a wall of spiritual defense around it so that the Enemy might find penetration impossible.

Some time ago the Lord asked the leaders of our church to intercede for six weeks. We prayed for the Assembly and for the city (about five hundred of us) for four to six hours four times a week. At the end of the six weeks, we were led to take the city for God. Three of the principal elders led teams of twenty to fifty brethren. One leader walked with his team from the East to the West of the city (fourteen kilometres), the other did the same thing with his team from North to South, and the third with his team walked from the lowest point in the city to the top of the highest mountain at the edge of the city. All three teams took about three hours for the walk and prayed as they walked, claiming the city and her inhabitants; all that was on their right and all that was on their left; all that was before them and all that was behind them was claimed for our Lord. We consider our city taken for the Lord. By systematic praying for each person, section by section, and by presenting the gospel from house to house, leading those who are ready to the Lord, baptizing those who believe, discipling them, and establishing assemblies in homes, we hope one day to complete not only the conquest of our city but also the building of the Body of Christ.

Glory be to the Lord!

Amen.

37
INTERCESSION FOR A NATION

Nations can be controlled by intercessors. There is a sense in which believers should be concerned with what is happening in their nation. If they are not involved and take control of all things through intercession, the enemy will have his way and all people will suffer, including the believers. The command of the Bible is.

> *"First of all, then, I urge that supplications, prayers, intercessions, and thanksgiving be made for all men, for kings and all who are in high positions, that we may lead a quiet and peaceable life, godly and respectful in every way. This is good, and it is acceptable in the sight of God our Saviour, who desires all men to be saved and come to the knowledge of the truth. For there is one God, and there is one mediator between God and men, the man Christ Jesus, who gave himself as a ransom for all, the testimony to which was borne at the proper time"* (1 Timothy 2:1-6).

The Bible here urges intercession for all men in general and for kings and all who are in high positions. The Bible then states clearly why there must be such intercession:

1. That there may be a quiet and peaceable life

2. That there may be godly living
3. That there may be respectful living
4. That all men may come to a knowledge of the truth

The ultimate aim of the intercession for a nation is that

all men might be saved and come to a knowledge of the truth.

This being so, we can infer that the intercession for the other aspects of national life has as the ultimate purpose the salvation of people.

There have been intercessors who have influenced the course of national history in various nations. Luther was one such man. John Knox was another. They changed nations through prayer.

About twelve years ago, precisely in the month of August 1977, the Lord led us to fast and pray every Wednesday for our nation. So mighty has been God's blessing on us that it is glaring evidence to the fact that God answers prayer. We are the richest, most prosperous, and most stable nation in this region of Africa. Even though our nation is in an economic crisis, we remain the most economically viable country in this region. We can look at the abundance of food supplies: yams, cassava, cocoyam, plantains, bananas, beans, maize and vegetables of all kinds, and fruits of all kinds as a part of the answers to our prayers. I remember that in 1977, as an associate professor of Organic Chemistry at the University of Yaounde, in order to have some food for my family, I was forced by life's hard realities to join everybody else in running to a truck with plantains for sale, jumping up into the truck, and holding fast to one or two bunches of plantains so as to be allowed to pay for them. This was a part of my morning exercise before I went to the university to teach. There was such scarcity that only those who jumped into the trucks fast enough and grabbed a bunch of plantains firmly were able to buy anything. I remember standing on a long line with my dear wife for over two hours in order to take our turns to buy palm oil. I will not forget the day she and I stood on a line for hours in order to enter a food store (Mideviv) in a part of Yaounde called Djoungolo. By the time that we finally got in, all the plantains, cocoyams, and bananas were gone. One of the frustrated people around said, "*At this rate, next year people will eat human flesh.*"

Glory be to God, we did not eat human flesh the next year. God called us to intercede and as we interceded and have continued to intercede, He has blessed the nation superabundantly. Today people beg to have their foodstuffs bought. We are producing more food than we can use. This year the reports say that there is more rice in store, rice grown in Cameroon, to meet the total needs of the nation for two years even if not one grain of rice is added to it. Food is being exported from our nation, including meat, to neighbouring countries: Nigeria, Chad, the Central African Republic, Congo, and Equatorial Guinea. Even our cash crops: coffee, cocoa, cotton, and tea are being produced in excess of international and national needs.

Another interesting thing is that, it is while we started interceding that our nation became a producer of crude oil.

Peace and stability have been superabundant. You can go to any part of this city at any time of the night walking without fear of being attacked. The relatively low level of crime is the result of answered prayers. The little crime that there is has been encouraged by one of the negative products of abundance - television. We did not have television at the time we started to fast and pray. As God brought prosperity, television came and amassed millions of worshippers who are glued to her screen daily and in the process learn crime from films produced in the developed nations. O Lord, stop this.

The Lord moved, in answer to our prayer, to enable a peaceful and voluntary handing over from one Head of State to another in our nation, a thing that is normal in the developed countries but very rare in Africa where bloody coup d'etats are the order of the day.

One thing of real significance that has come to us as an answer to intercessional prayers is the recognition of the State of Israel by our government. We prayed earnestly for that to happen, almost hoping against hope and for reasons that we do not feel free to state here, never included that topic among those we circulated. Remembering that God had promised to bless those who blessed Abraham's descendants and to curse those who curse them, we took sides with Israel and blessed her often, praying that our government would recognize her. Then the answer came suddenly in 1986. I still remember what we wrote in our book, <u>Knowing the God of Unparalleled Goodness</u> in April 1985, pleading that Israel would be recognized in answer to believing prayer. God has been faithful. Some African countries have recognized Israel and opened up diplomatic relations with her. Cameroon has done this. God will bless us for this!

Lastly, a major part of our intercession was that God would move in our land. He has moved. For some reasons that I cannot write about, we must keep quiet about the extent of God's penetration of the nation with the gospel and the planting of multitudes of small churches in homes. We can however say without fear that at the moment there are five prayer chains in the city of Yaounde where intercessors are crying out to God every hour of the day and night, nearly twenty-four hours each day, and that plans are afoot to raise the number of these chains first to ten and then to twenty and finally to fifty by A.D. 2000 (the Lord Jesus tarrying). The prayer chains have only one purpose - to pray for a revival from the Father on all who know the Lord Jesus all over the world and see one billion people come to the Lord and render to Him a total obedience in all things. We consider these prayer chains as

God's blessing to us in answer to intercession. At the moment, God has moved so that books, tracts, cassettes, and Bible correspondence courses are going free of charge from Cameroon to seventy-five countries of the world, in millions of copies. This, too, is God's answer to our prayers that He would bless our nation and use it to bless others.

In order that you may follow the development of our intercession for our nation, we are enclosing in the following pages all the prayer letters that were sent out as a part of the Fasting Intercessors for Cameroon. We believe that the Lord will show you something about intercession for a nation as you read them.

There are many other things that are being prayed for in detail for the nation. The outline that we suggested for the city is also applicable for the nation and we are applying it.

In the future, we shall not be content with fasting once a week. We shall have to fast for a week or weeks in addition to the Wednesday fast to accelerate the accomplishment of God's purpose in our nation.

To God be the glory, honour, and majesty. Amen.

NATIONAL CENTRE FOR EVANGELISM PRAYER

> *"... and the Lord saw it and it displeased him that there was no justice. And he saw that there was no man, and wondered that there was no intercessor..." (Isaiah 59:15-16);*

> *"The people of the land have used deceit and exercised robbery, and have vexed the poor and needy: Yea, they have oppressed the stranger wrongfully. And I sought for a man among them, that should make up the hedge, and stand in the gap before me for the land, that I should not destroy it; but I found none. Therefore have I poured out mine indignation upon*

them; I have consumed them with the fire of my wrath: their own way have I recompensed upon their heads, saith the Lord"(Ezekiel 22:29-31 KJV).

"If my people, which are called by my name, shall humble themselves, and pray and seek my face, and turn from their wicked ways, then will I hear from heaven, and will forgive their sin, and will heal their land" (2 Chronicles 7:14 KJV).

The Lord has led a number of us to see the need for mighty intercession in the power of the Holy Spirit for our government, our national leaders, the fertility of our land, and everything that affects the welfare of Cameroon, and the need for a mighty outpouring of the Holy Spirit in His convicting, convincing, converting power on all Cameroonians to prepare the body of Christ for the rapture.

We, therefore, feel that if Cameroonians would fast and pray, God will bless our nation in every way and the interests of Jesus in our land will be well taken care of.

We believe that fasting and prayer is the greatest power available to anyone under the sun. We want to wield this power and thereby control all that interests Jesus Christ and our nation.

If you are born again and have the interest of Jesus Christ and Cameroon at heart, we invite you to become one of the fasting intercessors for Cameroon. Such an intercessor will fast every Wednesday until 6 p.m and spend at least one hour in prayer either alone or in a small group with like-minded people. If you want to join in this nondenominational ministry, write to Joseph Mbafor, National Centre for Evangelism, B.P. 4092, Yaounde and he will send you suggestions for prayer every month.

God bless you as you fast and pray for Cameroon.

FASTING INTERCESSORS FOR CAMEROON, PRAYER AND PRAISE BULLETIN NO. 1

Praise the Lord for:

1. The peace and freedom enjoyed in our country, which makes it possible for the gospel to be preached everywhere.
2. The people being won daily into the kingdom of our Lord and Saviour.
3. An increasing desire for prayer and intercession among the lovers of Jesus Christ.
4. Many responses to this nondenominational ministry by people from all over the nation.

Pray for:

A. The government and the nation that:

1. The Lord may bless the Head of State, the president of the National Assembly, the Prime Minister in their service to the nation, giving them all wisdom and courage that is needed for God-fearing leadership.
2. The land may be blessed and its barrenness healed and crop-destroying diseases eliminated; for an increase in the fertility of the land that will result in more crops being grown for local use and export.
3. The spirit of laziness and corruption may be bound and eliminated from the nation.

B. The special interests of the Lord Jesus:

1. For a mighty outpouring of the Holy Spirit on all Cameroonians that will result in

2. the Born-Again believers living victorious Spirit-filled lives;
3. the nominal churchgoers coming to a genuine experience of conversion and total commitment to Jesus Christ; and
4. the heathens coming into contact with the message of salvation and turning to the Lord. (You should personally make a list of fifty born-again people; one hundred nominal Churchgoers and fifty heathens and pray for them by name as the Spirit leads.)
5. For all denominational leaders (make a list of them) that those who are not saved may come in humble repentance to the Lord and be saved and given courage to confess this publicly so that many may be blessed. That those who are saved may be filled with the Spirit and given courage to proclaim Christ without fear or favour.
6. That the Youth of this nation who are searching for meaning and are dissatisfied with "a form of religion that is powerless to deliver, save, and satisfy" will be won for the Lord Jesus who alone is the ultimate answer to life's questions.
7. That the Spirit of God will dislocate the power of all religions, systems, and philosophies that are a total or partial denial of the Lord Jesus who died on the Cross, rose from the dead, ascended into heaven, and is coming again.
8. For the raising of five hundred evangelists filled with the Holy Spirit and power (at least two from each tribe) for the urgent task of proclaiming the Gospel of God's love and forgiveness before the imminent return of our Lord and Saviour.

The Lord says,

"If my people who are called by mv name, shall humble themselves, and pray, and seek my face, and turn from their wicked ways; then will I hear from heaven, and will forgive their sin, and will heal their land" (2 Chronicles 7:14 KJV).

The Lord is counting on you to humble yourself, pray, and seek His face, repent and then He will do great things.

We invite you to join this ministry. It will involve fasting on Wednesdays until 3 p.m. and spending as much time as is possible in prayer either alone or in a small group of like-minded believers. When you start fasting and praying, please write to brother Joseph Mbafor, B.P. 6090 Yaounde, Cameroon.

God bless you richly.

FASTING INTERCESSORS FOR CAMEROON - PRAYER BULLETIN NO. 2

Praise the Lord for:

1. The Head of State and his subordinates for handling national affairs with wisdom that has resulted in the peace we now enjoy.
2. The various campaigns of evangelism being held nationwide and the harvest of souls for the Lord Jesus from these campaigns.
3. An increasing hunger among God's children for a close walk with the Lord Jesus.

Pray that:

A

1. The Lord will bless our land and cause it to become more fertile.

2. The Lord will destroy crop-destroying diseases.
3. The farmers will work hard and be blessed in their efforts.
4. There will be enough food at reasonable prices for all Cameroonians.

B

1. The Lord will enable all dishonest and corrupt people in our country to be caught by the appropriate authorities and brought to justice, irrespective of their position; and that Cameroonians may be delivered from a spirit of laziness.

C

1. The Lord may pour out His Holy Spirit in great might, as on Pentecost and that this may lead to the revival of believers and the conversion of millions of the unsaved.
2. That the Church may be brought back to the Bible and that once again Bible truth will characterize all Assemblies of true believers.
3. That the Lord will prepare His Body for His second coming by restoring all the nine gifts of the Spirit (1 Cor. 12:8-10) to each local Assembly and the ninefold fruit of the Holy Spirit (Gal. 5: 22,23) to each believer.
4. That the Lord will raise up five hundred Spirit-filled evangelists (two from each tribe) for the urgent task of making Christ known to every Cameroonian.
5. That the Lord will raise up one thousand Spirit-filled pastors for the indispensable task of building up the body of Christ to maturity.
6. That the Lord, will bless every medium being used for

Gospel proclamation—radio, cassettes, tracts, and the like and open up more doors where these are lacking.
7. That the Gospel Bookshops now in existence may be blessed by the Lord and that He may provide faithful men and finances to start similar bookshops in all the main towns of our country.
8. That the Lord may hold in check every person, system, philosophy that is a partial or total denial of Jesus Christ - crucified, buried, risen, and soon coming.

Fasting intercessors are born-again people who, irrespective of their denominational inclinations, believe that God meant business when He said,

> *"If my people who are called by my name, shall humble themselves, and pray, and seek my face, and turn from their wicked ways, then will I hear from heaven, and will forgive their sin, and will heal their land" (2 Chronicles 7:14 KJV).*

We are concerned that the Lord may bless this nation spiritually and materially.

We invite you to join us. Fasting Intercessors do not eat food on Wednesdays before 6 p.m. They spend as much time as they can have free on that day in prayer for these and other topics that the Lord will give them. If you are alone, you can begin to fast and pray; but it is better to look for at least one other believer with whom you can meet to pray at a set time on Wednesdays. Write to Joseph Mbafor, B.P. 6090, Yaounde, when you have started to fast and pray and he will send you the topics regularly as well as pray for you.

May the Lord bless you very richly.

FASTING INTERCESSORS FOR CAMEROON - PRAYER BULLETIN NO. 3

Praise the Lord for:

1. The Head of State and all who exercise political authority in our country because they do so with wisdom.
2. The peace which we are enjoying so freely.
3. The multitudes who are being won to the Lord Jesus Christ! throughout the nation.
4. All the open doors for the gospel throughout the nation.
5. The increasing thirst being born in the hearts of Cameroonians for the gospel of Jesus Christ.

Pray that:

A

1. The planning, preparation, and execution of the C.N.U. Congress of Bafoussam should be controlled and blessed by the Lord in such a way that it results in national peace, unity, and progress.
2. The forces of national security be made honest, hardworking and vigilant in order that they may discern and detect who the true enemies of the nations are and bring these up for trial.
3. The Lord would grant a spirit of discipline, honesty, and hard work to Cameroonian students and teachers so that better academic performances may be obtained at all levels.
4. The Lord will bless our soil and our farmers in such a way that the harvest will be abundant both for local consumption and for export.
5. The love and the fear of the Lord will sweep through the

nation as well as the mutual love and respect of each Cameroonian for the other.

B

1. The church, that is the Body of true believers will be united in
2. knowledge and love of the Lord Jesus,
3. obedience to the Lord Jesus and His Word,
4. love and service each of the other, and furthermore that Biblical truth would characterize all the local assemblies without any compromise.
5. The Lord would prepare His Body for the return of the Lord by pouring forth all the nine manifestations of the Holy Spirit (1 Corinthians 12:8-10), all the ministry gifts (1 Corinthians 12:27-31) and the motivational gifts (Romans 12:3-8) to all the assemblies and that the ninefold fruit of the Spirit (Galatians 5:22-23) would be given to each believer.
6. The Lord would raise up five hundred evangelists full of the Holy Spirit (at least two from each tribe) for the urgent task of making Jesus known to all Cameroonians .
7. The Lord would raise up one thousand pastors full of the Holy Spirit for the indispensable task of building up the Body of Christ.
8. The Lord would bless every tool that is being used for the proclamation of the gospel (tracts, booklets, books, cassettes, stickers, ctcetera) and that He may open doors for the gospel into areas that are not yet touched by the gospel.
9. The Lord would permit the carrying out of many evangelistic crusades throughout the nation, towns, and villages. Pray that the power of the Lord to save sinners, change lives, and that the filling with the Holy Spirit and

healing of the sick would accompany the proclamation of the gospel throughout the nations.

10. The Holy Spirit would move and cause at least twenty thousand people to be converted to Christ throughout the nation in 1980 and that each convert would continue firmly in the Lord and be filled with the Holy Spirit.
11. The Lord would raise up men and women of vision and consecration who will take the gospel of God's love and forgiveness to every part of the nation: North, East, South and West; that no place will be considered too far or too isolated as long as there are sinners for whom Jesus died and sinners whom He wants to save (Romans 15:20-21).
12. The Lord will enable evangelistic centres to be started in each village and town of the nation whose primordial task shall be evangelism; that the Lord will raise men filled with the Holy Spirit to lead these centres and that converts would be won to the Lord Jesus and not to any denomination whatsover.
13. Thousands of Cameroonian students, at all academic levels, will be won to the Lord Jesus.
14. The Lord would bless and strengthen all true spiritual leaders, giving to each a spirit of humility, meekness, and goodness but also giving to each a spirit of counge boldness, and authority in the name of the Lord Jesus; that the Lord would give each one of them a spirit of revelation and wisdom in Christ Jesus and a vision of the greatest need of the moment, which is the total evangelization of Cameroon in truth and power before the imminent return of the Lord Jesus for His Bride.
15. The Lord would put to nought every person, system, or philosophy that is a partial or total refusal of the Jesus crucified for our sins, and who was buried, resurrected, enthroned, and coming soon.

16. *Believers would recognize their authority as the children of God and use it against all the tricks and powers of the Enemy. The Lord Jesus said, "Behold, I have given you authority to tread upon serpents and scorpions, and over all the power of the enemy; and nothing shall hurt you" (Luke 10:19). He also said and continues to say, "Truly, I say to you, whatever you bind on earth shall be bound in heaven, and whatever you loose on earth shall be loosed in heaven. Again I say to you, if two of you agree on earth about any thing they ask, it will be done for them by my Father in heaven. For where two or three are gathered in my name, there am I in the midst of them" (Matthew 18:18-20).*

Fasting Intercessors are people who have completely turned their backs to all sin and have received the Lord Jesus as their personal Lord and Saviour. They are people who, regardless of their denominational inclinations, believe that God meant business and means business when He says,

"If my people who are called by my name humble themselves, and pray and seek my face, and turn from their wicked ways, then will I hear from heaven, and will forgive their sin and heal their land" (2 Chronicles 7:14).

Fasting Intercessors are people who do not want the Lord to say and do for Cameroon what He said and did in Israel when He said,

"The people of the land have practised extortion and committed robbery; they have oppressed the poor and needy, and have extorted from the sojourner without redress. And I sought for a man among them who should build up the wall and stand in the breach before me for the land, that I should not destroy it; but I found none. Therefore, I have poured out my indignation upon them; I have consumed them with the fire of my

wrath; their way have I requited upon their heads, says the Lord God" (Ezekiel 22:29-31 KJV).

Fasting Intercessors do not eat on Wednesdays before 18:00 hours. They fast and spend as much time as possible, when not at work, in prayer for the above prayer topics and any others that the Lord will put on their hearts. They pray in small groups, but even if you are alone you can begin to fast and pray. However, seek to be united to other fasting intercessors. Together, choose a convenient period on Wednesdays in order to gather together and pray together. When you have started to pray, write to Joseph Mbafor, B.P. 6090, Yaounde. He will make arrangements so that you may be able to obtain future bulletins. For those who are already fasting and praying, please kindly send us your names and addresses. We are about to establish a list of intercessors for 1980. Because some who once interceded no longer intercede, we want to know those who are interceding. So please kindly send us your name and address as a matter of urgency.

May the Lord bless your faithfulness in this ministry of intercession superabundantly.

Rejoice in the Lord!

FASTING INTERCESSORS FOR CAMEROON - PRAYER BULLETIN NO. 4

Praise the Lord for:

1. The success of the Bafoussam C.N.U. Congress.
2. The successful presidential elections and the overwhelming support that the Head of State received at the polls.
3. The new Cabinet.
4. The increasing productivity of our land.

5. Many doors being opened for the proclamation of the gospel of the Lord Jesus Christ as Saviour and Lord.
6. Hundreds of souls being won to the Lord Jesus Christ nationwide.
7. Many Local Assemblies being established for the care of believers.

Pray for the government and nation that:

1. The Lord will bless the Head of State during his current term of office; giving him good health, divine wisdom, a God-fearing heart and all other abilities that will enable him to lead the Cameroonian people satisfactorily.
2. That the Lord will bless the President of the National Assembly, the Prime Minister and all Ministers as they execute their God-given responsibilities.
3. That the Lord God will guide and oversee the preparation of the next five-year development plan of our nation.
4. That God will heal the land of the many diseases afflicting the nation so that the Cameroonian people are physically healthy. That God will enable the government to take the appropriate action against disease-forming habits like smoking, alcoholism, and laziness.
5. That irresponsible medical staff, be they doctors or nurses, will be spotted and severely punished.
6. That God will give our security and legal forces the courage and ability to apprehend all true embezzlers of public funds, all customs and tax defaulters, and the like and bring them to face the demands of the law without fear or favour, irrespective of who they are.

Pray for the Special Interests of the Lord Jesus

1. The Lord will pour out His Holy Spirit upon all Cameroonian flesh so that this will result in thousands being saved in the months ahead.
2. That all agents of the devil that are set up by him to oppose, hinder, or confuse the Gospel would be destroyed.
3. That God will put to nought and uproot completely out of every Cameroonian every system, philosophy, and ideology that is opposed to the Lord Jesus, the One Saviour and One Mediator.
4. That the Lord will open doors into all those tribes where the Gospel has never been preached in the power of the Holy Spirit. Pray that the Lord will convert some people from such tribes and use them for reaching their own people.
5. That Cameroonian youths in thousands will be radically converted to the Lord Jesus and that they will invest their youthful lives in serving Him and in building the nation. Pray that such youths will be reached with the whole counsel of God and not just partial truth.
6. Insist that the Lord will make it possible for the Gospel of Jesus Christ to be preached on the entire National Radio network by Spirit-baptised men and women. Claim an open door for the Gospel on each Provincial Station.
7. Ask and insist that the Lord should provide a permanent page on some leading national daily newspaper for the Gospel of Jesus Christ, written by Spirit-filled Believers.
8. Ask the Lord to make it possible for a magazine, that is solely committed to the Gospel of the Lord to be raised up.
9. Ask the Lord to bless the crucial ministry of Bible translation in Cameroon. Ask Him to eliminate and oppose all who are not truly converted who are ruining the Word by trying to translate it and that the Lord will

raise in their place true children of the kingdom with spiritual and literary gifts for the task.
10. Because the harvest is truly great and the labourers are few, pray to the Lord of the harvest that He will provide labourers by raising up five hundred national Spirit-filled evangelists and one thousand national Spirit-filled pastors.
11. Pray that truly converted Cameroonians will be delivered from greed and enabled by the Lord to give sacrificially for all the special interests of Jesus Christ, our Lord.

Fasting Intercessors are true believers in the Lord Jesus who, irrespective of their denominational inclinations, believe that God meant business when He said,

"If my people who are called by my name, shall humble themselves, and pray, and seek my face, and turn from their wicked ways, then will I hear from heaven, and will forgive their sin, and will heal their land" (2 *Chronicles 7:14 KJV*).

We are concerned that the Lord may bless this nation spiritually and materially.

We invite you to join us. Fasting Intercessors do not eat food on Wednesdays before 0 p.m. They spend as much time as they can have free on that day in prayer for these and other topics that the Lord will give them. If you are alone, you can begin to fast and pray; but it is better to look for at least one other believer with whom you can meet to pray at a set time on Wednesdays. Write to Voice of the Gospel, B.P. 6090, Yaounde when you have started to fast and pray and we will send you the topics regularly, as well as pray for you.

May the Lord bless you very richly.

FASTING INTERCESSORS FOR CAMEROON - PRAYER BULLETIN NO. 5: OCTOBER 1981

Praise the Lord for:

1. The peace being enjoyed in this nation.
2. The wisdom that God gave the Head of State and his advisers to handle the border problems with Nigeria and the misunderstanding with Gabon so that much bloodshed was avoided.
3. The oil deposits that have been found in Kribi.
4. The availability of food of all kinds in our nation at a time when many countries are close to starvation.
5. The doors that remain open to the proclamation of the glorious Gospel of our Lord and Saviour Jesus Christ.
6. The hundreds of souls that are being won for the Lord Jesus.
7. The increase in the teaching ministry of the Word from platforms, by literature, by cassettes, and so on, nationwide.
8. For increasing rediscovery of New Testament truths and practices and the commitment of many to believing and living these out as best as they are understood.

Pray for the government and nation that:

1. The Lord will protect the Head of State from all harm and give him the necessary wisdom, courage, love, and determination to take and effect the right decisions for national stability and prosperity.
2. God will bless the President of the National Assembly, the Prime Minister, all the ministers and Senior Civil Servants, giving them an ever-increasing sense of national commitment, so that their plans and actions will reflect a deep care for all Cameroonians.

3. All who are involved in national security will be honest, fair, vigilant, and hardworking and that they will weed out all true enemies of the nation (especially foreigners whose one purpose is to exploit and destroy) and bring them to justice with out fear or favour.
4. God will touch the hearts of lazy teachers in our educational system at all levels and make them into hardworking people. That God would enable corrupt teachers to be picked out and punished and that our educational system will truly reflect national aspirations. That corrupt students who cheat, buy marks and places will be disciplined with the view to correcting them.
5. That God will build a protecting wall round our nation so that evils like homosexuality, pornographic literature, drugs that lead to addiction, and every form of vice arc not brought in from "developed" nations to add to our own problems.

Pray for the special interests of the Lord Jesus that:

1. The Lord will pour out His Holy Spirit on all Cameroonians so that they are convicted of sin, righteousness, and judgment. Ask that the conviction of sin will be so deep and thorough that people will wail under conviction and cry out to the Lord Jesus who alone can save.
2. The Lord will heal all who are spiritually blind and all who are deceived and enable all of them to see Jesus Christ crucified, risen, ascended, and coming again. Pray that God will grant to millions of such men the power to become the children of God in Christ Jesus.
3. The whole counsel of God will be preached and taught by the lovers of the Lord and that no parts of the truth

would be left aside for fear of the religious and irreligious enemies of the gospel.

4. The Lord will grant a special door and special opportunities so that the youth of this nation is reached biblically, faithfully and in the power of the Holy Spirit with the one message that can make them whole and useful to God and men. Pray especially that the Lord will raise up a powerful ministry for sinners at all levels and that all the plans of the wicked one, to hinder this will be frustrated. Also pray that the illiterate, jobless, and working youth will be reached with the gospel and won over to the blessed Saviour.

5. Insist that the Lord will make it possible for the gospel of the Lord Jesus to be proclaimed on the entire national radio net work by Spirit-filled believers. Claim an open door for the Gospel on each Provincial radio station.

6. Ask and insist that the Lord provide permanent pages in leading daily newspapers for the Gospel of Jesus written by Spirit-filled believers.

7. The Lord will reveal His methods for reaching out to the many tribes in our nation where Christ has not yet been named and where there is not a single true believer. Pray that He will raise up the right people for that ministry and back them up in every way. Pray that the satanic powers holding these tribes under control and blocking the penetration of the Gospel there will be dislodged by powerful and persistent prayer and holy living.

8. The Lord will raise up quickly a magazine of good quality solely committed to proclaiming the gospel and building up the Church.

9. The Lord will unite all who love Him and obey Him in the one task of reaching Cameroon for Christ and building the Church of the Lord. Pray that false doctrines will be dispelled from among true believers and that non

biblical traditions will give away to the biblical-practices. Pray that imported foreign traditions that were brought along with the gospel by misionaries and nonbiblical African practices will be thrown away and replaced by the Word of God.
10. Ask the Lord to raise up the five hundred Spirit-filled pastors for the overripe national field and that these will faithfully reach out to the lost and prepare the Church to meet her Lord in the air.
11. Pray that truly converted Cameroonians will be delivered from the greed for money and luxury and that they will be enabled by the Lord to give sacrificially of their lives and property so that the Church in Cameroon will be self-supporting and self-propagating. Ask the Lord to remove from the minds of Cameroonians any thinking that makes them believe that foreign bodies, missions, churches will finance the work in this country and do it for us.

Fasting Intercessors are Believers in the Lord Jesus who, irrespective of their background, denominational affiliations, doctrinal inclinations, believe that God meant business when He said,

> *"If my people who are called by my name, shall humble them selves, and pray, and seek my face, and turn from their wicked ways, then will I hear from heaven, and will forgive their sin and heal their land"* (2 Chronicle 7:14 KJV).

If you are

1. God's person through the new birth in Christ,
2. prepared to humble yourself by fasting,
3. prepared to pray and seek God's face,

4. ready to turn away from all known sins and any others which the Lord shall reveal to you in future,
5. anxious that God will bless this nation spiritually and materially, then become a Fasting Intercessor by:
6. Setting each Wednesday as a day for national fasting from morning until 6 p.m.
7. Beginning to pray at your free time on Wednesday for these topics and others which the Lord shall show you.
8. Sharing this vision with some others who are like-minded and if they are willing, you should become a Fasting Intercessors Prayer Cell and together fix your time for joint prayer on Wednesday.
9. Writing to us at Voice of the Gospel, B.P. 6090, Yaounde, Cameroon, and we will pray for you and send you the next prayer bulletin.

May the praying, interceding Lord Jesus bless you mightily. We are eagerly waiting to hear from you. We love you.

FASTING INTERCESSORS FOR CAMEROON - PRAYER BULLETIN NO. 6

My beloved Brethren,

The Lord has asked me to have this ministry restarted. I plead with you to join me in fasting and praying for our nation. I humbly beg you to start a small group (of two people or more) who will fast and pray for the Republic of Cameroon each Wednesday. Please send me your name and those of the members of your prayer group. This will enable me to pray for you and send you prayer topics regularly.

The Lord bless you.

Praise

1. Praise the Lord for the peace that reigns in our country.
2. Praise the Lord for the political stability, which He has maintained for many years.
3. Praise the Lord for able leadership in government at different levels.
4. Praise Him for doors that are wide open for the proclamation of the Gospel of Christ all over the nation.
5. Praise Him for the many that He is transferring from the kingdom of Satan into the Kingdom of Jesus Christ.
6. Praise Him for many believers who are growing in grace and in the knowledge of Him.

Prayer

1. Ask the Lord to bless the Head of State and all who are in authority over us so that they will lead the affairs of the nation in a way that satisfies Him.
2. Pray that the Lord will control climatic conditions in the country so that rain and sunshine will come in the right proportions and times to ensure that the food production continues normally.
3. Rebuke the wicked spirits behind drought, crop diseases, disastrous winds, and put them under control all over the country.
4. Ask the Lord to protect the wealth of the nation from those who want to steal it and pray that national resources will be well used for the welfare of all Cameroonians.
5. Rebuke the wicked spirits behind greed, corruption, and wickedness and force these spirits under control in all places in the nation.
6. Judge the wicked spirits behind laziness and liberate all Cameroonians who are bound by them. Ask the Holy Spirit to instil a spirit of hard work, honesty, and concern

for others in the hearts of Cameroonians and all the other nationals who live in our land.

7. Ask the Lord to pour out His Holy Spirit in great might so that hardened sinners will be convicted of sin to such a depth that they will cry out for God.
8. Pray that all who are convicted of sin will turn to the Lord Jesus Christ who alone can save. Rebuke those demons that channel convicted people into Christless religious systems.
9. Pray that the Lord will open doors for the Gospel of Christ to reach all men, be they highly placed or lowly placed in our society. Rebuke those spirits that blind the hearts of those who are well placed in seeing their needs of repentance towards God and faith in the Lord Jesus.
10. Pray that the Lord will move in might and make it possible for the Gospel to be proclaimed regularly on all the radio stations of the nation. Pray that doors will be opened especially to those who have experienced Jesus Christ as the Saviour and are filled with the promised Holy Spirit to preach.
11. Pray that all who are truly converted will love the Lord in a supreme way.
12. Pray that all true believers will hate sin and radically terminate all activities in their lives that dishonour the Lord of Holiness.
13. Pray that all true believers will love each other and so fulfil the law of Christ.
14. Rebuke the wicked spirits behind "Denominationalism" and pray that the Lord will unite all who are His to serve the Lord Jesus and to serve Him only.
15. Pray that the Lord will open the eyes of all true believers to the truths in the Bible and that they will all be led to obey regardless of any denominational interests.
16. Pray that the saints will put on the character of Christ in

its fulness and that they will labour to be like Him in every way.
17. Pray that all the saints will seek the Lord and be filled with the Holy Spirit.
18. Pray that the Lord will restore all spiritual gifts to the Church. Rebuke the wicked spirit that teaches that the time for spiritual gifts is past.
19. Pray that spirit-filled believers will carry the glorious gospel to every village, tribe and town of our country and that they will proclaim the whole counsel of God without fear or favour. Pray especially for the tribes that are without Christian witness.
20. Pray that, the Lord will open the eyes of the believers in Cameroon to their responsibility to believers in other lands especially those who are being persecuted in Russia and the other lands and that we will do something for them.
21. Pray that the Lord will grant the believers to see the world as God sees it and thereby invest in the work of the Gospel as never before.
22. Pray that each believer will live in a moment-to-moment expectation of the return of the Lord Jesus. Ask the Lord to work so mightily in the hearts of His children so that they may put all of themselves and all that they have into the work of the gospel *NOW.* (This is the way to manifest a spirit that is eager for the return of the Lord).
23. Ask the Lord to raise up multitudes of people to fast and pray for Cameroon. Ask the Lord to unite such people in groups of twos or more.
24. Ask the Lord to protect this Ministry from the attacks of Satan and his agents. Do not forget to write and tell me that you will fast and pray for Cameroon. Why not write now? Why not enrol someone to pray with you? Why not look for that one today?

May the Lord direct your hearts to the love of God and to the steadfastness of Christ (2 Thessalonians 3:5).

"Therefore, my beloved brethren, be steadfast, immovable, always abounding in the work of the Lord, knowing that in the Lord your labour is not in vain" (1 Corinthians 15:58).

I greet you very warmly in the name of our Lord.

I love you.

I am waiting anxiously to hear from you.

FASTING INTERCESSORS FOR CAMEROON: B.P. 6090, YAOUNDE, CAMEROON - PRAYER BULLETIN NO. 7: APRIL 1985

(Seventh year of Ministry to the Lord, the Lord's people and the Cameroon Nation)

Topics for Praise and Thanksgiving

1. Praise the Lord that He has sustained us and enabled us to continue this ministry of fasting and praying for our nation for all these years.
2. Thank the Lord for the peace that He has given to our nation from year to year. Bless the Lord for all that He has done to frustrate the plans and attempts of Satan to destabilize the nation and bring disorder.
3. Thank the Lord for overseeing the affairs of the government at all levels, bringing down some and lifting up others according to His sovereign purposes.
4. Thank the Lord for giving our nation economic prosperity.
5. Thank the Lord for the abundant supply of food all over the nation; for heavy investments by the government in

agriculture and for climatic conditions that favour food production.
6. Thank the Lord for the advance of the gospel in the nation; for increasing books, tracts, personal evangelism, and other evangelistic methods.
7. Praise the Lord for the many who are coming to genuine life in Christ.
8. Thank the Lord for the doors being opened for gospel ministry by Cameroonians in the neighbouring countries, especially through literature.

Topics for Intercession

1. Ask the Lord to bless the Head of State and all He has placed in authority over us. Claim for all our leaders, hearts that are committed to the truth and to honesty in all its forms.
2. Ask the Lord to give the Head of State and all the other leaders of the nation the wisdom needed to seek solutions to all the problems facing the nation.
3. Judge corruption in all its forms - bribery, favouritism, nepotism, and so on - and ask the Lord to pull down all who practise such evils and raise honest people to their positions for the good of the nation.
4. Ask the Lord to move in might so that "Rigour and Moralization" would be applied to all phases of national life.
5. Judge the Satanic prince who brings drought upon nations and send him completely out of the Cameroon borders.
6. Judge the wicked spirit behind falsehood and lying in all aspects of national life and overthrow it. Release the Spirit of truth to invade lying men and liberate them.
7. Judge the wicked spirit behind laziness in all aspects of

national life and release the spirit of hard work in villagers, students, and workers at all levels.
8. Ask the Lord to guide policymakers to see new ways of orientating the economy so that jobs will be available for the unemployed who want to earn their living honourably.
9. Liberate the National Television from all who would want to use it to advertise immorality, crime, and all other things that advance Satan's kingdom. Open the national television for use in the proclamation of the gospel by Spirit-anointed preachers.
10. By violent prayer, create open doors on all the radio stations in the nation for the gospel preached by men who know and love the Saviour.
11. By prayer and waiting on God, identify the satanic prince that controls the people of your town or village and cast him out of his position of authority (You may need to fast for many days in order to effectively do this). Bind the "strong man" of your village or town and release all who are held in captivity by him. They are possibly held in the captivity of drunkenness, stealing, lying, sexual immorality in all forms, false religions of all kinds, and others. As you liberate those in captivity, expose them by prayer to the gospel that liberates and bring them to salvation in Jesus' name.
12. By prayer release the power of the Holy Spirit to move in might in your village or town. Pray for mighty torrents of revival to sweep through your village or town and bring multitudes of people to genuine repentance and faith in the Lord Jesus. Pray that any Catholics, Presbyterians, Lutherans, Apostolics, Baptists, Seventh Day Adventists, Assemblies of God people, Full Gospel Mission people, and the rest, who do not know the Lord Jesus be swept into the kingdom as the Holy Spirit moves in might.

13. Ask the Lord to open doors for evangelistic campaigns and crusades in your village or town. Pray that the Gospel will be preached in power and souls saved from sin and unto Jesus Christ. Be prepared to cooperate in soul-winning efforts, provided Christ is truly preached, regardless of who is organizing the campaign.
14. Ask the Lord to deliver you from a denominational spirit and prepare you to seek the Lord Jesus and His interest. Pray that other believers will be similarly delivered.
15. Ask the Lord to tear down denominational barriers that imprison believers separating them from the Lord and from each other. Ask the Lord to tear away nonbiblical denominational practices that bring in unnecessary differences that the devil exploits to his advantage. Rebuke the demons that advance denominationalism in the place of Christ and remove them from their places of authority. Pray that each believer will go out to look for the other believers who are imprisoned in denominations that confuse belonging to Jesus with be longing to the denominations.
16. By faith, usher that day in Cameroon when all who are the Lord's own will be united in love, faith, and service. Prayerfully advance the arrival of that day in Cameroon when all who are the Lord's in each village will meet together as the Lord's people, separated from the world and separated from all that is not of the Lord and so satisfy the heart of the Head of the Church - the Lord Jesus.
17. By faith ask the Lord to raise more apostles, prophets, evangelists, pastors, and teachers to champion the cause of Christ throughout the nation. Pray that when the Lord raises them (the Lord has already raised some) they will be men separated from self and separated unto the Lord and His work. Pray that they will be delivered from all attempts

to try and build their personal empires and be lost in the building up of the body of Christ. Pray that these ministers of God will minister according to the gifts that God has given them and thereby fulfil their ministries. Deliver them from the lust for power, positions, and ministries to which they have not been called by the Lord and which they are not equipped by the Holy Spirit to discharge.

18. Pray that the body of Christ in Cameroon would individually and collectively labour to evangelize the whole nation as rapidly as possible and by so doing accelerate the coming back of Jesus the King.

Fasting intercessors fast from Tuesday evening to Wednesday evening and meet individually or in small groups to pray on these topics and any others that they consider necessary. Join us and start to pray this Wednesday. Start a group in your home or place of work. Please send me your name and those praying with you.

God bless you abundantly.

FASTING INTERCESSORS FOR CAMEROON, B.P. 6090, YAOUNDE, CAMEROON - PRAYER BULLETIN NO. 8: JANUARY 1987

(Ninth year of Ministry to the Lord, the Lord's people, and the Cameroon Nation)

Topics for Praise and Thanksgiving

1. Praise the Lord that He has sustained us and enabled us to continue to fast and pray for our nation for over eight years.
2. Thank the Lord for the peace that He has continued to give our nation. Bless Him that he has upheld this peace

by His mighty hand even when the enemy of peace (the devil) has tried to disturb it.
3. Thank the Lord for our Head of State and all whom He has put in political and administrative authority over us. Thank the Lord for their health and wisdom in handling the affairs of the nation.
4. Thank the Lord for moving our Head of State to cause the Government to recognize the nation of Israel. This is surely one of the greatest achievements of our Head of State and it has surely put this nation in a position of favour before the Lord of Hosts.
5. Thank the Lord for giving our nation economic prosperity. Our economic situation makes us like an island that is blessed and surrounded by countries whose economies are in grave difficulties. There is no question about the fact that we are relatively in better economic prosperity than most countries in Africa. Give God glory for this.
6. Thank the Lord for abundant food, fruits, vegetables in most of the nation. Bless His name for blessing us in such a way that we are one of the very few nations in this continent who are able to feed ourselves.
7. Thank the Lord for good weather conditions all over the nation that enable us to live comfortably and carry out all kinds of agricultural projects.
8. Thank the Lord for the many people who are coming to a genuine experience of salvation and are learning to obey the Lord in all things.
9. Thank the Lord for the increase in instruments of evangelism and edification of the saints - Bibles, Christian literature, casettes, and so on, and for their impact on the nation for the glory of God.
10. Thank God for an increasing number of believers who are

being delivered from sin and are entering into a life of holiness and consecration unto the Lord.
11. Thank the Lord for enabling Bibles, books, tracts, correspondence courses, and preachers to go from our nation to other nations. Bless His name for the fruit that is being borne unto His glorified and enthroned Son. Praise His name that our economic prosperity has continued to place us in a situation where we can minister to other nations in this continent and other continents.

Topics for Intercession

1. Ask the Lord to bless the Head of State and all who assist him with all that they need to lead the nation in the way that God wants it led. Ask the Lord to protect them from every attack of the enemy. Pray that God will give them the best gift which is Jesus and then all the other gifts that they need.
2. Pray that, the Lord will oversee the implementation of the Sixth Plan by the Cameroonian people. Ask the Lord to touch all who are involved in its implementation to be honest in spite of themselves.
3. Pray that the fear of the Lord will fall upon the nation so that even those who do not know the Lord Jesus will act honestly out of a spirit-instilled fear of God. As you pray believe that nothing is too hard for God and that He is sovereign and can move anyone to do what He wants regardless of what the person's intentions were.
4. Judge the wicked spirit behind laziness in all aspects of national life and release the spirit of hard work among all Cameroonians at all levels.
5. Pray that the Lord will continue to bless our economy by enabling more mineral wealth to be discovered. Pray that He will cause more oil deposits to be found. Pray that

there will be increased cultivation of cash crops and that our products will fetch good prices on the world market.
6. Pray that the production of food will continue and that weather conditions will continue to favour agriculture. Judge the wicked spirits that are behind the advance of the Sahara desert, plant diseases, locusts, and all that the enemy would like to use to ruin our national agricultural products.
7. Pray that the Lord will continue to protect the planes of Cameroon Airlines from accidents. Pray that He would have mercy on us so that there are no future natural disasters like the one that took place at Lake Nyos. Pray particularly because such disasters are engineered by the devil in order to populate hell with people who have not yet been reached with the salvation of God in Christ.
8. Pray that God would deliver Cameroonians from the wicked spirit of complaining, gossip, and despair. Pray and bind the many lying spirits that the wicked one has injected into our nation.
9. Bind the demons behind drunkenness, adultery, fornication, greed, covetousness, impatience, selfishness, and other vices, and cast them out of the hearts of Cameroonians and out of our land.
10. Pray for a mighty outpouring of the Holy Spirit upon all who know the Lord Jesus as Saviour but are denying Him His throne as Lord in their lives so that they would be brought most rapidly to total consecration. Pray that the Holy Spirit would lead those believers who are consecrated to become even more consecrated so that there will be more lives in which Jesus Christ reigns in unquestioned majesty (Take time to sort out your personal consecration with the Lord).
11. Pray that the Holy Spirit would be poured out on all who know and love the Lord so that they would be convicted

deeply of all sins (sins of commission and sins of omission), repent, forsake all sin and be filled with the Holy Spirit.
12. Pray that the Bride of Christ would cooperate with the Lord so that she is rendered without spot or wrinkle. Pray that all who call themselves believers would face the Word of God that clearly teaches that all who continue in sin, including the sin of lying, will perish. Pray that all who live in secret sin will be delivered.
13. Pray that the many people whose repentance is false and whose conversion is spurious would be delivered from self- deception and come to the Lord Jesus for true salvation.
14. By violent prayer, tear down all the barriers that the devil and man have built to separate the children of God from each other. Be merciless as you remove such barriers. Pray that the Lord would gather His children around Himself and around each other. Pray that the Bride will be One in doctrine and that the demons that introduce nonbiblical doctrines and practices will be bound. Pray that the demons that cause believers to abandon parts of the Bible will grant honesty to God's children so that they will own up to their faults and failures, confess them to the Lord and to each other, abandon them and walk in honesty and truth so that the Lord's name will be glorified.
15. Pray that all the gifts of the Holy Spirit will be manifested more frequently among Cameroon believers to the glory of God and the edification of the Body. Pray that the ministry gifts of apostles, prophets, evangelists, pastors, and teachers will be fully restored to the Body of Christ in Cameroon and that the Body will recognize, thank God, and encourage these ministry gifts. Pray that the Holy Spirit will be given the liberty to raise all the

ministries that He wants to raise in Cameroon to the glory of God.
16. Pray that signs and wonders will follow the proclamation of the Gospel nationwide.
17. There have been many prophesies about the Gospel going from Cameroon to other lands. Pray that the Body of Christ will cooperate with the Holy Spirit so that these prophesies are fulfilled to the glory of God.
18. Pray that the Holy Spirit will move in a mighty way so that multitudes of Cameroonians are brought to the salvation of God.
19. Pray that the fruit of the Spirit: love, joy, peace, patience, and others, will mature in all who are the Lord's in Cameroon.
20. Pray that those tribes that have not been evangelised will be rapidly reached with the Gospel so that all those who love the Lord can pray with a good conscience saying, "Come, Lord Jesus."

Fasting Intercessors for Cameroon are people who have committed themselves to fast between 6 p.m. on Tuesday and 6 p.m. on Wednesday. They find time on Wednesday to pray individually or in small groups as the Lord leads them on these and/or other topics as the Lord may lead them. They believe that God answers prayers and that He rules in the affairs of men. So, they ask with faith and God is sure to answer. If you are standing with us in this ministry, please send us your name and address. We shall send future topics to you.

FASTING INTERCESSORS FOR CAMEROON, B.P. 6090, YAOUNDE, CAMEROON, PRAYER BULLETIN NO. 9-OCTOBER 1987

(Tenth year of Ministry to the Lord, the Lord's people, and the Cameroon Nation)

Topics for Praise and Thanksgiving

1. Praise the Lord that He has sustained us and enabled us to continue to fast and pray for the Cameroon Nation for over nine years.
2. Praise the Lord for the peace and stability that He has continued to shower on the nation.
3. Praise the Lord for our Head of State and all He has put in authority over us.
4. Praise the Lord for the abundance of food in our nation. There is food of all kinds. There is fish, meat, fruit, rice, and all types of food. God has really been good. Praise His wonderful hand that has done this.
5. Praise the Lord for the many roads that have been built recently in the nation, thus easing communication.
6. Praise the Lord for the present economic crisis. Thank Him for allowing it. Thank Him for the lessons He wants us to learn from it as a nation and as individuals. Praise Him for the measures that He is enabling the government to take in order to put the situation under control.
7. Praise the Lord that there have been no major accidents of any planes of the Cameroon Airlines nor ships of the shipping lines. Praise Him that the trains have continued to move with out major breakdowns or accidents.
8. Praise the Lord for all who are turning from sin and self to the Lord Jesus.
9. Praise the Lord for the gospel that is being preached all over the nation.
10. Praise the Lord for all who are increasingly becoming like the Lord Jesus in motive, thought, word, and deed.

11. Praise the Lord for the increasing number of people in whose lives the power of things has been broken permanently.
12. Praise the Lord for the increasing number of people who are fasting and praying for increasing lengths of time.
13. Praise the Lord for the gospel that is going from our nation to increasing numbers of countries worldwide through books, tracts, cassettes, and correspondence courses. Praise the Lord that He is enabling us to play a small part in the conquest of Planet Earth, for His glorious and soon-coming Son.

Topics of Blessing

1. Bless the Head of State, all in authority under him, and every Cameroonian.
2. Bless every Cameroonian with a saving knowledge of the Lord Jesus.
3. Bless the Sixth Economic Plan of the nation.
4. Bless the agricultural sector of the economy.
5. Bless every Cameroonian with an honest heart.
6. Bless every Cameroonian with deliverance from selfishness.
7. Bless every Cameroonian with deliverance from greed.
8. Bless every Cameroonian with deliverance from corruption.
9. Bless every Cameroonian with deliverance from sexual immorality and drunkenness.
10. Bless every Cameroonian with deliverance from laziness.
11. Bless every Cameroonian with a generous heart that seeks to give and give.
12. Bless every Cameroonian with a willingness to make sacrifices for the common good.

13. Bless the Cameroonian nation with peace, harmony, and economic prosperity.

Topics of Intercession

1. Pray that the Lord will give the Head of State the wisdom needed to handle the affairs of the nation in this period of crisis so that the will of God is accomplished and the nation blessed.
2. Pray that each Cameroonian will do all he can do to contribute to the solution of problems instead of passively criticising, complaining, and grumbling.
3. Pray that God will enable our crops to be sold on the world market and at good prices, especially our cocoa, coffee, cotton, petrol, and others.
4. Pray that farmers will not be discouraged and stop to produce, but rather that they will be strengthened to continue to farm while we wait for things to improve.
5. Pray that the Lord will guide and protect our resources from those who want to steal them in order to enrich themselves. Pray that all thieves and crooks will be discovered and that resources stolen be recovered and put into the coffers of the government.
6. Pray that there will continue to be good weather and an even distribution of rainfall all over the nation.
7. Pray that the Lord will prevent further natural disasters like the Lake Nyos incident from happening again.
8. Pray that as a nation we will be hospitable to the foreigners in our midst and generous to our needy neighbours in the nations that surround us.
9. Pray that each believer will love the Lord supremely and be faithful to Him at any cost.
10. Pray that each believer will grow in love towards other believers: forgiving, encouraging and praying for those

believers who might not have seen what he has been shown by the Lord. Pray that the Lord will act in a sovereign way nation wide, so that all who are His will become one in motive, thought, word and deed.
11. Pray that the Lord will enlarge the hearts of all who are His to include all whom He has included and to exclude all whom He has excluded.
12. Pray that the interests of the Lord Jesus, His holiness, His kingdom and His will, will take the place of any lower motive or goal of service.
13. Pray that all true believers will be delivered from the love of self and the power of sin. Pray that each true believer will enter into all of his inheritance in holiness and truth.
14. Pray that all of the truth of God's Word will be preached and lived and that nothing of it will be left out as unimportant. Pray that the thoughts, words, and actions of all true believers will be true and that each will be delivered from all lying and falsehood.
15. Pray that a Spirit-created fear of the Lord will fall on all who are His.
16. Pray that multitudes of believers who have backslidden over the years will be restored to the Lord.
17. Pray that the Holy Spirit will come upon all who are His mightily, leading to revival and spiritual freshness. Pray that as a result of that revival of the saints, millions of Cameroonians will be saved.
18. Pray that the Lord will raise up apostles, prophets, evangelists, pastors, and teachers, as well as the other needed ministers for the Cameroon Harvest. Pray that each will be appointed and anointed by the Holy Spirit and that each will seek the Lord fervently and serve Him in purity of heart. Pray that ministers will be sent from Cameroon into God's global harvest.

19. Pray that a spirit of true repentance will be in us all and upon us all.
20. Lord, deal with us and with our nation not according to Your wrath or justice (for we deserve to perish because of our sins), but according to Your mercy. Lord, for mercy we plead. Lord, in mercy, bless. Lord, in mercy bless us abundantly

Fasting remains from Tuesday evening to Wednesday evening. Arrange a time of prayer at your convenience. Encourage others to fast and pray. God bless you.

FASTING INTERCESSORS FOR CAMEROON, B.P. 6090, YAOUNDE, CAMEROON - PRAYER BULLETIN NO. 10: JANUARY 1989

(Twelfth Year of Ministry to the Lord, the Lord's People and the Cameroon Nation)

A Special Message to You

My Beloved Fasting Intercessor,

Praise the Lord!

We are now in the twelfth year of fasting intercession for our nation. We bless the Lord that He has kept the ministry going on from year to year and that He has added to the number of fasting intercessors for Cameroon. We bless the Lord that their commitment to the Lord and to the Lord's interests in Cameroon has grown and deepened. We praise the Lord that He has continued to bless the Cameroon Head of State and all who exercise authority under him. We bless the Lord for the peace and stability that the nation has known from the beginning unto now. We bless the Lord for the abundant food of all kinds that He has given us since we began to intercede. We bless the Lord for the gospel that is going out free of charge from our nation to many nations of the world (seventy-five countries at the moment) through books, Bible correspondence courses, tracts and cassettes. We bless the Lord for the many prayer chains that the Lord has raised in the nation where unceasing prayers are being offered to Him for His interests in Cameroon, Africa and Planet Earth. We bless the Lord for the increasing invitations for Cameroonians to minister Christ in other African countries and other continents. May He receive the honour and glory for this.

In spite of all these, the economic crisis that we prayed about in prayer bulletin No. 9 has persisted and is deepening. The government is labouring to bring things under control but the answer to the economic crisis in Cameroon is God's intervention. The Bible says,

"Unless the Lord builds the house, they labour in vain who build it; unless the Lord guards the city, the watchman stays awake in vain" (Psalms 127:1).

God must intervene in the Cameroon Nation and in the Cameroon economic crisis for real economic recovery to take place. This makes you, *the intercessory* to be the man or woman of the hour.

As the person of the hour we strongly recommend that you do the following:

1. Become more committed to fasting and praying for the nation .
2. Ensure that you fast and pray with us for the nation from Tuesday evening to Wednesday evening every week.
3. Set additional periods of fasting and praying for the nation as the Lord may lead you.
4. Recruit at least two more people to fast and pray for the

nation and ensure that they commit themselves to pray and that they actually pray.
5. Be entirely honest in all your activities so that you do not contribute in any way to the destruction of the economy of the nation by carrying out any dishonest deed.
6. Walk so close to the Lord Jesus and be absolutely consecrated to Him so that He will move and bless the nation because of you.
7. Refuse to be discouraged by what some people may be doing to destroy the nation. God's blessing of the nation does not depend on the corrupt or the wicked but on the righteous.

The Lord God says in His Word: "When I shut up the heavens so that there is no rain, or command the locust to devour the land, or send pestilence among my people, *if my people who are called by my name humble themselves, and pray and seek my face, and turn from their wicked ways, then will I hear from heaven, and will forgive their sin and heal their land*" (2 Chronicles 7:13—14). "*Run to and fro through the streets of Jerusalem, look and take note! Search her squares to see if you can find a man, one who does justice and seeks truth; that I may pardon her*" (*Jeremiah 5:1*). God will pardon the nation if He finds one person in it who does justice and seeks truth. We can say to God with a clear conscience that there are some in this nation who do justice and seek truth. On that basis we can ask the Lord to forgive and bless abundantly.

1. Actually intercede.

Pray As Follows

1. Lord, forgive the sins that the people of Cameroon have committed against You: the sins of corruption, hypocrisy, lying, deceit, falsehood, theft, pride, selfishness, self-

centredness, laziness, injustice, immorality, adultery, fornication, divorce, malice, witchcraft, sorcery, hardening of heart towards the Lord Jesus, despising of the gospel that saves, and so on.
2. Lord, change the hearts of all whom You have placed in authority so that they will turn from their sin to the Lord Jesus who saves. We pray with faith for, "Is there anything too hard for thee, thou Lord of hosts?"
3. Lord, grant perfect freedom to all Cameroonians so that they may hear the gospel of Jesus Christ and believe in Him from the extreme north to the extreme south and from the extreme east to the extreme west. Lord, take away all that prevents the gospel from reaching those who have never heard of it, especially among the unevangelized tribes.
4. Lord, grant that Jesus will be revealed as Saviour and Lord to all who only make a lip service of His Lordship.
5. Lord, grant that Your children will know deep and total deliverance from sin and that there will be a massive return to the Bible—a return to reading, studying, and obeying it.
6. Lord, grant that the gospel will continue to flow from Cameroon to other parts of Your world.
7. Lord, grant that Your children in this nation will live each day in glad expectation of the return of the Lord Jesus. Lord, grant that as they so expect His return, they will sacrifice their all to satisfy the heart of the soon-coming King in all ways.
8. Lord, there are multitudes in our nation who have heard Your gospel but taken it lightly. Lord, pour Your Holy Spirit on all such so that they will be quickened to turn from sin and self to the Lord Jesus.
9. Lord, there are some who are bitterly opposed to the gospel. Lord, in love and mercy reveal Yourself to them as

You revealed Yourself to Saul of Tarsus on the road to Damascus.
10. Lord, rend heaven and pour out Your Holy Spirit on every true believer in this nation so that each will be burdened to see this become a nation whose priority of priorities is that the Lord's name be hallowed, His kingdom come, and His will be done in Cameroon as it is in heaven.
11. Lord, bless the Cameroonian homes so that love and unity will replace hatred, separation, and divorce. Lord, grant that the marriages of those who know Your Son will become exemplary.
12. Lord, bless the children of those who know Your Son as their Lord and Saviour so that they, too, will come to a saving knowledge of the Lord Jesus.
13. Lord, grant that all who know the Lord Jesus, will enter into personal experience of the call of God to contentment, which says, "Keep your life free from love of money, and be content with what you have; for he has said, 'I will never fail you' " (Hebrews 13:5). Lord, do this so that there will be a clear difference between Your children's attitude to worldly things and that of those who are yet to believe.
14. Come, Lord Jesus.

Continue to Pray As Follows

1. Lord, bless the Head of State with perfect health and with wise and honest counsellors who are loyal to him and to the Cameroonian people.
2. Lord, grant that the Head of State will receive all the information that he needs in order to lead correctly. Lord, grant that people will not hide information that is vital from him.

3. Lord, grant that all who are in places of authority will know a new sense of commitment to utter hard work, discipline, and honesty.
4. Lord, grant that all Cameroonians will know a new sense of commitment to utter hard work, discipline, and honesty.
5. Lord, transform all whose attitude is one of always receiving, into people entirely committed to giving for the common good.
6. Lord, grant that every Cameroonian will be prepared (and actually) make sacrifices for the welfare of the nation. In the name of the Lord Jesus we rebuke that spirit that refuses to sacrifice at the personal level under the cover that some class of people should take the initiative and they would follow.
7. Lord, bless this nation by replacing lazy, corrupt, and self-centred employees by hard working, and self-giving Cameroonians at all levels.
8. Lord, reveal to our leaders Your strategy for economic recovery and give them the wisdom, courage, and all else that they need to implement it.
9. Lord, we pray that You will, out of love for us, deliver us from making the mistakes that other countries in economic crises made; mistakes that plunged them into darker times instead of recovery.
10. Lord, grant markets for our cash crops: coffee, cocoa, cotton, and the like.
11. Lord, enable us to sell our surplus food like rice, to neighbouring countries for mutual profit.
12. Lord, in Your love and mercy, grant that mineral wealth will be discovered in significant quantities: gold, diamonds, silver, et cetera, in our country. Lord, You make these things. You know where they are. Lead our explorers to them. Lord, grant that new oil wells will be

discovered on shore and offshore so that the resources from oil are not depleted.
13. Lord, give us creative hearts so that we may apply ourselves to using local materials to solve our problems instead of looking to other nations to do things for us. Lord, deliver each Cameroonian from a spirit of continuous dependence on other nations. Lord, grant that we will believe that we can, for You have made us able.
14. Lord, take away any spirit of despair from Cameroonians. Lord, grant a spirit of hope since You are going to bless the nation.
15. Lord, continue to give us peace, stability, and security for these are necessary for careful planning and careful execution .
16. Lord, You are our answer to the crisis and we look to You for Your answer.
17. Lord, You are the unfailing answer. Our hope is in You. Amen.
18. Lord, deal with us and with our nation not according to what he have done but according to Your mercy. Lord, show us Your mercy. Lord, in mercy bless abundantly. O Lord, bless for we ask in the name of our Lord and Saviour Jesus Christ.

Fasting remains weekly (from Tuesday evening to Wednesday evening). Arrange a time of intercession at your convenience. Encourage others to fast and pray. Lead a prayer group of two, three, or more people and in the group fast and pray.

May the Lord bless you and reward you mightily in the expectation of a prosperous Cameroon: spiritually, socially and economically!

INTERCESSION FOR A CONTINENT

Even as a city and a nation need to be interceded for, each continent needs to be interceded for very specially. When I look at the map of the world, I am fully aware of the fact that God intended the continents to exist as indeed they do. He was the One who caused the geological movements that separated the Planet Earth into the continents that exist today.

We shall base this chapter on intercession for a continent on intercession for the continent of Africa. We are going to do this not because we believe Africa to be a superior or inferior continent, but because we are currently involved in interceding for the continent of Africa in a specific way and that of the other continents only in a general way - as a part of Planet Earth.

There is another reason why I must use Africa as an example. The reason is that when I went to secondary school in 1960, I soon became caught up with a great desire, a passion, a goal. That goal was to see Africa liberated from colonialism and neocolonialism. I would lie in my bed and dream about the day when Africa would be free from wicked foreign rule and exploitation and from wicked internal rule and exploitation. I believed then that the answer lay in education. I said to myself, *All that is going on is because our people cannot read and write. That is why the white man has come and divided us and is ruling us. It is because we do not know how to read and write that we exploit each other, kill each other, and commit all the evils that we are committing against each other.* I thought that when illiteracy would be wiped out completely in all of Africa and many Africans have been educated to obtain degrees up to doctorates, things would change.

It was then, in 1961 that I decided that I must obtain a Ph.D. by the year 1972 so as to contribute to the liberation, not just of a part of Africa, but of the entire continent. Dr. Kwame Nkrumah of Ghana was to me the ablest African leader to lead us into the new day of freedom. In high school, I was a founder-member of the Nkrumanist Society and when he was overthrown in 1966 before my Advanced Level examination, I carried out a twenty-one day partial fast, protesting his overthrow and yearning that he would come back to the helm of power in Ghana and so lead the African revolution. I do not know what would have happened to me had two events not taken place in my life. The first of these and the most important is that on October 1, 1966, during my first week at university (Fourah Bay College, Freetown, Sierra Leone) I met the Lord Jesus and He knocked me out. I yielded to Him and determined to be His slave for all my life. The second thing that happened was that I discovered that university people, be they lecturers or students, were fundamentally selfish. They were just as self-centred as the primitive villager, the only difference being that they had an unusual capacity to hide what their real selves were. I then found that the literate African was just as bound as the illiterate one. I found that mere knowledge of facts could not liberate. As I began to grow in the knowledge of the Lord, I found that the deeper problem of the African was not political or racial. The African was under the bondage of the colonialism of sin and the neocolonialism of self. I came to discover that the only hope for Africa lay in the deliverance from these. I found that education could not set a man free from sin and self. I found that a man could be the holder of a Ph.D. in some area of learning but also be a poor hopeless drunkard who in addition, commits adultery and embezzles money. I found that those who came to the Lord Jesus and received Him as their Saviour and Lord were immediately liberated from the colonialism of sin and that as they continued to walk with Him, He also liberated them from the neocolonialism of self. I know and I am fully persuaded that Jesus is the answer to Africa. I am also persuaded that He is the only answer to Africa. In Fact He is God's answer to the whole world. Because I have borne Africa for so long on my heart, I know that I must fast and pray that she would become what God intended her to become.

Fasting Intercession for Africa was born in August 1988 after some of us completed a forty-day fast during which we prayed for holiness in the sexual realm among the people of God the world over. A few of us have started fasting for God's special move in Africa. We are praying for a continental move of God that will purge the Churches in Africa of the following sins that hold her in greater bondage than any force in human history:

1. Adultery
2. Fornication
3. Pride
4. Jealousy
5. Self-exaltation
6. Financial indiscipline
7. Dishonesty
8. Hypocrisy
9. The love of money
10. The love of power
11. Laziness

12. Vanity
13. Tribalism
14. Prayerlessness

The sanctification of the believers in Africa is priority number one, for if all the believers or even 25 percent of the believers on the continent walked in purity and holiness before God, everything would be different.

We are also praying, with fasting, that God will raise up in the churches in Africa true apostles, prophets, evangelists, pastors, and teachers in place of the many self-styled apostles, prophets . . . who know nothing of a deep fear of God nor of purity and holiness, yet they carry these titles and lord it over ignorant people.

We are also praying that the African leaders and men of substance will stop draining national resources and hoarding them in personal accounts in Europe and other countries. We arc crying out to God to raise statesmen on the continent to replace those leaders who know neither the art of leadership nor the sacrifice for the people that is basic for successful leadership.

The last thing that we are currently fasting and praying for has to do with the population of the continent. The Lord asked Adam to

"Be fruitful and multiply, and fill the earth and subdue it" (Genesis 1:28).

Unfortunately, many Africans misunderstood this Scripture to read, *"Be overfruitful and overmultiply and overpopulate [overfill] the earth and let it subdue you."*

There are slightly over 5 billion people in the world today with the continent of Africa accounting for around 600 million of these. This is about 12 percent of the world's population. In the year two thousand, there will be around 870 million people in Africa compared with a world total of 6.25 billion, which means that Africa will contain 14 percent of the world's population. By the year 2025 when the world's population will be around 8.5 billion people, there will be around 1.58 billion people in Africa or 18.6 percent of the world's population. If you consider the fact that Northern Europe will go from its present population of 83 million to 85 million by 2025, and that Western Europe will go from its present population of 155 million to 152 million by 2025, then it is obvious that Africans are over reproducing and things will be extremely difficult in the future.

We have divided Africa into regions for prayer and we are praying. We are pleading with God that He will raise up five hundred thousand people who will fast and pray for Africa. We will soon launch a program to raise these intercessors.

We have included on the enclosed sheets the population of the various countries and regions as they were last year and as they are estimated by the United Nations to be in A.D. 2000 and in A.D. 2025.

An African apostle, prophet, evangelist, pastor, and teacher ought to know how large his task will be in the years ahead (should Jesus tarry) and so plan accordingly.

Some of us are already crying out to God to enlarge our hearts to contain the additional 970 million (nearly 1 billion) more people who will be on this continent in our lifetime (should our Lord tarry). Will you not pray with us? Will you not team up with us to fast and pray every Thursday for God's move and God's victory in Africa? Would you not write to us of your interest and commitment? You do not have to be an African. Just one who is interested in God's Africa. God bless you indeed. Amen.

You may be led to begin to fast and intercede for another continent. Why not do it? Why not dream to do great things for our

God? Why not put your all into attempting great things for our God? Is the Lord saying to you, "Take My Asia for Me"?

WORLD CONQUEST FOR CHRIST

		1988	2000	2025
	World Total	15,112,298,000	6,251,055,000	8,466,516,000
	Africa	609,718,000	872,234,000	1,580,984,000
	Eastern Africa	182,956,000	269,185,000	523,025,000
1.	British Indian Ocean Territory	2,000	2,000	2,000
2.	Burundi	5,147,000	7,283,000	13,100,000
3.	Comoros	487,000	710,000	1,323,000

4.	Djibouti	383,000	552,000	1,070,000
5.	Ethiopia	44,727,000	61,206,000	112,269,000
6.	Kenya	23,100,000	37,581,000	77,616,000
7.	Madagascar	11,238,000	16,562,000	32,984,000
8.	Malawi	7,884,000	11,706,000	22,804,000
9.	Mauritius	1,077,000	1,240,000	1,480,000
10.	Mozambique	14,845,000	20,445,000	34,368,000
11.	Reunion	575,000	685,000	875,000
12.	Rwanda	6,755,000	10,144,000	18,079,000
13.	Seychelles	67,000	75,000	84,000
14.	Somalia	7,106,000	9,803,000	18,903,000
15.	Uganda	17,189,000	26,285,000	55,198,000
16.	United Rep. of Tanzania	25,397,000	39,572,000	84,784,000
17.	Zambia	7,851,000	12,197,000	25,466,000
18.	Zimbabwe	9,125,000	13,135,000	22,621,000

Central Africa		65,589,000	93,498,000	179,645,000
1.	Angola	9,481,000	13,295,000	24,731,000
2.	Cameroon	10,674,000	14,787,000	26,178,000
3.	Central African Republic	2,771,000	3,765,000	6,815,000
4.	Chad	5,401,000	7,337,000	13,245,000
5.	Congo	1,888,000	2,635,000	4,964,000
6.	Equatorial Guinea	420,000	561,000	991,000
7.	Gabon	1,094,000	1,620,000	2,927,000
8.	Sao Tome and Principe	106,000	149,000	284,000
9.	Zaire	33,755,000	49,349,000	99,512,000

Northern Africa		135,210,000	181,481,000	275,020,000
1.	Algeria	23,841,000	33,247,000	50,291,000
2.	Egypt	51,453,000	66,710,000	93,976,000
3.	Libyan Arab Jamahiriya	4,232,000	6,500,000	12,846,000
4.	Morocco	23,910,000	31,366,000	44,368,000
5.	Sudan	23,797,000	33,610,000	59,594,000
6.	Tunisia	7,809,000	9,821,000	13,284,000
7.	Western Sahara	169,000	228,000	362,000

Southern Africa		39,118,000	51,172,000	78,023,000
1.	Botswana	1,198,000	1,804,000	3,364,000
2.	Lesotho	1.676,000	2,354,000	4,949,000
3.	Namibia	1,760,000	2,354,000	4,949.000
4.	South Africa	33,747,000	43,332,000	63.232,000
5.	Swaziland	737.000	1,116,000	2.206,000
Western Africa		186,845,000	276,898,000	525,271,000
1.	Benin	4,448,000	6,561,000	12,987,000
2.	Burkina Faso	8,529,000	12,025,000	22,678,000
3.	Cape Verde	358,000	518,000	886,000
4.	Ivory Coast	11,612,000	18.547,000	39,842,000
5.	Gambia	812,000	1,116,000	1,850,000
6.	Ghana	14,130,000	20,418,000	37,031,000
7.	Guinea	6,540.000	8,879,000	15,710.000
8.	Guinea Bissau	945,000	1.244,000	2,165,000
9.	Liberia	2,396,000	3,543,000	7,241,000
10.	Mali	8,824,000	12,658,000	24,142,000
11.	Mauritania	1,916,000	2,685,000	4,962,000
12.	Niger	6,688,000	9,750,000	18,940,000
13.	Nigeria	105,471,000	159,149,000	301,312,000
14.	St. Helena	6,000	10,000	19,000
15.	Senegal	6,978,000	9,668,000	16,364,000
16.	Sierra Leone	3,946,000	5,399,000	9,641,000
17.	Togo	3,247,000	4,727,000	9,500,000

39

INTERCESSION FOR PLANET EARTH

God so loved the world!

God still loves the world. He is the Creator of the world and His interests are tied with the people in His world. His heart's desire is that none should perish but that all should reach salvation. The Bible says,

> "The Lord is not slow about his promise as some count slowness, but is forbearing toward you, not wishing that any should perish, but that all should reach repentance" (2 Peter 3:9).

There is no question about the fact that God desires the salvation of every one who is upon the earth. First of all He did not create man to perish. The fall was man's introduction into the purpose of God and not a part of the initial design. In the initial purpose of God, man was to live in deep and increasing fellowship with Him, eat of the tree of life, and live for ever in deeper fellowship with God. Man unfortunately rebelled and fell away. However, God did not give up. In His love, God sent the Lord Jesus to die on the cross for the sins of the world. The price that the Lord paid on the cross in Christ was for every human being who had ever lived, who is living, and who will ever live on planet Earth. God loves every human being and desires their repentance and their salvation.

Since God requires that people cooperate with Him through intercession, He desires that while some will intercede for individuals and others for cities and nations, some will intercede for continent or Planet Earth, depends on two factors. **The first** of these is the call of God. The Lord has called some to intercede for individuals and others to intercede for continents and the whole Planet. Each one must seek the Lord and receive from Him the spheres of his labours as an intercessor. To choose merely on personal preferences is to fail utterly. **The second**, is that God will only call a man to intercede for a continent if he has a continental vision and for Planet Earth if the person has a world vision. If someone has had his heart so enlarged by the Lord that he can carry the world on it and bring it to the Lord in prayer, such a one might be called to intercede for the whole world. It is not a matter of carnal ambition, but of God giving someone power to see.

The person who is wrapped up with himself may be able to pray for himself. The person who is wrapped with a small village may be able to pray for that village. The one who rises high enough with God may see God's vision for a nation and thereby pray for a nation whereas the one who rises high enough will see that God is interested in His purpose in all of the world and may be able to intercede for the whole world.

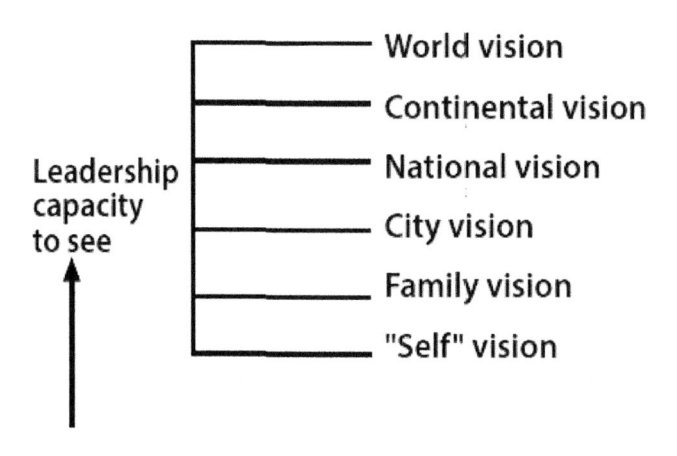

```
                        ┌────── World vision
                        ├────── Continental vision
    Leadership          ├────── National vision
    capacity            ├────── City vision
    to see              │
       ▲                ├────── Family vision
       │                └────── "Self" vision
       │
```

It should not necessarily be thought that the person who is called upon to intercede for a planet is necessarily more spiritual than the one who is called upon to intercede for an individual. Anna, the prophetess interceded so that God's Christ might come into the world. She invested nearly sixty years into that one task and accomplished what could not otherwise have been accomplished. She reached out to the whole world by reaching out to the world's Saviour.

Some of us have been led to intercede for God's interests on Planet Earth. The Lord led us to this only recently. We call ourselves Fasting Intercessors for Planet Earth. We fast every Friday.

Our goal is to labour to ensure that the power of Satan is broken the world over and that multitudes are transformed to love the Lord Jesus supremely. We are still waiting on God for details, but for now we have begun to intercede generally for each country of the world. We are using the accompanying outline and praying for country after country. We have begun to use the prayer topics outlined in the excellent book published by World Evangelisation Crusade, *Operation World*. We believe that this is just the beginning and we are asking God to raise 5 million believers from all over the world who will pray for God's move in full power and majesty all over His world. We are inviting others to join us in fasting and praying for God's total victory all over the world - in every place where the curse is found.

I have personally decided to have 187 minutes of prayer retreat every Friday. I will intercede for each country for one minute and trust that the Lord will lead me in this. We shall send out prayer letters to all intercessors for planet Earth and in that way encourage the intercessors to pray particular things through. There are a number of ways in which someone can intercede for Planet Earth using the lists that follows:

1. He can pray for ten countries each day.
2. He can decide to put one hour of intercession for Planet Earth each day and just pray for a particular country as the Spirit leads him and for the topics that the Spirit will lay on his heart.
3. He can have a six-hour retreat once a week to intercede country by country according to the guidelines given in *Operation World*.
4. He could take one theme, like Christian homes or the holiness of the Church and pray it through for each country. On the other hand he can make a list of the Heads of States of each country and pray for their salvation.

Each person must move ahead as he is led by the Lord and each group of people must move ahead as they are led by the Lord. However, fasting intercessors for Planet Earth will be people who share God's burden and God's vision for all for whom His Son died, and who will consequently put in their total being in intercession so that all of the interests of Jesus Christ are accomplished.

Praise the Lord.

INTERCESSORS FOR PLANET EARTH

Africa

Eastern Africa

1. British Indian Ocean Territory
2. Burundi
3. Comoros
4. Djibouti
5. Ethiopia
6. Kenya
7. Madagascar
8. Malawi
9. Mauritius
10. Mozambique
11. Reunion
12. Rwanda
13. Seychelles
14. Somalia
15. Uganda
16. United Republic of Tanzania
17. Zambia
18. Zimbabwe

Central Africa

1. Angola
2. Cameroon
3. Central Africa Republic
4. Chad

5. Congo
6. Equatorial Guinea
7. Gabon
8. Sao Tome and Principe
9. Zaire

Northern Africa

1. Algeria
2. Egypt
3. Libyan Arab Jamahiriya
4. Morocco
5. Sudan
6. Tunisia
7. Western Sahara

Southern Africa

1. Botswana
2. Lesotho
3. Namibia
4. South Africa
5. Swaziland

Western Africa

1. Benin
2. Burkina Faso
3. Cape Verde
4. Ivory Coast
5. Gambia
6. Ghana
7. Guinea
8. Guinea Bissau

9. Liberia
10. Mali
11. Mauritania
12. Niger
13. Nigeria
14. Saint Helena
15. Senegal
16. Sierra Leone
17. Togo

Europe

Eastern Europe

1. Bulgaria
2. Czechoslovakia
3. German Democratic Republic
4. Hungary
5. Poland
6. Rumania

Northern Europe

1. Channel Islands
2. Denmark
3. Faeroe Islands
4. Finland
5. Iceland
6. Ireland
7. Isle of Man
8. Norway
9. Sweden
10. United Kingdom

Southern Europe

1. Albania
2. Andorra
3. Gibraltar
4. Greece
5. Holy See
6. Italy
7. Malta
8. Portugal
9. San Marino
10. Spain
11. Yugoslavia

Western Europe

1. Austria
2. Belgium
3. France
4. German Federal Republic
5. Liechtenstein
6. Luxembourg
7. Monaco
8. Netherlands
9. Switzerland

Asia

Eastern Asia

1. China
2. Hong Kong
3. Japan
4. Korea

5. Democratic People's Republic of Korea (North Korea)
6. Republic of Korea (South Korea)
7. Macau
8. Mongolia

South-eastern Asia

1. Brunei Darussalam
2. Burma
3. Democratic Kampuchea
4. East Timor
5. Indonesia
6. Laos People's Democratic Republic
7. Malaysia
8. Philippines
9. Singapore
10. Thailand
11. Vietnam

Southern Asia

1. Afghanistan
2. Bangladesh
3. Bhutan
4. India
5. Islamic Republic of Iran
6. Maldives
7. Nepal
8. Pakistan
9. Sri Lanka

Western Asia

1. Bahrain

2. Cyprus
3. Democratic Yemen
4. Gaza Strip (Palestine)
5. Iraq
6. Israel
7. Jordan
8. Kuwait
9. Lebanon
10. Oman
11. Qatar
12. Saudi Arabia
13. Syrian Arab Republic
14. Turkey
15. United Arab Emirates
16. Yemen

Latin America

<u>The Caribbean</u>

1. Anguilla
2. Antigua and Barbuda
3. Bahamas
4. Barbados
5. British Virgin Islands
6. Cayman Islands
7. Cuba
8. Dominica
9. Dominican Republic
10. Grenada
11. Guadeloupe
12. Haiti
13. Jamaica
14. Martinique

15. Montserrat
16. Netherlands Antilles
17. Puerto Rico
18. Saint Kitts and Nevis
19. Saint Lucia
20. Saint Vincent and the Grenadines
21. Trinidad and Tobago
22. Turks and Caicos Islands
23. U.S. Virgin Islands

Central America

1. Belize
2. Costa Rica
3. El Salvador
4. Guatemala
5. Honduras
6. Mexico
7. Nicaragua
8. Panama

Oceania

Australia-New Zealand

1. Australia
2. New Zealand

Melanesia

1. Fiji
2. New Caledonia
3. Papua New Guinea
4. Solomon Islands

5. Vanuatu

Micronesia

1. Guam
2. Kiribati
3. Nauru
4. Pacific Islands

Polynesia

1. American Samoa
2. Cook Islands
3. French Polynesia
4. Niue
5. Samoa
6. Tonga
7. Tuvalu
8. Wallis and Futuna Islands

U.S.S.R.

America

South America

1. Argentina
2. Bolivia
3. Brazil
4. Chile
5. Colombia
6. Ecuador
7. Falkland Islands
8. French Guiana

9. Guyana
10. Paraguay
11. Peru
12. Surinam
13. Venezuela

North America

1. Bermuda
2. Canada
3. Greenland
4. Saint Pierre and Miquelon
5. United States of America

PART 7

40
A FULL-TIME MINISTRY OF INTERCESSION

The amount of time that a person consecrates to a thing betrays his evaluation of that thing. If people see the importance of intercession, they will give themselves increasingly to it. They may start by giving one hour a day to it and soon they will go to two hours. This will continue until they find that they cannot effectively discharge the burden on their hearts in two hours. They will begin to intercede for three hours a day and then they will go on to intercede for five hours each day. As the burden grows, they will discover that they need more time to invest into intercesion. They will therefore cut off the time that was spent in atending parties and visiting friends and relatives and invest this in intercession. This may enable them to intercede for an average of five hours each day. Seeing the needs of the Lord and receiving increasing revelations and burdens from Him, they will decide to spend their week-ends in intercession. This will enable them to invest an average of seven hours daily in intercession.

Having seen the Lord's needs and tested of His goodness in answering intercessional prayers, they will convert all public holidays into days of intercession and they will also convert their annual and terminal holidays into periods of intercession. Such a person will take his leave, depart from home to a lonely place, and there, pray. He will separate himself from every other duty and every other request and give himself to the most important work on Planet Earth. Such a person may thereby find that he is praying an annual average of nine hours a day. He may find that this satisfies all his needs. In that case he can continue that way for the rest of his life, interceding for nine hours each day.

On the other hand he may find that the nine hours are not enough. He needs to spend more time before the Lord. He needs to pray and wrestle more and more so that God's interests are accomplished. He may find that there is no other way to increase his time of intercession. He will therefore ask himself, "Why am I working in this office?" The answer may come, "I am working in this office in order to earn my living." The question may further arise, "Is it the right investment of time, seeing it from the perspective of eternity, to invest eight hours every day, five days a week into earning my living when these hours could be invested in intercession and so give me an additional average of six hours of intercession a day? Will it not be better to give up my job and invest an average of fifteen hours each day in prayer? Will this not make a greater impact on God's purpose?"

The question may then arise, *"How will I feed, house myself, clothe myself, and meet all my other financial needs?"* The voice of the Lord may be heard saying, *"Can I not supply your needs?"* Does the confession of the apostle,

> *"And my God will supply every need of yours according to his riches in glory in Christ Jesus" (Philippians 4:19),*

not apply to you? "How did the apostles of My time have their needs met? How have the needs of My apostles of this era been met? How have the needs of all My other servants who have served Me directly in the work been met? Can I not do for you what I have done for them? Will you trust Me?" The answer may then come, "Lord, I will trust You. I will move out in faith and invest all my life in intercession and trust You to supply all my needs."

Such a person will resign his job and give himself to the task of intercession. He will intercede for twelve, fifteen, and at crisis hours, he will intercede for eighteen, twenty-one and perhaps twenty-four hours a day. Such a person will decide not to get married if he is single, for such a life has no place for the distractions of a wife and children. He will give up his right to have a wife and produce children so that he may fulfil the burden on God's heart. He will, in this way, separate himself from common people who marry. He will do it not because marriage is bad but because he is preoccupied by something that is more important than marriage. He is in the full-time ministry of intercession. When this happens, no one should be surprised about it. It has happened before. The Bible says,

> *"And there was a prophetess, Anna, the daughter of Phanuel, of the tribe of Asher, she was of a great age, having lived with her husband seven years from her virginity, and as a widow till she was eighty-four. She did not depart from the temple, worshipping with fasting and prayer night and day"* (Luke 2:36-37).

She might have been married at sixteen. She was, therefore, widowed at twenty-three. She, therefore, entered her full-time ministry of fasting and intercession between the ages of twenty-three and twenty-four, and at eighty-four she was still at it.

She gave up everything! She gave up everybody! She gave up her total being to the Lord and to intercession. She was a woman apart. She was a great woman. May God raise others like her.

The Lord does supply the needs of such women. First of all, He supplies their emotional needs. In the second place, He supplies their material needs. It is obvious that a woman like Anna did not have many material needs. However, whatever were her needs, they were supplied her.

A local Assembly that supplies the needs of the teaching elders will also have her eyes open to supply the needs of those who are in the full-time ministry of intercession. She would test and try their motives, preparation, and maturity for the ministry and if found faithful, they will be set aside for it and backed up with prayer and fasting. She will supply their needs that will include a quiet place where to live and pray and the other things that they need to live. Such will intercede and their intercession will help meet the needs of God and the needs of the local Assembly.

There will be many who will grumble at such acts of separation unto intercession. Many unbelievers will complain. Relatives will be shocked! Some believers will murmur but the Lord will rejoice and be their unfailing companion and that is all that matters.

Glory be to His holy name.

Amen.

41
INTERCESSION

In the Father's good pleasure
He's ordained intercession
And then invited those who would
To stand now in the gap.

He could have established
That without intercession
His will might yet be established
On earth as in heaven.

Yet that pathway He did not choose,
But set forth a divine law
That unless men interceded,
He would not do many things.

So unchanging is this law
That it is binding on all;
Even the Son right on the throne
Must intercede night and day.

The Son understands this law
And bearing the Church on His heart Since
His return to the throne,
Does nothing but intercede.

The Father waits for the Redeemed
To follow in His steps
And make daily intercession
Life's most important work

My Lord, My God and My King
I give myself to Thee
And now make intercession
My life's one priority.

O blessed Holy Spirit
You intercede in me;
Help me daily in this work
As I labour in Thee.

Blessed Father of glory,
Hearken to my intercessions
And grant the requests of my heart
As I labour with Thine Christ.

— *YAOUNDE, 10 APRIL 1988*

VERY IMPORTANT!!!

If you have not yet received Jesus as your Lord and Saviour, I encourage you to receive Him. Here are some steps to help you,

ADMIT that you are a sinner by nature and by practice and that on your own you are without hope. Tell God you have personally sinned against Him in your thoughts, words and deeds. Confess your sins to Him, one after another in a sincere prayer. Do not leave out any sins that you can remember. Truly turn from your sinful ways and abandon them. If you stole, steal no more. If you have been committing adultery or fornication, stop it. God will not forgive you if you have no desire to stop sinning in all areas of your life, but if you are sincere, He will give you the power to stop sinning.

BELIEVE that Jesus Christ, who is God's Son, is the only Way, the only Truth and the only Life. Jesus said,

> "I am the way, the truth and the life; no one comes to the Father, but by me" (John 14:6).

The Bible says,

"For there is one God, and there is one mediator between God and men, the man Christ Jesus, who gave himself as a ransom for all" (1 Timothy 2:5-6).

"And there is salvation in no one else (apart from Jesus), for there is no other name under heaven given among men by which we must be saved" (Acts 4:12).

But to all who received him, who believed in his name, he gave power to become children of God..." (John 1:12).

BUT,

CONSIDER the cost of following Him. Jesus said that all who follow Him must deny themselves, and this includes selfish financial, social and other interests. He also wants His followers to take up their crosses and follow Him. Are you prepared to abandon your own interests daily for those of Christ? Are you prepared to be led in a new direction by Him? Are you prepared to suffer for Him and die for Him if need be? Jesus will have nothing to do with half-hearted people. His demands are total. He will only receive and forgive those who are prepared to follow Him AT ANY COST. Think about it and count the cost. If you are prepared to follow Him, come what may, then there is something to do.

INVITE Jesus to come into your heart and life. He says,

"Behold I stand at the door and knock. If anyone hears my voice and opens the door (to his heart and life), I will come in to him and eat with him, and he with me " (Revelation 3:20).

Why don't you pray a prayer like the following one or one of your own construction as the Holy Spirit leads?

> "Lord Jesus, I am a wretched, lost sinner who has sinned in thought, word and deed. Forgive all my sins and cleanse me. Receive me, Saviour and transform me into a child of God. Come into my heart now and give me eternal life right now. I will follow you at all costs, trusting the Holy Spirit to give me all the power I need."

When you pray this prayer sincerely, Jesus answers at once and justifies you before God and makes you His child.

*Please write to us (**ztfbooks@cmfionline.org**) and I will pray for you and help you as you go on with Jesus Christ.*

THANK YOU
For Reading This Book

If you have any question and/or need help, do not hesitate to contact us through **ztfbooks@cmfionline.org**. If the book has blessed you, then we would also be grateful if you leave a positive review at your favorite retailer.

ZTF BOOKS, through the Book Ministry of Christian Missionary Fellowship International (CMFI) offers a wide selection of best selling Christian books (in print, eBook & audiobook formats) on a broad spectrum of topics, including marriage & family, sexuality, practical spiritual warfare, Christian service, Christian leadership, and much more. Visit us at **ztfbooks.com** to learn more about our latest releases and special offers. **And thank you for being a ZTF BOOK reader.**

We invite you to connect with more from the author through social media (**cmfionline**) and/or ministry website (**ztfministry.org**), where we offer both on-ground and remote training courses (all year round) from basic to university level at the **University of Prayer and Fasting (WUPF)** and the **School of Knowing and Serving God (SKSG)**. You are highly welcome to enrol at your soonest convenience. A **FREE online Bible Course** is also available.

We would like to recommend to you the next book in this series: Praying With Power

Lord, teach us how to pray…

With these well-known words, the disciples acknowledged there was much to learn from the master about prayer and praying. As a keen student of these subjects, who has sat long at the master's feet, *Professor Fomum* has learned and practiced much. Even today, the master is able to teach us through this faithful disciple who has searched deep and wide within the pages of scripture.

As a scientist, the author puts the Lord Jesus's prayer life under a microscope and draws certain quantifiable guidelines. This *"Textbook"* on praying is replete with charts and diagrams. *Professor Fomum* draws on **Jesus' prayer life and teaching on prayer to help enrich the prayer of today's disciples**.

The original title of this book is self-explanatory. *With Christ in the School And Ministry of Payer*. However, the current title brings out the results of applying what we learn from the Master's School of prayer. *Professor Fomum* invites us to enroll with him - a lifelong learner - in the Lord's School of praying.

To enroll in the Master's programme on praying all you need to do is read and apply what you learn from this extraordinary book.

ABOUT THE AUTHOR

Professor Zacharias Tanee Fomum was born in the flesh on 20th June 1945 and became born again on 13th June 1956. On 1st October 1966, He consecrated his life to the Lord Jesus and to His service, and was filled with the Holy Spirit on 24th October 1970. He was taken to be with the Lord on 14th March, 2009.

Pr Fomum was admitted to a first class in the Bachelor of Science degree, graduating as a prize winning student from Fourah Bay College in the University of Sierra Leone in October 1969. At the age of 28, he was awarded a Ph.D. in Organic Chemistry by the University of Makerere, Kampala in Uganda. In October 2005, he was awarded a Doctor of Science (D.Sc) by the University of Durham, Great Britain. This higher doctorate was in recognition of his distinct contributions to scientific knowledge through research. As a Professor of Organic Chemistry in the University of Yaoundé 1, Cameroon, Professor Fomum supervised or co-supervised more than 100 Master's Degree and Doctoral Degree theses and co-authored over 160 scientific articles in leading international journals. He considered Jesus Christ the Lord of Science ("For by Him all things were created..." – Colossians 1:16), and scientific research an act of obedience to God's command to "subdue the earth" (Genesis 1:28). He therefore made the Lord Jesus the Director of his research laboratory while he took the place of deputy director, and attributed his outstanding success as a scientist to Jesus' revelational leadership.

In more than 40 years of Christian ministry, Pr Fomum travelled extensively, preaching the Gospel, planting churches and training spiritual leaders. He made more than:

- 700 missionary journeys within Cameroon, which ranged from one day to three weeks in duration.
- 500 missionary journeys to more than 70 different nations in all the six continents. These ranged from two days to six weeks in duration.

By the time of his going to be with the Lord in 2009, he had preached in over 1000 localities in Cameroon, sent over 200 national missionaries into many localities in Cameroon and planted over 1300 churches in the various administrative provinces of Cameroon. At his base in Yaoundé, he planted and built a mega-church with his co-workers which grew to a steady membership of about 12,000. Pr Fomum was the founding team-leader of Christian Missionary Fellowship International (CMFI); an evangelism, soul-winning, disciple making, Church-planting and missionary-sending movement with more than 200 international missionaries and thousands of churches in 65 nations spread across Africa, Europe, the Americas, Asia and Oceania. In the course of their ministry, Pr Fomum and his team witnessed more than 10,000 recorded healing miracles performed by God in answer to prayer in the name of Jesus Christ. These miracles include instant healings of headaches, cancers, HIV/AIDS, blindness, deafness, dumbness, paralysis, madness, and new teeth and organs received.

Pr Fomum read the entire Bible more than 60 times, read more than 1350 books on the Christian faith and authored over 150 books to advance the Gospel of Jesus Christ. 5 million copies of these books are in circulation in 12 languages as well as 16 million gospel tracts in 17 languages.

Pr Fomum was a man who sought God. He spent between 15 minutes and six hours daily alone with God in what he called Daily Dynamic Encounters with God (DDEWG). During these DDEWG he read God's Word, meditated on it, listened to God's voice, heard God speak to him, recorded what God was saying to him and prayed it through. He thus had over 18,000 DDEWG. He also had over 60 periods of withdrawing to seek God alone for periods that ranged from 3 to 21 days (which he termed Retreats for Spiritual Progress). The time he spent seeking God slowly transformed him into a man who hungered, thirsted and panted after God. His unceasing heart cry was: "Oh, that I would have more of God!"

Pr Fomum was a man of prayer and a leading teacher on prayer in many churches and conferences around the world. He considered prayer to be the most important work that can be done for God and for man. He was a man of faith who believed that God answers prayer. He kept a record of his prayer requests and had over 50, 000 recorded answers to prayer in his prayer books. He carried out over 100 Prayer Walks of between five and forty-seven kilometres in towns and cities around the world. He and his team carried out over 57 Prayer Crusades (periods of forty days and nights during which at least eight hours are invested into prayer each day). They also carried out over 80 Prayer Sieges (times of near non-stop praying that ranges from 24 hours to 120 hours). He authored the Prayer Power Series, a 13-volume set of books on various aspects of prayer; Supplication, Fasting, Intercession and Spiritual Warfare. He started prayer chains, prayer rooms, prayer houses, national and continental prayer movements in Cameroon and other nations. He worked with leaders of local churches in India to disciple and train more than 2 million believers.

Pr Fomum also considered fasting as one of the weapons of Christian Spiritual Warfare. He carried out over 250 fasts ranging from three days to forty days, drinking only water or water supplemented with soluble vitamins. Called by the Lord to a distinct ministry of intercession, he pioneered fasting and prayer movements and led in battles against principalities and powers obstructing the progress of the Gospel and God's global purposes. He was enabled to carry out 3 supra – long fasts of between 52 and 70 days in his final years.

Pr Fomum chose a lifestyle of simplicity and "self- imposed poverty" in order to invest more funds into the critical work of evangelism, soul winning, church-planting and the building up of believers. Knowing the importance of money and its role in the battle to reach those without Christ with the glorious Gospel, he and his wife grew to investing 92.5% of their earned income from all sources (salaries, allowances, royalties and cash gifts) into the Gospel. They invested with the hope that, as they grew in the knowledge and the love of the Lord, and the perishing souls of people, they would one day invest 99% of their income into the Gospel.

He was married to Prisca Zei Fomum and they had seven children who are all involved in the work of the Gospel, some serving as missionaries. Prisca is a national and international minister, specializing in the winning and discipling of children to Jesus Christ. She also communicates and imparts the vision of ministry to children with a view to raising and building up ministers to them.

The Professor owed all that he was and all that God had done through him, to the unmerited favour and blessing of God and to his worldwide army of friends and co-workers. He considered himself nothing without them and the blessing of God; and would have amounted to nothing but for them. All praise and glory to Jesus Christ!

- facebook.com/cmfionline
- twitter.com/cmfionline
- instagram.com/cmfionline
- pinterest.com/cmfionline
- youtube.com/cmfionline

ALSO BY Z.T. FOMUM

Online Catalog: https://ztfbooks.com

THE CHRISTIAN WAY

1. The Way Of Life
2. The Way Of Obedience
3. The Way Of Discipleship
4. The Way Of Sanctification
5. The Way Of Christian Character
6. The Way Of Spiritual Power
7. The Way Of Christian Service
8. The Way Of Spiritual Warfare
9. The Way Of Suffering For Christ
10. The Way Of Victorious Praying
11. The Way Of Overcomers
12. The Way Of Spiritual Encouragement
13. The Way Of Loving The Lord

THE PRAYER POWER SERIES

1. The Way Of Victorious Praying
2. The Ministry Of Fasting
3. The Art Of Intercession
4. The Practice Of Intercession
5. Praying With Power
6. Moving God Through Prayer
7. Practical Spiritual Warfare Through Prayer
8. The Ministry Of Praise And Thanksgiving
9. Waiting On The Lord In Prayer
10. The Ministry Of Supplication

11. Life-Changing Thoughts On Prayer (Volume 1)
12. The Centrality Of Prayer
13. Life-Changing Thoughts On Prayer, (Volume 2)
14. Life-Changing Thoughts on Prayer (Volume 3)
15. The Art of Worship
16. Life-Changing Thoughts on Prayer (Volume 4)
17. Life-Changing Thoughts on Prayer (Volume 5)
18. Prayer And A Walk With God
19. From His Prayer files
20. Learning To Importune In Prayer
21. Prayer and Holiness
22. Prayer and Spiritual Intimacy
23. Pray or Perish
24. Prayer Crusades Vol. 1
25. Prayer Crusades Vol. 2
26. Prayer Crusades Vol. 3

PRACTICAL HELPS FOR OVERCOMERS

1. Discipleship at any cost
2. The Use Of Time
3. Retreats For Spiritual Progress
4. Personal Spiritual Revival
5. Daily Dynamic Encounters With God
6. The School Of Truth
7. How To Succeed In The Christian Life
8. The Christian And Money
9. Deliverance From The Sin Of Laziness
10. The Art Of Working Hard
11. Knowing God - The Greatest Need Of The Hour
12. Revelation: A Must
13. True Repentance
14. Restitution - An Important Message For The

Overcomers
15. You Can Receive A Pure Heart Today
16. You Can Lead Someone To The Lord Jesus Today
17. You Can Receive The Baptism Into The Holy Spirit Now
18. The Dignity Of Manual Labour
19. You Have A Talent!
20. The Making Of Disciples
21. The Secret Of Spiritual Fruitfulness
22. Are You Still A Disciple Of The Lord Jesus?
23. The Overcomer As A Servant Of Man

SPIRITUAL LEADERSHIP

1. Vision, Burden, Action
2. Spiritual Aggressiveness
3. Leading A Local Church
4. The Leader And His God
5. You, Your Team And Your Ministry
6. Leading God's People
7. Basic Christian Leadership
8. The Character And The Personality of The Leader
9. Revolutionary Thoughts On Spiritual Leadership
10. Laws Of Spiritual Leadership
11. Spiritual leadership in the pattern of David

GOD, SEX AND YOU

1. Enjoying The Premarital Life
2. **Enjoying The Choice Of Your Marriage Partner**
3. Enjoying The Married Life
4. **Divorce And Remarriage**
5. A Successful Marriage; The Husband's Making
6. A Successful Marriage; The Wife's Making

RECENT TITLES BY THE ZTF EDITORIAL TEAM

1. Spiritual Fragrance (Volume 1)
2. Qualifications For Serving in The Gospel
3. Prerequisites For Spiritual Ministry
4. Power For Service
5. The Art Of Worship
6. Issues Of The Heart
7. In The Crucible For Service
8. Spiritual Nobility
9. Roots And Destinies
10. Revolutionary Thoughts On Spiritual Leadership
11. The Leader And His God
12. The Overthrow Of Principalities And Powers
13. Walking With God (Vol. 1)
14. God Centeredness
15. Victorious Dispositions
16. The Believer's Conscience
17. The Processes Of Faith
18. The Missionary As A Son
19. You, Your Team And Your Ministry
20. Prayer And A Walk With God
21. Leading A Local Church
22. Church Planting Strategies
23. The Character And The Personality of The Leader
24. Deliverance From The Sin of Gluttony
25. The Spirit Filled Life
26. The Church: Rights And Responsibilities Of The Believer
27. Revolutionary Thoughts On Marriage
28. Learning To Importune In Prayer
29. Jesus Saves And Heals Today
30. God, Money And You

31. Meet The Liberator
32. Salvation And Soul Winning
33. The Salvation Of The Lord Jesus: Soul Winning (Vol. 3)
34. Soul Winning And The Making Of Disciples
35. Victorious Soul Winning
36. Making Spiritual Progress (Vol. 4)
37. Life Changing Thought On Prayer (Vol. 3)
38. Knowing God And Walking With Him
39. What Our Ministry Is
40. Practical Dying To Self And The Spirit-filled Life
41. Leading God's People
42. Laws Of Spiritual Leadership
43. From His Lips: Compilation of Autobiographical Notes on Professor Zacharias Tanee Fomum
44. The School of Soul Winners and Soul Winning
45. The Complete Work of Zacharias Tanee Fomum on Prayer (Volume 1)
46. Knowing and Serving God (Volume 2)
47. Walking With God (Volume 1)

PRACTICAL HELPS IN SANCTIFICATION

1. Deliverance From Sin
2. The Way Of Sanctification
3. Sanctified And Consecrated For Spiritual Ministry
4. The Sower, The Seed And The Hearts Of Men
5. Freedom From The Sin Of Adultery And Fornication
6. The Sin Before You May Lead To Immediate Death: Do Not Commit It!
7. Be Filled With The Holy Spirit
8. The Power Of The Holy Spirit In The Winning Of The Lost

MAKING SPIRITUAL PROGRESS

1. Vision, Burden, Action
2. The Ministers And The Ministry of The New Covenant
3. The Cross In The Life And Ministry Of The Believer
4. Knowing The God Of Unparalleled Goodness
5. Brokenness: The Secret Of Spiritual Overflow
6. The Secret Of Spiritual Rest
7. Making Spiritual Progress, Volume 1
8. Making Spiritual Progress, Volume 2
9. Making Spiritual Progress, Volume 3
10. Making Spiritual Progress, Volume 4

EVANGELISM

1. God's Love And Forgiveness
2. The Way Of Life
3. Come Back Home My Son; I Still Love You
4. Jesus Loves You And Wants To Heal You
5. Come And See; Jesus Has Not Changed!
6. 36 Reasons For Winning The Lost To Christ
7. Soul Winning, Volume 1
8. Soul Winning, Volume 2
9. Celebrity A Mask
10. The Winning of The Lost as Life's Supreme Task

UNCATEGORISE

1. Laws Of Spiritual Success, Volume 1
2. The Shepherd And The Flock
3. Deliverance From Demons
4. Inner Healing

5. No Failure Needs To Be Final
6. Facing Life's Problems Victoriously
7. A Word To The Students
8. The Prophecy Of The Overthrow Of The Satanic Prince Of Cameroon
9. Basic Christian Leadership
10. A Missionary life and a missionary heart
11. Power to perform miracles

WOMEN OF THE GLORY

1. **The Secluded Worshipper**: The Life, Ministry, And Glorification Of The Prophetess Anna
2. **Unending Intimacy**: The Transformation, Choices And Overflow of Mary of Bethany
3. **Winning Love:** The rescue, development and fulfilment of Mary Magdalene
4. **Not Meant for Defeat**: The Rise, Battles, and Triumph of Queen Esther

ZTF COMPLETE WORKS

1. The School of Soul Winners and Soul Winning
2. The Complete Works of Zacharias Tanee Fomum on Prayer (Volume 1)
3. The Complete Works of Zacharias Tanee Fomum on Leadership (Volume 1)
4. The Complete Works of Z.T Fomum on Marriage
5. Making Spiritual Progress (The Complete Box Set of Four Volumes)

OTHER TITLES

1. A Broken Vessel
2. The Joy of Begging to Belong to the Lord Jesus Christ: A Testimony

ZTF AUTO-BIOGRAPHIES

1. From His Lips: About The Author
2. From His Lips: About His Co-Workers
3. From His Lips: Back From His Missions
4. From His Lips: About Our Ministry
5. From His Lips: On Our Vision
6. From His Lips: School of Knowing & Serving God

DISTRIBUTORS OF ZTF BOOKS

These books can be obtained in French and English Language from any of the following distribution outlets:

EDITIONS DU LIVRE CHRETIEN (ELC)

- **Location:** Paris, France
- **Email:** editionlivrechretien@gmail.com
- **Phone:** +33 6 98 00 90 47

INTERNET

- **Location:** on all major online **eBook, Audiobook** and **print-on-demand** (paperback) retailers (Amazon, Google, iBooks, B&N, Ingram, NotionPress, etc.).
- **Email**: ztfbooks@cmfionline.org
- **Phone**: +47 454 12 804
- **Website**: ztfbooks.com

CPH YAOUNDE

- **Location:** Yaounde, Cameroon
- **Email:** editionsztf@gmail.com
- **Phone:** +237 74756559

ZTF LITERATURE AND MEDIA HOUSE

- **Location:** Lagos, Nigeria
- **Email:** zlmh@ztfministry.org
- **Phone:** +2348152163063

CPH BURUNDI

- **Location:** Bujumbura, Burundi
- **Email:** cph-burundi@ztfministry.org
- **Phone:** +257 79 97 72 75

CPH UGANDA

- **Location:** Kampala, Uganda
- **Email:** cph-uganda@ztfministry.org
- **Phone:** +256 785 619613

CPH SOUTH AFRICA

- **Location:** Johannesburg, RSA
- **Email:** tantohtantoh@yahoo.com
- **Phone:** +27 83 744 5682

Printed in Great Britain
by Amazon